Failure Is NOT an Option

THIRD EDITION

In memory of Grandma Sarah who refused to give up
on me when others had lost faith. You assured that
failure would not be an option for your grandson.
You are the reason I have PERSEVERED.

To my firstborn daughter Sarah: You have been the joy
and an inspiration for this and earlier editions of this book.
May your light shine brightly and deeply touch those who most need it.

To Ava and Virginia: Thank you for your love and patience
throughout the writing of this book . . . and so much more!

To Nancy and Zenobia: Your love and friendship has been a constant,
sustaining factor through thick and thin. "Thank you" doesn't run deep enough.

ALAN M. BLANKSTEIN

Foreword by Pedro A. Noguera

Failure Is NOT an Option®

6 Principles That Advance Student Achievement in Highly Effective Schools

THIRD EDITION

A JOINT PUBLICATION

CORWIN
A SAGE Company

FOR INFORMATION:

Corwin
A SAGE Company
2455 Teller Road
Thousand Oaks, California 91320
(800) 233-9936
www.corwin.com

SAGE Publications Ltd.
1 Oliver's Yard
55 City Road
London EC1Y 1SP
United Kingdom

SAGE Publications India Pvt. Ltd.
B 1/I 1 Mohan Cooperative Industrial Area
Mathura Road, New Delhi 110 044
India

SAGE Publications Asia-Pacific Pte. Ltd.
3 Church Street
#10-04 Samsung Hub
Singapore 049483

Printed in the United States of America

Library of Congress Cataloging-in-Publication Data

Blankstein, Alan M.

Failure is not an option : 6 principles that advance student achievement in highly effective schools / Alan M. Blankstein. — Third edition.

pages cm.
"A joint publication with the HOPE Foundation."
Includes bibliographical references and index.

ISBN 978-1-4522-6827-9 (pbk.)

1. School improvement programs—United States. 2. Academic achievement—United States. 3. Educational leadership—United States. I. Title.

LB2822.82.B53 2013
371.2'07—dc23   2012043976

This book is printed on acid-free paper.

Acquisitions Editor: Debra Stollenwerk
Associate Editor: Desirée A. Bartlett
Editorial Assistant: Mayan White
Production Editor: Melanie Birdsall
Copy Editor: Janet Ford
Typesetter: C&M Digitals (P) Ltd.
Proofreader: Cheryl Rivard
Indexer: Sheila Bodell
Cover Designer: Rose Storey
Permissions Editor: Adele Hutchinson

Certified Chain of Custody
Promoting Sustainable Forestry
www.sfiprogram.org
SFI-01268

SUSTAINABLE FORESTRY INITIATIVE

SFI label applies to text stock

15 16 17 10 9 8 7 6 5 4 3

Contents

List of Resources

Resources also available for download at
http://www.corwin.com/failureisnotanoption3

Foreword

Schools are increasingly under enormous pressure to achieve goals that are important to the functioning of a modern democratic society. However, schools are not typically provided the resources or support they need to fulfill their mission, and for that they are frequently subject to scathing criticism.

We want our schools to provide students with the skills they will need to contribute to the competitiveness of the economy in the 21st century, but we judge schools by the scores students obtain on standardized tests, and the tests typically do not encourage critical thinking or creativity, attributes that are vital to economic success. We want our schools to educate every child regardless of their background and close the achievement gaps, but more often than not we ignore the unmet social needs of children—health, housing, nutrition, and so on—needs that have an impact on learning and child development. Finally, we want our schools to be safe and to protect the lives of the children we entrust to them, even though we do little to shield children from the violence that pervades the media and our society.

While many policy makers have chosen to blame public schools and the educators who work within them but do little to provide support, Alan M. Blankstein's *Failure Is Not an Option* offers a different approach. In these pages, readers will find concrete and comprehensive suggestions for what they can do to meet the ambitious goals that have been set for them. This thoughtful and creative book addresses all of the elements that educators must consider if they are to create schools that will meet our society's needs in the 21st century. With his bold pronouncement that "failure is not an option," Blankstein clearly describes the strategies and steps that educators can take to realize this ambitious goal.

In the first four chapters, Blankstein clearly and convincingly establishes the foundation for courageous action. He not only explains why failure is not an option, he also shows how courageous leadership can inspire others to meet this challenge. With vivid examples that demonstrate what genuine success looks like, he offers guidance that educators will find invaluable as they address the complex challenges confronting their schools. Blankstein identifies 10 common routes to failure that educators will readily identify with, and then he suggests what to do about them, using concrete examples from schools that have undergone transformation. He also explains why and how professional learning communities are so essential to successful and sustainable reform.

The next six chapters address topics that are critical to school reform: mission, achievement for all, collaborative teaching, using data to make decisions, active engagement of the community, and sustained leadership for continuous improvement.

Each of these topics is presented with clear and thoughtful ideas, interesting vignettes and case studies, and practical techniques for addressing difficult issues. Educators will find that the techniques presented in the Resources section are invaluable and worth referring to over and over again. Throughout the book, Blankstein poses challenging questions and then proceeds to outline solutions to each of the challenges.

At a time when schools are increasingly expected to do more with less, to overcome enormous challenges with minimal guidance or support, *Failure Is Not an Option* will be embraced by educators as a potent resource. Blankstein understands the nature of the challenges confronting educators today, and, drawing on the best ideas from research and classroom practice, he offers strategies for effective action. For those on the front lines of reform, who understand that this generation of children cannot afford to wait until our policy makers finally understand that it takes more than slogans and bold exhortations to educate every child, this book couldn't have come at a better time.

—*Pedro A. Noguera*
New York University

Preface

The Year of the Dragon

I write this book during the unusually propitious, yet challenging, Chinese Year of the Dragon. The mythical, sacred dragon and its qualities have particular relevance to the struggles educators now face. It has personal relevance for me as well.

When my daughter Sarah was five and school was out, I offered a daily curriculum based on choices she made the evening before. She had witnessed my daily martial arts practice many times, and perhaps just to please me, one evening she finally asked to explore China and Kung Fu. We attended a local Dragon Boat Festival, watched a group perform a Lion Dance, and then met with their Kung Fu master. Sarah wanted to know about Chinese dragons.

The earliest Chinese sign for the dragon depicted a horned reptile with teeth, scales, and sometimes paws and appeared between inscriptions on bones and turtle shields during the Yin and Shang dynasties. The dragon is often portrayed as a large, scaly reptile, which can become dark or bright, can increase or decrease its size, and can fly into the sky in the spring and live under the water in the fall.

Having divine and/or magical powers, the Chinese dragon is perceived as capable of almost any feat. Yet its focused determination, courage, and rootedness are what allow for its adaptability and flexible approach to challenges. When two dragons are together facing opposite directions, they form the symbol of Yin and Yang, covering the entirety of existence. Therefore, it is no surprise that the first Ming emperor decreed that the five-clawed dragon would be his emblem. It became a capital offense, punishable by execution of the offender's entire clan, if anyone other than the emperor himself ever used the completely gold-colored, five-clawed *Long* dragon.

Like the Chinese dragon, educational leaders at all levels—from classroom to district and state or province—are now called on to address myriad challenges in creative and flexible ways, while remaining rooted in their core purpose. This expectation is easier said than done. The good news is that the answer lies within. This book is meant to help you find those resources, align and organize them around what is most meaningful and energizing for you and your community, and then sustain the success that naturally follows.

As a result of the new demands and rapid changes of the 21st century, this third edition of *Failure Is Not an Option*® is offered up to help the reader

- Root in what is most meaningful to the entire learning community;
- Focus and succeed with limited resources;
- Tap the leadership within the school and district in new and sustainable ways;
- Make cohesion out of cacophony, which leads to effective teaching and enhanced student learning.

This book does NOT present another list of things to do. Rather, it presents a new and highly effective way to organize the best of what is already happening in your schools. The entire learning community can use this book to guide more productive conversations, commitments, and focused outcomes for 21st century learning.

While most books focus on the *"what"* and the *"how"*—*What* should I do, and *how* should I do it?—this third edition of *Failure Is Not an Option*® also addresses the two questions often ignored yet crucial to success: *Why* am I doing this, and *who* do I need to be to succeed?

Perhaps more than in any other profession, educators pursue their calling for a noble reason. Indeed, what could be more compelling than undertaking a profession that *literally* places the future of *children* in your hands?

Educators don't have the distractions of fame and fortune to cloud their thinking about *why* they are here! So there must be another reason—a more profound *why* that leads to all the hours of toil, the deep concerns for the success of young people, the countless evenings and weekends attending plays and ball games.

In light of the barrage of attacks that *public* education and all those involved with it regularly endure, reconnecting with this *why* is imperative to sustaining one's passion and focus. Standing up for why we are in this field is essential to our personal and professional well-being. Equally important, it is imperative for our very future—and that of our children. In this, failure is indeed not an option.

What's New?

This third edition of *Failure Is Not an Option*® maintains its roots, while adapting specific applications to the opportunities and challenges of the 21st century. In particular, it includes:

- Powerful engagement cultures and strategies for students and staff
- A case study on maintaining a collaborative culture in the face of new teacher evaluations and merit pay
- A section on RtI implementation and guidelines
- New case studies of school and districtwide improvement efforts for 21st century education and project-based learning
- A section on how to build relational trust even while addressing tough issues
- A score of new tools and processes for developing a high-performing leadership team
- New information from Pedro Noguera on family and community engagement (Chapter 9)
- Real-life examples from districts across the country that exemplify best practices in building the capacity to *implement* Common Core and other new initiatives
- Video segments to show the six principles of *Failure Is Not an Option*® in action, available at www.corwin.com/failureisnotanoption3
- "Think It Through" questions about the video content to prompt individual reflection or discussion with colleagues
- Reproducible, field-tested forms in the Resources section to help apply the book's examples to your own situation
- Group questions at the end of the book to encourage further investigation into critical issues, and to assist in collaborative work with colleagues to promote change

Practicing Courageous Leadership

The demands of the 21st century are enormous, and in countries like the United States and the United Kingdom, they are taking their toll on educators. New mandates call for professionals to change their standards, their evaluation systems, and their levels of success, while resources are being diverted to prisons and other for-profit ventures (M. P. Williams, 2002). All this while support for those educators on the front lines wanes. "While analysts describe a wave of teacher bashing in the United States, and a 'war on teachers' in England, nations that have a strong professional ideal for teaching deliberately celebrate teachers, teaching, and education" (Darling-Hammond & Lieberman, 2012).

It would be ideal to change this operating dynamic for working educators. However, many people, this author included, do not see that happening in the short term. In a recent meeting hosted by the National Center on Education and the Economy, Robert Swartz from the National Center for Teaching Thinking (NCTT) was asked when America would be like so many other nations in the world that are ahead of us in international assessments based on their investment in and value of education. He said bluntly: "I don't see that happening in America." Courageous leadership is called for now more than ever to navigate this treacherous terrain while staying focused on what is most important. New strategies are being introduced (e.g., "buffering" staff from outside distractions) that are proven both in the literature and in our fieldwork to have a positive influence on student achievement (Leithwood, Patten, & Jantzi, 2010; Seashore Louis, Leithwood, Wahlstron, & Anderson, 2010). These strategies are discussed in Chapter 2.

Similarly, choosing a galvanizing purpose that strategically moves the enterprise forward is critical. As Nietzsche said: "I can bear almost any HOW, if I have a WHY." Getting to the WHY worth fighting for is an essential first step to enduring and overcoming the challenges posed. The specifics on how to use levers to align and improve everyone's efforts around a purpose that has meaning for them are shared in Chapters 1 and 5.

Unleashing the Teacher Leadership Within

Our work of the past two decades began with bringing quality guru W. Edwards Deming into the educational arena to help explore and translate what was being called total quality management (TQM)—to his dismay, incidentally—into the educational arena. Through a series of national forums engaging virtually every major educational leader at the time, as well as CEOs and government leaders, we helped launch what is now commonly called the "Professional Learning Community" (PLC) through Solution Tree, a company that I founded and directed for more than a decade.

The lessons learned in actualizing this work in schools and districts in North America and South Africa—as well as two decades of learning about how PLCs, leadership, and school networks have evolved—are the focus of the HOPE Foundation and at the core of this book. One big lesson is that even in the most challenged schools in the poorest of nations, good instruction is under way. In other words, the answer is in the room, to a great extent. The leadership challenge is in galvanizing, organizing, and scaling the excellence that already exists.

For most of the last century, education in the Western world assumed the hierarchical structures found in corporations. For example, principals became "headmaster" of the school. Even today, our professional associations are all divided by professional title, and training is provided to each profession separately by their association or union. Even the flow of federal funding reinforces this segmentation of work by profession, for example, in grants for "turnaround" principals with the expectation that since principals are critical to success, one can be dropped into a *mission impossible* school and save the day.

The reality is that a small but growing body of research (Hargreaves & Fullan, 2012; McLaughlin & Talbert, 2006; Portin, Knapp, Dareff, Feldman, Russell, Samuelson, & Yeh, 2009; Seashore Louis, Leithwood, Wahlstron, & Anderson, 2010; Wallace Foundation, 2011) confirms what we have experienced for more than a decade: effective leadership starts with a leader who can create an effective leadership *team.*

This skill is not taught in schools of education nor in almost any professional development experience. If it *were* "taught," it would by definition be out of context—akin to teaching swimming while standing next to the pool.

The real lessons over the past decade about what it means to create, build, leverage, and sustain a high-performing team are more than *described* in this book. Specifically, many of the processes necessary to create these teams are provided for actual implementation. Reproducible forms are also included for practical use in the Appendices.

Building a Culture of Relational Trust and Lateral Accountability

Trust in schools—between and among adults—is essential to any significant academic gain among students (Bryke & Schneider, 2002; Bryke, Sebring, Allensworth, Luppescu, & Easton, 2010). In addition, while it is simple to mandate structural changes ("Everyone will meet for their PLC team meetings at 9 a.m.!"), what happens in those meetings is all about the relations and culture. While more difficult, changing a culture is a more sustainable legacy that any leader would want to leave, and the one with the greatest impact on performance (Barth, 2006; Fullan, 2011). We are currently working with our colleague, Ben Waxman, who leads a network in a cluster of 250 New York City schools, and he put it another way:

> You can have the best program for literacy, math, or anything else, and if you have a bad culture it will fail. The opposite is also true: if you have a great culture, almost anything you do will eventually succeed. (personal conversation, Columbia Teachers College, October, 2012)

This edition of FNO *(Failure Is Not an Option®)* demonstrates how to build that high-performing culture. In addition, it provides tools necessary to build it across a network of schools in order to achieve both lateral support and accountability. As described in this book, the "networking" of schools serves to close the gaps between those schools and to sustain the success of the entire district, region, state, or province.

The Structure of This Book

This third edition offers clear guidance to help school leaders, staff developers, instructional coaches, educators, and administrators create successful, sustainable, high-performing schools. The material presented here is intended to assist the entire learning community, from the boardroom to the classroom, to outside partners.

Failure Is Not an Option® begins in Chapter 1 with an overarching moral purpose for schools: *sustaining success for all students because failure is not an option* (Fullan, 2001a). This provides coherent direction for our work and answers the question "*Why* are we in this profession?"

Addressing the *who* question, the succeeding chapter formalizes what we have discovered to be the mental framework of thousands of highly successful leaders. We call it the courageous leadership imperative. The components of this imperative are described in Chapter 2, and specific examples and processes for developing this kind of courageous leadership are provided. Leaders of every variety can produce short-term gains in student achievement. A courageous leadership imperative, however, is necessary to *sustain* significant gains. This is especially true under challenging circumstances. Leaders who adopt the five axioms that compose this imperative are more likely than others to successfully adapt to shifts in educational spending, priorities, personnel, and policies. Ultimately, it is the internal strength of the leader and the school community that act as ballast, rudder, and engine for the ship during stormy weather.

Chapter 3 gives a realistic depiction of the common factors that have derailed many change efforts. What is of more importance is that it offers specific processes and strategies for keeping initiatives on track.

Chapter 4 provides an extensive research base to answer the *what* question. With relational trust as the foundation, it offers six principles for creating and sustaining a learning community. These principles are drawn from more than a decade of research on the topic and 20 years of practical experience in the field. The research referenced in Chapter 4 is clear: building this type of learning community is our best hope for sustained school success. How this community is defined, constructed, and sustained—as well as how to build a foundation of trust— is addressed beginning in Chapter 4.

Finally, we address the *how to* question in Chapters 5 through 10. In these chapters, we provide field-tested processes for creating professional learning communities where failure is not an option. Specifically, these chapters offer a detailed look at the six guiding principles that make up the heart of *Failure Is Not an Option®:*

- Common mission, vision, values, and goals (Chapter 5)
- Achievement for all students through prevention and intervention systems (Chapter 6)
- Collaborative teaming focused on teaching for learning (Chapter 7)
- Data-based decisions for continuous improvement (Chapter 8)
- Active family and community engagement (Chapter 9)
- Building sustainable leadership capacity (Chapter 10)

As you see in Chapters 9 and 10, thankfully some of the foremost researchers and writers in our field have shared their expertise with us to provide some of this clarity. These chapters feature compelling contributions from Pedro Noguera and the team of Dean Fink and Andy Hargreaves, respectively, and in Chapter 8 we draw heavily from our work with Jay McTighe and Ken O'Connor.

Finally, this book builds on more than two decades of intensive work with educational leaders to reshape school cultures for *sustained* student success. As noted, our work began with W. Edwards Deming in

Figure P.1   Structure of This Book

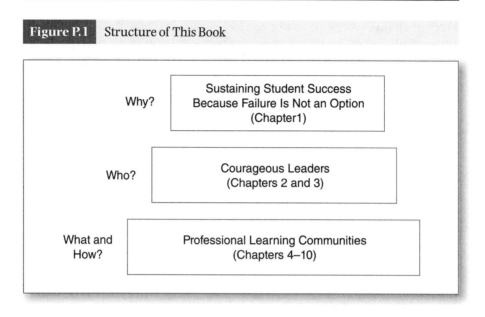

Why?	Sustaining Student Success Because Failure Is Not an Option (Chapter1)	
Who?	Courageous Leaders (Chapters 2 and 3)	
What and How?	Professional Learning Communities (Chapters 4–10)	

1988 and continued with the work of Peter Senge, Michael Fullan, Andy Hargreaves, Maurice Elias, Shirley Hord, Dennis Sparks, Pedro Noguera, James Comer, Tom Sergiovanni, and thousands of school leader-practitioners who have been at the forefront of creating true learning communities.

Limitations of This Work

We approach the task of this book with both caveats and conviction. The first major caveat is that there is no *formula* for success.

In many cases, educational principles that have been passed down through generations must be replaced with processes for creating *new* approaches to success using data, past experience, a willingness to reconsider all assumptions, and the climate for challenging one another's assumptions toward reaching a widely understood and commonly desired outcome. Through the process, courageous leadership is necessary to maintain a sense of hope and optimism, composure, and urgency.

Formulas for success are suspect. As Peter Drucker (1992) stated, the reason we have so many *gurus* is because we can't spell *charlatan*. That being said, we *do* share some convictions and experience regarding "best practices" for reculturing schools and districts toward sustainable student achievement, guiding principles for success, and using time-tested truths about leadership and implementation of initiatives, while taking into account the complexity of change. The trick is sorting all this out, being accurate and precise without oversimplifying, and providing specific steps for action in the face of intricate challenges. That's the balancing act this book aims to perform.

Moving Forward

Throughout this book, we draw from an array of literature and practice from all areas, including organizational development technologies, educational change, PLCs, practice and research, enlightened corporate approaches to leadership development, youth psychology, and enduring wisdom of the past. Ironically, the single most important element for success in any endeavor is often omitted from books such as this. While it is easy to focus on what *others* need to do, or on how to *structure* an organization, or on what *policies* need to be handed down to staff members, the *real* determinant of success will no doubt be *you!* You, the reader of this book. This book grapples with the thorny issue of *intro*spection to assure *external* results. Make no mistake about it: Failure Is Not an Option begins with *you!*

Acknowledgments

Obuntu is a concept and word that has great value in South Africa. Obuntu means that we are inextricably bound to one another and is roughly translated as "I am because you are." Similarly, it has become apparent to me that those who have supported me personally in fundamental ways have also supported this work. They are named below, along with the professionals who have contributed directly to this book.

Before Failure Was Not an Option . . .

My grandmother Sarah was there for me as an infant when no one else was. She later taught me what courage, compassion, and commitment look like. She, the Jewish Child Care Agency, and God were no doubt responsible for my surviving infancy and early childhood.

When I was 13, Harry Haun befriended my mother. While their relationship did not endure, he has been a friend, supporter, and father figure to me ever since.

At age 17, I met Dr. Myland Brown, who made it possible for me to attend college through a grant from the Educational Opportunity Program that he administered. He has been mentor to hundreds of young people, and I was able to find him again and show my gratitude by joining others who were honoring *his* academic success as the Black Distinguished Alumni of Ball State in 2001. We have been in close touch since then.

At the age of 18 and in college, I befriended Reneé Fleming. She has since galvanized the world as the most renowned opera diva of our time. Yet she still remembers her "early fans" and has been a constant supporter. She is now Honorary Board member of the HOPE Foundation.

In 1981, I met Africans for the first time while studying French in Canada. Adama Sy, Oumar Dicko, and Kadi Ly (whom I met years later) changed my life by introducing me to the love, grace, warmth, and dignity of Malians—even in the face of extraordinary poverty. While students together, we shared meals from the same bowl in the warmth of their homes. All of them have since advanced to the top tiers of leadership in Mali to help their countrymen and -women, and they remain among my closest friends.

In 1988, I met the current Executive Director of the HOPE Foundation and my best friend of more than 20 years. Nancy Shin contributed directly and in many more important ways to this work. She, along with her husband and my teacher, Jeff Pascal, gave me invaluable direction and guidance. In addition, Nancy's support, friendship, and unwavering commitment have made the past 20 years of the HOPE Foundation's success possible—and joyous!

Since we met in 1989 when Melanie was working for Chancellor Richard Green in New York City, Melanie and Phillipe Radley have been like surrogate parents and have always been available and shown up during the tough times in particular! In the same year, 1989, I met and began mentoring with quality guru W. Edwards Deming, whose brilliance altered the course of events in Japan, and later the world.

In 1994, shortly after apartheid ended in South Africa, I had the honor of meeting one of our world's great spiritual and moral leaders, Archbishop Desmond Tutu. Although his calendar, life, and heart would seem to have been too full for *one more thing*, he graciously became Honorary Chair to the HOPE Foundation, and continues to provide inspiration for me on a personal level.

Our Board of Directors comprises some of the most talented, brilliant, and committed people I have ever met, and this isn't a superficial analysis— I have known some of them since I was in graduate school! They include Felicia Blasingame, Maurice Elias, Marilyn Hartman, Barbara Huff, Fred Mathews, Larry Rowedder, Bill Scott, and Paul Stafford.

Failure Is Not an Option®, First Edition

The first book was born out of a conversation I had over breakfast with Tom Koerner, a wonderful person and committed educational leader, who is the Executive Director Emeritus of the National Association of Secondary School Principals. He encouraged me to write the work, and

I did so over the next three months. Maurice Elias (mentioned above, but never mentioned enough for all he has done for this field!) put me in touch with Faye Zucker, who became my editor and brilliantly navigated a rapid publication process of the work through Corwin. Along with others named above and below, these people played a critical role in bringing this work to fruition.

Contributors to *Failure Is Not an Option*®, Third Edition

As with the first edition, this book has been graced by some of the great researchers and practitioners in our field. I am grateful to Andy Hargreaves, Dean Fink, and Pedro Noguera for their significant contributions. In addition, we drew heavily from a project under way with Jay McTighe, and informed by Ken O'Connor in order to update Chapter 8.

Case stories and insightful commentary were contributed by practitioners whose insights, commitment, and years of experience in creating learning communities through the Failure Is Not an Option process were inspiring. They include Cindy Anderson, James Baiter, Lydia Beer, Marcy Bestard, Dan Bickel, Nancy Brantley, Laura Cain, Kari Cocozzella, Martin Creel, Linda D'Acquisto, Dan Domenech, Tania Dupuis, MaryEllen Elia, Sandro Garcia, Barbara Gillian, Paul Gordon, Heather Greicicius, Laura Hill, Colleen Kobi-Berger, Dennis Littky, Susan Lothamer, Lillian Lowry, Jim May, John E. McKenna, Anne McKinney, Ernest Morrel, Mike Morris, Bob Morrison, Marcus Newsome, Nancy Noel, Diane Pelkington, Kristen Pelster, Debra Pitts, Carolyn Powers, Mike Pringle, Chris Rasor, Mike Reed, Reggie Rhines, Wendy Robinson, Charlie Rose, Christopher Ruszkowski, James Scaife, Christine Sermak, Tom Sherman, Nancy Shin, Duane Thurston, Jim Vaszauskas, Mary Pat Venardos, Tony Wagner, John Wilson, and Marion Wilson. Thank you for taking the time to not only implement the program but also to share your successes and challenges with others.

Some of the most exciting work now unfolding is under way within a network of some 200 NYC schools in the CEI-PEA cluster directed by Sy Fleigel. Along with his extraordinary team, including Bill Calovito, Walter O'Brien, and Harvey Newman, and network leaders like Ben Waxman, Joseph Blaize, Ben Soccodato, Lucile Lewis, Ellen Pavda, Nancy Ramos, Gerard Beirne, and Mae Fong, Sy has been able to provide true courageous leadership and advanced professional development in one of the toughest U.S. urban districts to navigate.

Reviews of early iterations of this work from Mary Dietz, Ken O'Connor, Carol Tomlinson, Dennis Sparks, Paul Houston, Sharon Kagan, David Osher, Father Val Peter, Alma Harris, and Louise Stoll were extremely incisive, encouraging, challenging, and greatly appreciated! Thank you for bearing with me under, at times, difficult time constraints.

Numerous practitioners weighed in on this work as well, and their advice challenged me to deeply examine and consider many changes to the work. They include Jennifer Walts, Calanthia Tucker, Carol Anne Russler-Boyer, Carol Godsave, Dr. Jo Ann Pierce, Ronald Gorney, Phyllis Wilson, Marilyn Rogers, Peggy Saunders, Rosemary Manges, Diane Williams, Trudy Grafton, Barbara Gillian, Mary Dietz, Wendy McVicar-Lew, David McAdam, Kari Cocozzella, Deborah Wortham, Carolyn Powers, Ed Dawson, Gail Cooper, John McKenna, Linda Jonaitis, and Mike DiDonato.

This book was put on a fast and smooth track to publication thanks to Corwin's new and dynamic editorial director, Lisa Shaw . . . I certainly would have spent this past summer another way without you! Thanks for fanning the flames.

My senior acquisitions editor, Debra Stollenwerk, did a fantastic job of finding superb support in Renee Nicholls as editor, and Mary English as researcher. The only downside of finally completing this book is having to end the work on it together with you! It has been like a cool breeze to work with Melanie Birdsall—thank you as that was needed at this point of finalizing the book! I am paraphrasing and co-opting the axiom "Behind every superb woman, there are a couple of pretty fantastic guys!" in order to acknowledge Mike Soules, David McCune, and Blaise Simqu as amazing supporters. And of course, behind such men is again an exceptional woman. In this case, I am referring to Sara Miller McCune, for whom failure has never been an option!

Publisher's Acknowledgments

Corwin gratefully acknowledges the contributions of the following individuals:

Valerie Chrisman
Assistant Superintendent
Educational Services
Ventura County Office of
    Education
Camarillo, CA

Barbara Hayhurst
Special Education Teacher
Lakevue Elementary School
Nampa, ID

Joy Rose
High School Principal (Retired)
Westerville City Schools
Westerville, OH

Dr. Monica L. Uphoff
Educational Consultant
Corinth, TX

Dr. Linda R. Vogel
Associate Professor and
Leadership Department Chair
University of Northern Colorado
Greeley, CO

About the Author

Alan M. Blankstein is the founder and president of the HOPE Foundation (Harnessing Optimism and Potential through Education), a not-for-profit organization whose honorary chair is the Nobel Peace Prize winner Archbishop Desmond Tutu. The HOPE Foundation's decade-long track record of building highly effective school leadership teams has been validated by three external studies to advance student achievement.

Blankstein helped launch the "professional learning communities" movement through the HOPE Foundation, first by bringing W. Edwards Deming and later Peter Senge into the educational arena, and then by publishing seminal works on the topic through Solution Tree, which he founded in 1987 and directed for 12 years. His *Failure Is Not an Option®: Six Principles That Guide Student Achievement in High-Performing Schools* won the National Staff Development Council's Book of the Year award. With more than 350,000 copies in circulation, it is now the gold standard in creating and sustaining learning communities.

Along with Paul Houston, Blankstein is senior editor of the 13-volume series, *The Soul of Educational Leadership*. His most recent publication, *The Answer Is in the Room: How Effective Schools Scale Up Student Success*, has already met with international acclaim.

Blankstein has authored, edited, and coauthored a total of 16 books and more than 25 professional articles. In addition, he has delivered keynote addresses throughout the United Kingdom, South Africa, the Middle East, and Canada, as well as for virtually every major educational organization in the United States.

A former "high risk" youth, Blankstein began his career in education as a music teacher and has worked since 1983 in youth-serving and educational organizations such as the March of Dimes and Phi Delta Kappa. He has served on the advisory board of the Harvard International Principals' Center, as a board member for the Federation of Families for Children's Mental Health, as cochair of the Community Network at Indiana University's Neal Marshall Black Culture Center, and as advisor to the Faculty and Staff for Student Excellence (FASE) mentoring program. He also served as a trustee of the Jewish Child Care Agency, where he was once a youth in residence.

CHAPTER 1

Why Failure Is Not an Option

In times of drastic change, it is the learners who inherit the future. The learned usually find themselves beautifully equipped to live in a world that no longer exists.

—Eric Hoffer, 1972, *Reflections on the Human Condition*

Knowing what works plays a very important role in school improvement, but alone it is not enough. There are questions about building capacity to implement what works, (and to) measure, check, and adapt to changes.

—Sarah D. Sparks quoting John Q. Easton

On August 5, 2010, a mine in Copiapó, Chile, caved in leaving 33 men trapped 2,300 feet (700 meters) below the surface. Their leader and crew foreman, Luis Urzana, leveled with them early on: their chances of survival were slim to none. Indeed, death was a common companion to miners in Chile, where for the past decade an average of 34 people died annually. Yet something different was to happen this time.

Aboveground, the new minister of mining, Laurence Golborne, had taken office. Lacking any knowledge of mines, Golborne nonetheless was a confident leader. On August 5, his life and that of the 33 miners trapped underground became inextricably bound, and his leadership was to be tested well beyond anything he had imagined. While unable to communicate with each other, Golborne and Urzana shared a common crisis, a similar leadership style, destiny, and faith. As one miner, Florencio Avalos, later offered: "As a group, we had to keep faith. We had to keep hope. We had to believe we would survive" (Govan & Laing, 2010).

Yet, initially, panic broke out underground. Some of the younger miners threw themselves on the ground in despair. Others were anxious to explore escape routes. It was determined that roles would be assigned for maintenance of the area; preservation of the food supply (their rations were 2 teaspoons of tuna, a morsel of peach, and a biscuit every two days); creation of a water supply via digging underground water sources; and search for escape routes. They determined to make decisions democratically and every person would get one vote. No one was to be left alone as each day someone would invariably need group support to make it through.

Early the next morning aboveground, Golborne informed Chilean president Pinera of the situation and flew to the mining site. This was a risky move, as the government was not yet a part of this crisis and going there could change that dynamic. In fact, on his return, Golborne was informed by an advisor that no minister of mines had ever gone to the site of a mining accident.

Indeed, one of the first critical decisions that had to be made aboveground was the role the government would play and whether getting involved at all made sense. When Golborne returned from his initial visit to the mine, he was surrounded by a group of advisors. "It was a big political risk that the president involved himself directly in the rescue," one advisor recalled. "If things went well, it would be great, but, the downside—if things went bad—was enormous" ("Empresarios colombianos," 2010).

Others noted that the president wasn't even popular in that region and that it was politically volatile for him to be seen as in charge there. Did Golborne even have the expertise to navigate this crisis? In short, it was dangerous to get deeply involved, much less take responsibility for the rescue!

The crisis took on a life of its own with virtually every major governmental department joining the fray. Golborne had to manage hundreds of volunteers; coordinate across dozens of governmental agencies; meet with the miners' relatives, to whom he promised total transparency and status reports every two hours; tend to the miners' health; deal with the growing media attention; and determine how to lead a rescue effort in an arena he knew nothing about. His approach was to allow the experts to meet, shape the dialogue with questions, ultimately leading to the best decision.

On August 7 at 3 p.m., the two lead rescuers returned to the surface in utter despair: A new cave-in had occurred, blocking the ventilation shaft. "They must be dead," explained one. "[And] if they are not already dead, they will die."

True to his word, Golborne went out with megaphone in hand to meet the miners' relatives. He began sharing the news but then saw two daughters of former football player Frank Lobos, who was one of the trapped miners. They began crying silently, teardrops streaming down their faces. "I broke down. I could not continue speaking," he said. Then one of the relatives shouted: "Minister, you can't break down. You have to give us strength!"

"That was the turning point for me," Golborne said. Likewise, President Pinera committed totally to the rescue, despite the political risks to his presidency and against the advice of countless members of his staff, who said, "Don't get close to this mine; it is going to end in tragedy!" President Pinera finally shared with his staff: "Even if there is one chance in a million of finding them alive, I shall do whatever is necessary to rescue them because it is my duty as president of Chile, and I believe that with God's help, with the help of many, with technology, and an unshakable faith, we will achieve a miracle." He later met with relatives and told them, "We are going to search for them as if they were our children" ("Empresarios colombianos," 2010).

After a total of 69 days since the mine first collapsed, with organizations from throughout the world contributing their expertise (including the NASA team that had helped bring the Apollo 13 men home safely), some 1 billion television viewers worldwide watched 33 men emerge from a mine shaft of doom. Failure was not an option for all who had committed to the safe return of these men to their families. The nation of Chile, likewise, was uplifted by this belief, this commitment, and this "miracle" (Jordán, Koljatic, & Useem, 2011).

Failure Is *Not* an Educational Option

Many educators would intuitively agree: Failure is not an option for today's students, either—at least not one that we would conceivably choose. Although clearly, students *may* fail, and indeed many do, the consequences are generally too dire to *allow* for such an option. Students who don't make it through high school earn substantially less in wages and may have far greater rates of incarceration and drug abuse than their peers. By contrast, even quality childcare leads to four times the rate of matriculation in 4-year colleges in adulthood versus a random control group that received poor childcare (Pungello & Ramey, 2012).

Rosa Smith, a former superintendent of Columbus, Ohio, schools who is now a nationally recognized educational leader, had an epiphany one morning when she read some statistics about the U.S. prison population. Some 75% of the prison population, she found, is Latino or African American, and 80% are functionally illiterate. She felt a new sense of purpose: her work was no longer about teaching math or science, but about saving lives!

The ability to articulate such a clear and compelling message to all educational stakeholders—inside and outside of the school building—is the beginning of defining what Michael Fullan (2001a) refers to as "moral purpose." Leaders who tap this clear sense of purpose in themselves and others are addressing the beginning of what we refer to in this book as the *courageous leadership imperative*.

Many leaders have yet to discover their moral purpose or develop their courageous leadership abilities. A popular keynote presenter, Rick DuFour, recounts his reaction to a superintendent who challenged the importance of educating *all* children to *high* standards. The superintendent told DuFour, "This isn't brain surgery. No one is going to die here! Some kids advance a little, some a lot. Isn't that the way it goes?" DuFour retorted that this cavalier attitude reminds him of a little office building he once saw in a small town. On the office door were posted two signs: "Veterinarian" and "Taxidermist." Printed underneath were these words: "Either way you get your dog back!"

Failure is not an option for public schooling, either.

Leaders in Western society have long articulated the close tie between a strong public education system and democracy itself (Dewey, 1927; Glickman, 2003; S. J. Goodlad, 2001; Putnam, 2000; Ravitch, 2011). Schools are clearly for the common good, and they serve as the gateway to, and potential equalizer for, economic and life success for millions of underserved children.

As Michael Fullan (2003a) states, "A high-quality public school system is essential, not only for parents who send their children to these schools but also for the public good as a whole" (p. 4). Diane Ravitch (2011) explained it this way: "Education is key to developing human capital. The nature of our education system—whether mediocre or excellent—will influence society far into the future. It will affect not only our economy, but also our civic and cultural life" (p. 223). Failure is no more an option for the *institution* of public education than it is for the children within that institution.

Yet we have seen countless threats to public schools in recent years. They include the rise of vouchers, even for private and religious schools (Cavanagh, 2012; Walsh, 2002), although the evidence indicates that on the whole these schools do no better, and often perform worse, than regular public schools (Bowen, Cooley Nelson, Lake, & Yatsko, 2012; Raymond, 2009). Another threat includes the concerted entry of large, for-profit corporations into the public education arena where "the flow of venture capital into the K–12 education market has exploded over the past year, reaching its highest transaction level [$10 billion] in a decade in the United States" (Ash, 2012). This entry into the for-profit realm is also evident in Canadian Education (Davis, 2012).

This siphoning off of public funds to private ventures is most troubling in the rise of the for-profit prison industry, where executives gauge the number of prison cells to build based on literacy rates from the *second* grade (Williams, 2002)! David Lawrence (2009) points out that

> a child who can read by the third grade is unlikely ever to be involved with the criminal justice system [while] four of five incarcerated juvenile offenders read two years or more below grade level. Indeed, a majority of them are functionally illiterate.

This direct trade-off between education and prison populations couldn't be more stark and disheartening. In response to the deepest recession in 30 years in the United States, 2009 funding for K–12 and higher education declined; however, in that same year, 33 states spent a larger proportion of their discretionary dollars on prisons than they had the year before (NAACP Report, 2009).

As the global recession forces educators to compete for scarce resources with health care, the military, and other sectors of the economy, it often appears that *public* policy itself is harmful to *public* education. A greater level of courage and commitment is needed now—more than ever before—to meet these and other grave challenges.

> The country that uses this [financial] crisis to make its population smarter and more innovative . . . is the one that will not just survive but thrive down the road. We might be able to stimulate our way back

to stability, but we can only invent our way back to prosperity. And for this there is no script—only a heart of courage and a hungry mind. (Friedman, 2009, p. WK8)

Indeed, that is what this book is about: an approach to develop the collective will and capacity for higher levels of student success than previously imagined. We are all in these uncharted waters together. Developing collective commitment to our children and faith in our actions—even in the absence of full information—is essential to brave the storm.

The Significance of the Book's Title: The Passion to Persevere

As all good educators know, failure will and should occur as part of one's learning experience. In fact, researchers at the University of Pennsylvania are beginning to link small failures among young people with larger successes in life (Tough, 2011), and a willingness to risk failure may be linked with creativity (Robelen, 2012). So what is the significance of the book's title? *Failure Is Not an Option®* is about perseverance—about not giving up on what is most vital to us. As researcher Angela Duckworth noted, "People who accomplished great things . . . often combined a passion for a single mission with an unswerving dedication to achieve that mission, whatever the obstacles and however long it might take" (Tough, 2011). As seen in the opening vignette about the Chilean mining disaster, and further explored below, what you believe is often what you get. Consequently, leaders who develop a Failure Is Not an Option mentality can actually enhance outcomes (Dweck, 2006; Walton & Dweck, 2011).

How did the minister of mines, the president of Chile, and the 33 trapped miners persevere under such dire circumstances and unrelenting odds during the crisis? What are the elements of this kind of courageous thinking and action, and how does one develop them? How can leaders harness the urgency of the situation, yet maintain composure with lives at stake and the whole world watching? What kind of organizational culture allows both for the open commentary from "naysayers" and for the ability to quickly move beyond those initial reactions to concerted teamwork? This book addresses these questions with a unifying framework for action to help schools improve their leadership and collaboration, invigorate their teaching in response to current data, and, ultimately, assure that all students succeed.

Lessons Learned From Leaders in the Field

Many extraordinary practitioners have advanced the field since the first edition of this book was released in 2004, and we have been honored to work with some of them in a sustained manner. It is humbling and exciting to see what many of the 350,000 readers of the combined first and second editions of *Failure Is Not an Option*® have done to give these texts additional life and energy through the creative and effective ways in which they have actualized them. Some have taken pieces of the book to make adjustments in their work. Others have moved their entire schools, districts, provinces, and regions forward in a sustained manner, often with the support of the HOPE Foundation (www.hopefoundation.org).

The latter group has certainly pushed the envelope with their concerted and courageous implementation of the six principles embodied in this book. Many of these leaders have taken on a kind of "second order change" (Heifetz, 1999; Stoll & Temperley, 2009), tackling challenges for which there are no known script or easy answers. The subsequent chapters of this book explore the six essential principles that have created a solid foundation for thousands of highly successful leaders using *Failure Is Not an Option*®. The rest of this chapter is dedicated to five new lessons that have emerged over the past few years thanks to the dedicated and sustained use of these principles by colleagues in the field.

Lesson 1: Connect With Your Core

In the opening of this chapter, there came a turning point for Laurence Golborne, minister of mines, when he saw the children of one of the trapped miners begin to cry. After that, there was no turning back. This reaction occurs for many, and the catalyst often involves a deep connection to one's core values inspired by a personal relationship or contact. Consider this example from one of the great leaders of our time:

> During apartheid, the apartheid government was obsessed with turning South Africa into a haven for whites. But this was hindered by an awkward fact: blacks outnumbered whites 5 to 1.

With cunning, the government decided to parcel out South Africa according to ethnicities. The whites, though only 20% of the population, were allocated 87% of the most arable land, while blacks, forming 80% of the population, got only 13%. South Africa's population had, however, mixed together over several decades to occupy the same land, and trying to separate them was like trying to unscramble an omelette. I once visited a resettlement camp. A little girl lived in a shack with her widowed mother and sister. I asked, "Do you have any food?" and she said, "We borrow food" (and later added): "We drink water to fill our stomachs."

These children were not going hungry because there was no food. South Africa was a net exporter of food. No, they were starving by deliberate government policy . . . that incident made me decide to call for sanctions. I would tell her story until apartheid was overthrown. (personal conversation with Archbishop Desmond Tutu; Blankstein, 2011)

Outrage over injustice, advancement of the human condition, desire to help those most in need. Any of these (and more), combined with a personal connection, can serve as a catalyst for great forward movement. What is yours? What is it for your entire learning community? In the following chapters, you will see how to enhance the likelihood that such connections are formed within the school and with external members of the learning community.

Next, consider how one overriding idea strategically chosen and aligned to the "core" of the leader and thousands of employees produced a practical plan to turn around one of America's Fortune 500 companies.

Connecting in Action

Alcoa was in disarray when Paul O'Neill assumed leadership. The company had overextended itself. Profits were down, and employees were disgruntled. The previous CEO had tried to mandate improvements and 15,000 employees had gone on strike, bringing dummies dressed as managers to parking lots and burning them. One person joked that they "were all like a family—the Manson family, but with the addition of hot molten" (Duhigg, 2012, p. 105).

O'Neill researched the company, met with countless employees, and then called a meeting to announce the game plan for reform to an anxious group of investors and employee reps. "I want to talk to you about worker safety," he began. "Every year, numerous Alcoa workers are injured so badly they miss a day of work . . . I intend to make Alcoa the safest company in America. I intend to go for zero injuries" (Duhigg, 2012, p. 98).

The investors, board of directors, attorneys, bankers, and others in the room were ready to move on from that topic: get on to profits, inventories in aerospace, and the like. They failed to see the brilliance in O'Neill's focus.

While worker safety was essential to O'Neill, it also was the top priority for the previously disgruntled workers. Once these workers felt their deepest concerns were adopted by O'Neill, they wholeheartedly committed to that safety vision that he had so clearly and simply articulated. This in turn called for systems adjustments throughout all of their work processes—the *same* systems adjustments that led to the resignation of O'Neill's predecessor when he tried to bring them about through *mandate* (Duhigg, 2012).

It is easy to skip this critical step of connecting to core. When dealing with education, so much is dictated by outsiders. Even a school's mission seems to be determined by others than by those charged with living it. Yet within this environment there is still room to maneuver.

One successful superintendent in Ysletta, Texas, tapped into a unifying need and commitment on behalf of the almost entirely Hispanic population of students, 80% of whom were on the Free and Reduced lunch program. Collectively, they came up with this mission statement: *Every student will graduate fluent in at least two languages and enter an institution of higher academic learning.* This statement resonated with the community and turned what was previously seen as a deficit into a strength.

Marcus Newsome, while superintendent of Newport News Public Schools, took considerable time following his appointment to learn about the work that was under way and the people who were committed to it. He helped them name their focus: a "committed community of learners." With this lever, they began a system of closing achievement gaps between their schools through what emerged as a "paired school model," which later served as a model of change in the United Kingdom (Hargreaves, 2010; Hargreaves & Fink, 2005).

Students whose biggest complaint about school is that "it's boring!" also need to connect with their core passions and interests. Kristen Peltzer, principal of Ridgewood Middle School, in Arnold, Missouri, has revamped the school so that "now students run this building." One small example is called the Aftershock elective, which is taken by up to 25 eighth-grade, high-risk girls. Last year, the girls decided to launch a schoolwide anti-bullying education day. They organized the entire day of speakers, curriculum, peer-to-peer lessons, and topics to address in coordination with a very comprehensive system of student-ledgroups. While students enhanced their academic writing, speaking, and math skills, they also developed 21st century skills of presentation, collaboration, organization, critical thinking, and leadership. Most importantly, student engagement is off the charts in this school, which has seen a rise in proficiency in math and language arts from 30% to more than 70%.

More about Ridgewood School is provided in Chapters 2, 6, and 8. Connecting with your core is also a feature of Chapter 2. It is emphasized here as well because it is so critical to sustainable success—especially in such challenging times—and is so often left out of the educational landscape.

Lesson 2: Articulate and Act on Beliefs

> There are few things more powerful than the commitment of the group.
>
> —Fullan, 2011, p. 85

Once the "core connection" is made, it becomes easier to state a clear and compelling commitment. For O'Neill, it was zero injuries; for Archbishop Tutu, it was the end of apartheid, and for President Pineras, it was "whatever is necessary to rescue them." They all had a Failure Is Not an Option (FNO) mentality.

The FNO mentality has in and of itself shifted the conversation significantly in thousands of identified schools and districts. Stringfield, Reynolds, and Schaffer (2008) outlined highly reliable organizations, where failure would mean disaster and therefore is almost completely mitigated. Similarly, the concept of FNO has led school leaders and their teams to create places where, as the children in one district put it: "Success is the only option!"

Ideas and single statements alone certainly do not change school systems. As noted previously, however, they have been an essential starting point for many, many leaders. Marion Wilson, principal of PS 375, Jackie Robinson School, in a tough part of Brooklyn, New York, decided with her staff that Failure Is Not an Option and "Excellence is the only option," thus beginning a journey in which they went from being a "D" school to an "A" school in her three-year tenure. In the fall of 2011, her school was named one of the top five in New York, and although it has since slipped, the staff has made plans to turn this around.

The power of clarifying and articulating intentions cannot be underestimated. As Dennis Sparks (2007) writes, "Knowing what we want and being proud of it increases the likelihood we will achieve the results we seek" (p. 8).

The Power of an Idea: A New Start

When Shawn Smiley first became principal of Shaumburg Elementary School in Fort Wayne, Indiana, he told his new staff that failure was not an option (personal communication, 2009). As teacher and leadership team member Diane Pelkington recalls:

> We had to find a way to succeed. Shawn made it very clear that he was not going to accept failure in our building anymore. Just hearing that and having a leader who believed, truly believed that, helped everybody else get onboard. It gave us that same desire to make our building a strong building once again. I was so impressed. I had not heard that before—"failure is not an option"—so I clearly remember that moment.

This determination on the part of the principal and school staff to ensure success across the board had significant consequences, as can be seen by the school scores for current reading levels below.

Grade	Quarter 1	Quarter 4
Kindergarten	51%	97%
First	80%	84%
Second	46%	67%
Third	61%	75%
Fourth	48%	63%
Fifth	48%	70%

Source: Shawn Smiley, Nancy Noel, Susan Lothamer, Chris Rasor, Diane Pelkington, Colleen Kobi-Berger, Lydia Beer, Marcy Bestard, and Deb Hyatt, personal communication, 2009.

Note: These were percentages of students per grade level reading at grade level; Grades K–3 were measured from DIBELS and Grades 4 and 5 were taken from Scholastic Reading Inventory (measured in LEXILE).

The idea that no child will fail is still relatively new:

The old mission was about providing access for all to basic education and access for a relatively elite to university education. . . . The new mission for schools is to achieve 90–95 percent success. (Fullan, Hill, & Crévola, 2006, pp. 1–2)

In fact, the 21st century school mission may go well beyond 95% proficiency to fully engaging students in authentic, project-based learning. Some districts are also redefining "success" to include what happens *after* graduation. (Find more on this subject in Chapter 5.)

Once this tenet of no failure becomes the clear picture of a core group of leaders, it begins to spread and develop in a manner that reflects the character of the new owners. For example, the teachers participating in the Courageous Leadership Academy at Shambaugh Elementary School in Fort Wayne, Indiana, developed their own institute for the district based on similar information and titled it "Failure Is Not an Option . . . One Student at a Time."

Value-based commitments tend to be unwavering, and eventually they must connect to commitments by the larger group, fueled by their belief in what can be achieved. ("Hope" may not be a strategy, but a strategy without hope is going nowhere fast!) An essential depiction of the power of belief in one's teaching ability has been well documented around *collective teacher efficacy* (CTE) or *collective confidence*: "relatively recent evidence demonstrates a significant positive relationship between CTE and student achievement . . . the effects on achievement of CTE exceed the effects of Socio Economic Status "(Leithwood, Patten, & Jantzi, 2010, p. 677). Creating this CTE among the staff becomes one of the most critical tasks of the school and district leadership, as described in Lesson 3 below.

When a learning community agrees that success is the only option for their students, they must come to terms with a whole new set of actions required to support this new agreement for a no-fail school (Blankstein, 2007; Corbett, Wilson, & Williams, 2002). Indeed, convictions and commitments require capacity to carry them out. Yet the clear articulation of these commitments is the necessary precursor to any substantive change.

Lesson 3: Unleash the Leadership Within

It has been understood for at least a decade that the role of the principal is critical to a school's success. The principal is the most potent factor in determining school climate, and a direct relationship between visionary leadership and school climate and culture is imperative to support teacher efforts that lead to the success of the instructional program (Leithwood & Seashore Louis, 2012; Wallace Foundation, 2010b, 2011).

Moreover, an extensive survey of leaders in education and policy listed principal leadership as among the most pressing matters in public education (Simkin, Charner, & Suss, 2010). Put more succinctly, "leadership is second only to classroom instruction among school-related factors that affect student learning in school" (Wallace Foundation, 2011).

The key insight from our work this past decade, however, is that the research that pins the success of schools on the powers of the principal— the "Head Master" if you will—masks what really guides the school's success. It is not the leader but rather the leader*ship* that determines sustainable success of the school (Fullan, 2012; Hargreaves & Fullan, 2012; Wallace Foundation, 2011). And the leader who can foster great leader*ship* will have sustained success. Still, it is important to remember that this is relatively new terrain.

Professional organizations focus on segmenting and targeting their members' needs by job title, and funding streams emerge to reinforce this same tendency (e.g., to develop new leaders, or "turnaround principals"). However, the real gains we have experienced in the educational field this past decade embody the development of powerful leadership *teams* that actually do their work together, using specific tools to have different types of conversations that lead to commitments, actions, lateral support, and accountability to outcomes.

Effective leaders, therefore, (1) intuitively root themselves and their learning communities in their core beliefs or common purpose, and then (2) build the team that can shape the culture to (3) support *collective teacher efficacy* (CTE), which (4) sustains student success.

It is often the case that the bottom three Cs on the diagram in Figure 1.1 are arrived at by chance, or are skipped altogether in a rush to bring about teacher efficacy and student success. At best, this will lead to short-term or episodic success, as the foundations for sustainability are not in place. At worst, it can lead to pushback or revolt on the part of staff, as it did in the Alcoa example above.

Consider the following scenario reported by Karen Seashore Louis (2008): "The busy and well-respected principal, eager to find new resources for her school, attended a workshop in which the work of DuFour and Eaker was discussed. Arriving back at school, she announced that they would be implementing PLCs (Professional Learning Communities) and assigned

Figure 1.1 Five Cs of Sustaining Student Success

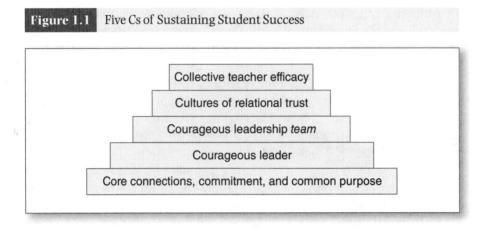

teachers to cross-grade-level work groups to analyze the school's literacy data" (p. 44). Not surprisingly, the staff was not prepared to follow. As Seashore Louis reminds us, "Culture cannot be permanently altered in a short time frame of one school year" (p. 48).

Unleashing the leadership within the school building and district requires a different approach than most leaders ever received in training. In an effort to maintain control yet modify tactics, many leaders fall back on obtaining "buy in," another term for getting others to see *our* light. Chapters 5, 7, and 10 provide specific tools to facilitate the development of high-performing teams, using an inside-out process in which the team members don't "buy into"; rather, they "own the outcome." Or as one teacher shared: "I used to work here; now I help run the school!"

Lesson 4: Create Cultures of Relational Trust

> The first couple of times the teachers went in [to observe other classrooms], they did so empty-handed. It was just to build trust. The protocol was to follow up with an e-mail just saying something positive that was noted during the visit. We didn't call it "instructional walks"; we called it "peer-to-peer." This was all to build trust before we got into specific strategies for instructional improvement.
>
> —Duane Thurston, principal,
> Mary Orr Intermediate School, Mansfield, TX

Probably the most important and most difficult job of the school-based reformer is to change the prevailing culture . . . ultimately a school's culture has far more influence on life and learning in the schoolhouse than the state department of education, the superintendent, the school board, or even the principal can ever have.

—Roland S. Barth, 2001a, *Learning by Heart*

While there are many quick solutions that focus on techniques of collecting and analyzing data or changing teaching strategies, the enduring payoff comes in shifting school culture and basing that in relational trust (Blankstein, 2007, 2010; Bryk & Schneider, 2002; Bryk, Sebring, Allensworth, Luppescu, & Easton, 2010).

"You can have the best program for literacy, math, or anything else, and if you have a bad culture it will fail. The opposite is also true: if you have a great culture, almost anything you do will eventually succeed." Echoing this quote by Ben Waxman in the Preface, everyone we spoke with in our fieldwork concurred with the research: cultures of high trust among adults in the school yield the greatest benefit for student success. Contrarily, without relational trust, there will be no student achievement gains (Bryk & Schneider, 2002; Bryk, Sebring et al., 2010). Of the 21 correlates between a principal's responsibilities and student academic achievement identified by Marzano, Waters, and McNulty (2005), fully 12 of them are directly related to relationships the principal has with his entire learning community. Richard Elmore (2000) recommends that principals "rely more heavily on the face-to-face relationships than on bureaucratic routines . . . the most powerful incentives reside in the . . . relationships among people in the organization."

Yet despite all the evidence, many are still dismissive about making relational trust an agenda item, equating it with "singing *Kumbaya*" or going to the forest for trust walks. And while there may well be a place for these two activities as well, it would not go to the core of what practitioners need to succeed, nor is that what we are advocating. In the words of Christine Sermak, principal of the Williamston Middle School at Ingham Intermediate School District, "We can do all these mini-feel-good sessions and share personal stories, but it doesn't get to the root and heart of what would take us to the next level as a building." (See her story in Chapter 7.)

Knowing one another is certainly critical to advancing the work. Tom Sherman of Mattoon Community School District in Mattoon, Illinois, recalls,

At our initial meeting, we had 20 people in the room representing the 5 building leaders, some teacher leaders, and the district. It became evident within the first 30 minutes that even among the 20 of us, we didn't know each other, let alone the 600 staff members in our districtwide project. The relationship piece was huge! (personal communication, 2009)

Developing an affinity for one another also helps. Creating entire "Firms of Endearment," where employers "love their employees," is even better (Fullan, 2008). Yet trust is also built on taking tough actions in a fair, truthful, and databased manner. Allowing everyone their dignity through difficult times of change makes success more likely.

Trust Is Built on Truth

It is also important to recognize that trust is built on truth. As Principal Shawn Smiley recalls,

I had been looking at grade-level data at the end of Quarter Two. I have three sections of kindergarten, and one classroom was not moving as I knew they could. I got the three grade levels' data sheets and marked out the teachers' names and asked for a meeting with the grade-level team.

Later, as the low-performing teacher and I sat in my office and discussed the grade-level data sheets, she noticed that one classroom was not performing as the others had. She noticed the trends, identifying factors, and lack of growth in areas where growth is expected, relative to the amount of growth she had seen in the other two classes. She looked at me, smiled, and asked, "What is this teacher doing?"

I replied, "You tell me." Then she knew it was her class. She felt as though she had cheated her students. She felt terrible about what she had done. . . . She never intended to let her students slide under the radar.

> From that day forward, she was no longer closed off from outside help. She was a regular contributor to collaboration. We saw a fire that I, in my short time here, had not seen to date. She had fired herself and hired a new self. I had a brand-new kindergarten teacher from that day forward. (personal communication, 2009)

This principal combined pressure and support very effectively. Being caring, compassionate, and patient—especially in the midst of crisis, high demand, and the pressures of time—is not wimpy. It is courageous, and it is hard. Consider the following about relationships that came from a tough corporate CEO, speaking to Ivy League business school students:

> How many of you have taken courses on how you talk with an employee you are firing? How do you talk with a person who comes to your office late at night to tell you that her daughter is sick, and she won't be in the following day? . . . As managers and leaders of people, those are the kinds of questions that one deals with probably 80% of the time. (Bryant, 2009, p. 2)

These are the words of the vice chairman of Wal-Mart stores, Eduardo Castro-Wright, who is likely not advocating singing *Kumbaya*. This dichotomous thinking of either soft or hard, either relationships or results, is one of the challenges we face in creating a common language of leadership and a common language of success. Once we get past that, we still need to meet the challenge of building capacity. Where does one learn the soft skills that lead to the hard outcomes?

As Mary Ellen Elia, superintendent of Hillsborough Public Schools in Florida, indicated: "Educators need to be impatient yet leaders need calm impatience (that is, a sensitive way to communicate impatience). Interpersonal relationships are huge. Some just already have it. If you could teach it . . . ?!" (personal communication, August 14, 2012).

A systematic approach to this is needed and some field-tested tools for how this is accomplished are provided throughout this book, especially in Chapters 4 and 5. With these tools, readers can enhance their pool of qualified new leaders.

Lesson 5: Tap the Answers in the Room

Some 50 leading experts in education surveyed across two continents agreed that excellent teaching is under way in virtually every school and district in the world (Blankstein, 2011). "Everywhere we see pockets of groups achieving success on some level" (Hargreaves & Fullan, 2012, p. 44). The problem is that these are generally what Tony Wagner refers to as "random acts of excellence."

Successful Processes

Part of the challenge in tapping the wisdom in the room involves having a process for doing so. Every endeavor has three components, as illustrated in Figure 1.2.

In schools, the *product* is learning by using an agreed-upon set of measures. The *process* to achieve that product includes pedagogy, creation of positive school climate, and so forth. The *people* are all those involved with the process. To tap the answers that lie within a school and make excellence the norm, we must create a solid process that brings people together to achieve a commonly defined aim or outcome.

For example, once a leadership team has clarified its purpose, defined its protocols and values, and determined its vision and specific

Figure 1.2   Three Parts to Every Project

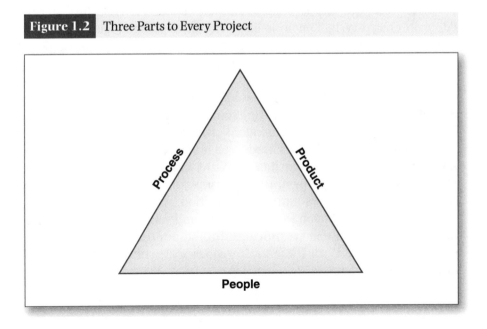

SMART goals, it will soon get to the topic of instruction. But how can they agree on what good instruction look like? What is the *process?* When different teachers are asked to grade the same paper, they usually give it widely varying grades. In addition, there is little correlation between the grades given on schoolwork and the results students receive on standardized tests (Tom Guskey, speaker from the HOPE Conference, 2012). One process tool for agreeing on total clarity of a definition of "good" instruction calls for a leadership team to define good instruction based on members' experiences. When did they last see good instruction? What did it look like? What were the behaviors of the teachers that correlated with good instruction? What role did the students play? (Refer to Resource 1: Creating a Common Rubric to Define Excellent Instruction, for a list of questions and an entire process that drives the creation of a rubric for evaluating "good" instruction.)

Once a team spends several quality hours defining excellent instruction and boiling it down to five factors within a rubric they create, guess what they want to do with the rubric? Yes . . . use it! There are additional steps to the process of defining and then scaling excellent teaching, but the point is there is a *process* for doing this (see Case Story 1 below). Leaders who root in their core purpose—and who develop leadership teams with the tools and processes to bring about a culture of trust focused on developing teacher efficacy—will be able to sustain student success across the entire school, district, or region of schools.

Research-Based System and Framework for Action

For many, the six principles of *Failure Is Not an Option®* that make up the heart of this book have provided the framework, system, and common language for cohesive action that is "highly correlated with student achievement gains" (Brown, Choi, & Herman, 2011). These schools and districts use the principles not as a checklist of to-dos, but as a means of organizing the best of what they already do. As Figure 1.3 shows, each principle works with the others as part of a system so that if a school wants to ensure that no students fall through the cracks (Principle 2), then they meet as a collaborative team (Principle 3) and make data-based decisions (Principle 4) rooted in their mission and goals (Principle 1). Having a common language and framework for action is essential in order to tap the wisdom in the room as well as to build sustainable leadership capacity to deal with myriad shifting challenges, as exemplified in Case Story 1.

Figure 1.3   FNO Principles as a System

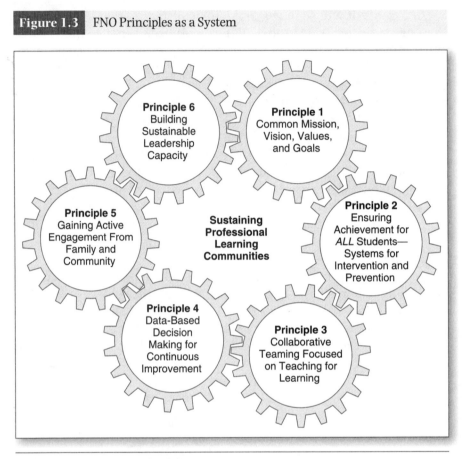

Case Story 1

Maintaining a Collaborative Learning Community While Introducing Teacher Evaluation and Merit Pay

In 2012, Fort Wayne Community Schools (FWCS) in Indiana decided to take on the challenge of piloting the state's forthcoming teacher evaluation system, called RISE. Both the risks and rewards have been great. Due to several key factors, the district has succeeded in navigating some treacherous waters and retains the collaborative culture they built over the past decade.

Laying the Ground for Collaboration

About six years ago, the district set out to build a collaborative community to support the "Three Ps" of "Precision, Personalization, and Professional Community in pursuing their Moral Purpose" (Fullan, 2001a). The district then came into contact with the "Six Principles that Guide Student Achievement in High-Performing Schools" (Blankstein, 2004, 2010), and they did a beta test in the six schools that volunteered to begin the work in what was called the "Courageous Leadership Academy."

The process they used involved networking those six schools together and using a new construct for advancing conversations within and across the schools. For example, teacher-leader teams discussed good instruction and how to recognize it when it was present. At the end of each meeting, the leadership teams created "reentry plans," which allowed them to bring the process back to the schools. This expanded the collaboration and excitement for the initiative.

Based on the outcomes of these six schools, FWCS leaders decided to use the process and the Academy with all of their 51 schools. The entire district now uses the same language to describe success in detail, quickly evaluate it, and make adjustments based on that evaluation. Moreover, they now have structures and systems for quickly sharing best practices across the district and making those practices the norm. This can range from simple tactics practiced by a teacher to keep students engaged throughout the day to the more complex process of establishing a collaborative work environment for teachers. FWCS recognized long ago the value of daily collaboration, and they collectively established time for this within the teachers' workday.

The environmental changes made in FWCS were rooted in its strong moral purpose to "educate all students to high standards." With a clear focal point set by Superintendent Dr. Wendy Robinson in 2003, staff members knew the direction in which they should head. Trust built as the school board established a clear mission, a strong vision, and three key goals aligning all efforts from the boardroom to the classroom. With the development of a Balanced Scorecard, there was and is now transparency of district activity and achievement with the community.

Trust, collaboration, and communication are at an all-time high in this district, which is on its way to making Adequate Yearly Progress (AYP) for the third time in as many years, although for this diverse district this requires achieving success levels in 37 categories. One of the biggest challenges to come, and now listed as a top agenda item for the district, is the introduction of a new teacher evaluation system and corresponding pay for performance.

The Challenge

The teacher evaluation in Indiana is similar to the one that is being introduced in most states in America. It calls for observable performance measures and a student data rating. Next year, pay for performance will also be attached to the evaluations. As Project Manager Laura Cain notes, "We have built our common language, collaboration, and cohesion these past few years. We need to ensure that we continue this culture of collaboration that allows teachers to help each other get better. We have an amazing teacher workforce that is having conversations about children and student achievement every day. That collaborative culture is a big part of why we had consistent growth in student achievement" (personal communication, 2012). As new teachers and administrators enter the system, this becomes an even greater challenge. Here are some of the strategies the district is using:

- **Move toward the danger.** Fort Wayne had the option to take on this teacher evaluation pilot or duck. Consistent with their district leaders' disposition, they decided to take the lead instead of waiting for the new systems to be foisted on them. In this way, they started a year earlier, determined the extent and nature of the challenges, and shaped the final evaluation program to be implemented next year throughout the state.

- **Maintain trust by communicating fully and transparently.** The trust built over the years and described briefly above has been maintained by real-time sharing by the district leadership with all staff any information from the Department of Education (DOE). "This is the reality of our world now. There is competition of choice externally. So we must collaborate internally," Dr. Robinson told her staff (personal communication, 2012). The teacher-leader teams have been one mechanism for communicating and processing complex issues like teacher evaluation.

- **Focus on the work.** Fort Wayne planned its introduction of the new evaluation program by working through the particulars in advance of it affecting anyone's salary. Teacher contracts were already signed and would not be affected in any way for more than a year prior to beginning the pilot. As a result, everyone knew they were able to focus on the work—not the conflict that might arise were they to "go live" with a new system in a way that could affect salaries. As a result, the focus was on success for everyone, and how that could be obtained.

- **Rename, reframe, and own the initiative.** Many evaluation systems coming from the state are seen as onerous and are indeed divisive. This district has as its ethos this statement: "We did it the Fort Wayne Way." Consistent with this, they renamed the challenge and what it meant in terms that made sense for them. "We don't have a choice as to whether we will have teacher evaluation," Laura Cain said to a group of teacher leaders and their principals, "but we can decide whether we are going to let it tear us apart" (personal communication, 2012). In addition, terms like Student Learning Objective (SLO) were seen as negative and renamed "Goals of student achievement."

- **Meet new demands with support.** FWCS collectively decided that 70% of the principals' time would be spent on instruction. To accomplish this, the systems and constructs mentioned above became supports focused on helping reorganize people's time and the principals' effectiveness. The district also brought in instructional coaches to support teachers' professional growth.

- **Create consistent instructional processes.** As noted, FWCS uses a support system that establishes principals as instructional leaders. Starting the first day of school, the process includes frequent and quick classroom visits by principals to provide immediate feedback to teachers, as well as longer visits that are used to further provide support to teachers to improve their instruction. Throughout the year, teachers are given written and oral feedback from their principal to become better educators. The system is considered a support system and not a final evaluation until the end of the year. This work began in the district's eleven schools that piloted reform initiative and was later used in other schools as part of FWCS' participation in the teacher evaluation pilot. This gave FWCS a two-year head start on establishing a system that favors support and collaboration instead of a punitive evaluation process.

- **Engage staff formally and continuously.** Sessions with teacher leaders focused on this new priority, and surveys were used prior, during, and after the yearlong pilot. Teachers reported both positive aspects of the new evaluation and things that need to be changed. The district continues to work collaboratively to make this program successful for all their staff.

Source: Laura Cain, Dan Bickman, and Wendy Robinson, personal communication, 2012.

Moving Forward

As this chapter emphasizes, failure simply cannot be an option as we work to guide all students through the challenges of the 21st century. Moreover, there are ways to succeed even in the toughest of times. As the Chilean disaster points out, it begins with an "inside-out" approach rooted in your core purpose. From there, the lead team gets in synch on processes to support collective teacher efficacy to sustain student success. In Chapter 2, courageous leadership is further defined and serves as the foundation for the rest of the work to be done to exemplify Failure Is Not an Option.

CHAPTER 2

Courageous Leadership for School Success

The ultimate measure of a man is not where he stands in moments of comfort, but where he stands at times of challenge and controversy. Courage faces fear and thereby masters it; cowardice represses fear and is thereby mastered by it. We must constantly build dikes of courage to hold back the flood of fear.

—Martin Luther King, Jr.

Having courage in my heart helps me to get through tough times. Courage is a key to life.

—Justin Reyes, fifth grader,
in Elias et al., 2008, *Urban Dreams:
Stories of Hope, Resilience, and Character*

Leaders across disciplines and throughout time have seen *courage* as the essential human virtue. Consider this small sampling:

Courage is the mother of all virtues because without it, you cannot consistently perform the others.

—Aristotle

Without courage, all other virtues lose their meaning. Courage is, rightly esteemed, the first of human qualities, because . . . it is the quality that guarantees all others.

—Sir Winston Churchill

Courage may be the most important of all virtues, because without it one cannot practice any other virtue with consistency.

—Maya Angelou

Courage, the footstool of the virtues, upon which they stand.

—Robert Louis Stevenson

Leadership has for centuries been closely associated with courage. Richard I, king of England from 1189 to 1199, was renowned for his courage and dubbed by troubadours "Richard the Lionhearted." Likewise, recent Western interpretations of courage have associated it with war, battle, and fallen or surviving heroes. Yet the word itself comes from the French root *coeur,* or "heart," and the concept of courage traditionally corresponded to acts of the heart.

King Richard was renowned for almost single-handedly wiping out opposing armies. It is likely, however, that today's 21st century school leader has an even more demanding task—one that is too big to do alone! As with the Chinese dragon from the preface, this chapter will root us in the timeless concept of courage, adapting it to the 21st century need of building a courageous leadership *team*—a theme introduced in Chapter 1 and carried forward throughout this book.

Reclaiming Courage

Having heart was among the greatest virtues in many early Native American societies, and courage was systematically developed in young men (who were, not coincidentally, called "braves"). "The greatest brave was he who could part with his cherished belongings and at the same time sing songs of joy and praise" (Standing Bear, 1933). Eastman (1902) recounts that his grandmother encouraged him to give away what he cherished most, his puppy so that he would one day become "courageous and strong." These young braves were taught to face their inner fears of loss. Many would later extend this courage to the ultimate loss—sacrificing their lives for members of their tribe, especially children and their elders, who were unable to defend themselves. To make a sacrifice for children was natural and consistent with many Native American cultures, yet to give up one's life was an extreme depiction of courage.

Eddie Belleroe, a Cree elder from Alberta, Canada, recalled a conversation with his aging grandfather. He asked, "Grandfather, what is the purpose of life?" After a long time in thought, the old man looked up and said, "Grandson, children are the purpose of life. We were once children and someone cared for us; now it is our turn to care" (Brendtro, Brokenleg, & Bockern, 1990, p. 45).

Many educators regularly make sacrifices and face fears on behalf of children. We at the HOPE Foundation work with these educators globally. For example, we know a principal who fought with the bus driver's union to create an ever-changing, flexible bus schedule that serves itinerant and homeless children. We work with thousands of teachers who daily put their practice on the line in an unwavering commitment to children who are years behind their grade level.

Every day, all these teachers, and their students, face the very real possibility of failure. Rudy, another courageous colleague, recently ran a big-city school district. One day he met with one of his principals to ask why the children in his school were consistently underperforming. The principal took Rudy to the window of his office, pointed to the children entering the school, and said, "You see those poor kids? Most of them have one parent, if that; they can't read; and they probably don't even speak the language. They just aren't going to make it!" Rudy fired the principal that day, although the political consequences were serious. In another large school district working with us, the leadership analyzed the strengths and needs of 34 elementary schools. Acknowledging that they could no longer settle for the dim improvement results they'd experienced, they decided to "get the right person on the right bus," which resulted in eight principal changes and seven assistant reassignments within one year. That was followed by one resignation and one retirement but a net gain as the needs of each building now matched the strengths of the principals and assistant principals for the buildings. Transition meetings followed to clarify expectations and smooth the change process, and the entire school community then realized how serious the district was about improvement.

The day after a major earthquake hit Haiti in January 2010, Melissa McMullan's students at JFK Middle School in Port Jefferson Station, New York, couldn't concentrate on their social studies work. Overwhelmed by all their questions about victims in Haiti and moved by her own viewing of the evening news, she revamped the curriculum to address their "core" needs, interests, and passions. The interdisciplinary unit she created led to partnerships with people traveling to Haiti; McMullan herself took an 18-hour trip to Haiti and Skyped back to her classroom. Ultimately, the courageous decision to do what students needed led to a schoolwide shipment of 1.5 tons of donated shoes, clothing, and toiletries (students did all the packing, weighing, invoicing, and problem solving); and the opening of a new school in Haiti (Flanigan, 2012). Full student engagement, communitywide involvement, and high-level 21st century learning skills were outcomes of the courageous leadership of this teacher.

Even as this chapter is being written, tens of thousands of students and educators are gathering in Hong Kong streets to protest a politically driven revision of their history proposed for all school children. No doubt they face grave risks (Bradsher, 2012).

The courageous actions described above are not calculated in terms of personal risk or gain. These professionals have a courageous leadership imperative (CLI), defined as acting in accordance with one's own values, beliefs, and mission—even in the face of fear, potential losses, or failure. These educators acted in accordance with their hearts. They do what they have to do because of who they are and what they value. They do it because of the young people whom they are charged to protect, nurture, and help develop into successful young men and women. Developing such courageous leadership individually and organizationally, and leveraging it to assure sustained student success, is the subject of this chapter.

When Failure Is Not an Option

Following a conversation with Archbishop Desmond Tutu, Nobel Peace Prize laureate, we asked his personal assistant, Oupa Seane, if fear of failure ever influenced them in their struggle against apartheid. Oupa responded,

> We never considered failure. Even though we were under apartheid, we had some African neighbors who were doing even worse than us! We drew strength from one another; we would reminisce and conceive of a brighter future for our country . . . a day when everyone could eat, lodge, and have other basics of life; a day when we could create a space program that would rival NASA in the U.S. While so many of our brothers died, we never considered defeat. (personal correspondence, 2003)

What makes it possible for people facing such horrific odds against success to persevere until ultimate victory? If they can do this under such circumstances, are there lessons for teachers who face daily struggles in the classroom, or school administrators looking down the barrel of steep budget cuts, or superintendents and district personnel dealing with massive turnover?

Developing a "Failure Is Not an Option" Philosophy

In a three-year study documenting schools that embraced a philosophy of "all children can learn and it's my job that they do," Corbett, Wilson, and Williams (2002) discovered Granite Junior High School. Despite the poor urban location, the students' success rate on standardized tests compared favorably with wealthier schools in the district—due in great part to the staff's consensus position that every assignment by each student must be completed at a level sufficient to earn a B. In essence, all assignments received one of the following:

A—Above and beyond.

B—The basics. You know your stuff.

I—Incomplete. You need time and support.

To earn an A, students needed to complete extra-credit work. To attain a B, they needed to meet the quality standards clearly defined in advance by each teacher. Teachers had to address many structural challenges to make this philosophy work, including how to handle the open-endedness of the incompletes. According to the study,

The ninth-grade teachers established the end of each marking period as the deadline for assignments . . . while the other two grades continued with the more open-ended approach . . . ninth grade also resorted to using Cs and Ds [still avoiding Fs]. (Corbett, Wilson, & Williams, 2002, p. 86)

Granite Junior High School embraced a common philosophy, behaved in accordance with that philosophy (culture), and created structures and teaching strategies to accommodate it. In the traditional school's equation of Time + Efforts = Learning, the time spent on students and the teaching efforts (including alternative pedagogies) are shifted only marginally in response to students who don't learn. At Granite Junior High, however, learning became the constant; time and instructional approaches became the variables that could be manipulated in order to assure student success.

Source: Adapted from *Engaging Every Learner* (Blankstein, 2007, p. 13) and *Effort and Excellence in Urban Classrooms* (Corbett et al., 2002).

A Test of Courage

Courage is a natural virtue—but it's also a virtue that can be developed. Although we tend to mystify this "mother of all virtues" (Aristotle) and idealize it in the realm of conflict and war, as noted previously, acts of courage can be found regularly in daily life. Indeed, " . . . we demonstrate this virtue more often than we realize. Sometimes . . . by what we refuse to do" (Elias, Ogburn-Thompson, Lewis, & Neft, 2008, p. 11). But it's important to take note that courage can be *developed.*

One's capacity for courageous action can be quickly gauged by this informal test that has been given to more than 5,000 educational leaders since 2002. Imagine that you are in a new town or city and are on your way to shop at a nearby mall. As you approach the mall, you discover that it is on fire. You do not know the nature of the fire only that it began shortly before you arrived. There are no fire trucks in sight.

Would you enter the mall? Most of us would say "No!" Our instincts tell us that it would be foolish to do so. There is a difference, after all, between foolish behavior and courage. Under what circumstances, if any, *would* you enter the mall? Would you enter if . . .

1. a big sale is going on?

2. people are in the mall (who might be trapped)?

3. children are in the mall (who might be trapped)?

4. your children are in the mall?

None of those we surveyed said "Yes" to Question 1, though some laughed. About 5% of those surveyed said "Yes" to Question 2.

An additional 25% responded positively to Question 3. Every person who was asked Question 4 emphatically answered that they would enter that mall to save their own children.

Although we do not claim that this is a scientifically administered survey of educational leaders, it does provide an interesting glimpse into the nature of courage and what evokes that virtue. For example, no one surveyed responded to Question 4 with another question. Questions about particulars *did* arise when those surveyed were asked to respond to Question 3 ("How many children are there?" "Has the fire department already been notified?" "Do I know where the entrance is?" and so on). This implies that the need for specific "skills," "strategies," and "how to" information may diminish as the relevance of the task at hand grows for the individual.

The lesson is, in part: "People are willing to make sacrifices if they see the reason why. . . . People need to know the stakes are worth it" (Heifetz & Linsky, 2002, p. 94). In short, where there's a will, there's a way. Conversely, where there's no will, there may also be no way!

The need to *act* can be more compelling than the *fear* of action, its consequences, or possible failure. Countless examples—from the Chilean mine disaster to the struggle against apartheid, from the educators cited previously, and from our own research—indicate that this is the case. Courageous leaders can learn to develop their own internal fortitude as well as learn to tap and develop a courageous leadership imperative throughout their organization.

Building the Courageous Leadership Team

Building the courageous leadership *team* is the critical strategy for success and it is a process addressed throughout this book. While more details are provided in subsequent chapters, the elements involved include:

- **Selecting the leadership team.** The leadership team must be representative of the entire learning community. Even naysayers are needed as long as they are open to having their concerns addressed and are not CAVE people (Citizens Against Virtually Everything).
- **Constituting the team.** This gets back to the team's core purpose (why they are in existence) and must be clarified.

- **Developing meaningful protocols.** Such protocols go beyond superficial matters such as "starting on time"; they also deal with how to address conflict, how to make decisions, and how to act on them.
- **Focusing on goals and battles that are important enough to win, and meaningful enough to matter!** Initially, depending on the efficacy of the team, it may require many quick and small wins to gain momentum, motivation, and mastery.
- **Finding success: a treasure hunt versus a witch hunt.** Remember, the answer is in the room (Chapter 1), and the goal is to create the context for it to be possible to find the answer and to bring it to scale.
- **Building in feedback loops, transparency, and deeper levels of conversation.** It is essential to look beneath the surface to ensure that you reach the heart of the matter.
- **Setting up the infrastructure to make all the above an embedded organizational "habit."** This is worth the initial time and investment because it saves time and energy in the long run and ensures consistent success.

The bottom line is that it is imperative to engage the heart or courage of people throughout an organization:

As the strategy unfolds, leaders must pay close attention to whether they are generating passion, purpose, and energy . . . on the part of principals and teachers. Failure to gain on this problem is a surefire indicator that the strategy will fail sooner than later. (Fullan, 2003a, pp. 62–63)

The Courageous Leadership Imperative

The CLI not only begins with the desired end in mind, but also requires a resounding *commitment* to that end. The link between success in a given endeavor and our belief in our *ability* to succeed has long been established (Bandura, 1986; Dweck, 2006; Goddard, Hoy, & Hoy, 2000; Goleman, 1995; Kleitman & Gibson, 2011; Love & Kruger, 2005; Mattern & Shaw, 2010; Porter, Murphy, Goldring, Elliott, Polikoff, & May, 2008; Seashore Louis, Leithwood, Wahlstron, & Anderson, 2010; Sternberg, 1996).

"The research literature over the past quarter century has consistently supported the notion that having high expectations for all, including clear and public standards, is one key to closing the achievement gap and for raising the overall achievement of all students" (Porter et al., 2010, p. 13).

Research on highly reliable organizations (HROs) takes this concept of positive expectations and belief systems a step further. These HROs embrace the core concept that *failure is not even an option.* In fact, for these organizations, failure would mean disaster, as they are responsible for such things as clean water, electrical power supplies, and air traffic control. One study of two types of HROs—air traffic control towers and regional electrical power grids—considered applying "HRO response" to meeting the demand for high-quality instructional services for *all* students. This study indicated the strong likelihood that what was learned from HROs can be applied to work in schools (Stringfield, Reynolds, & Schaffer, 2008).

Rossi and Stringfield (1997) wrote, "We found much support for the HRO construct [for potential use in schools] and for its dependence on an established network of high-quality relationships among all stakeholders" (p. 6). Among the cited principles of HROs were

- The central goals are clear and widely shared.
- All staff in HROs share a belief that success is critical and that failure to achieve core tasks would be absolutely disastrous.
- HROs build interdependence among all staff. (Rossi & Stringfield, 1997, pp. 6–7)

Our interviews with thousands of school leaders over the past two decades have yielded findings similar to those immediately above. We found that those administrators who hold an unshakable belief in the ultimate success of their staff and students have far better results than those who do not hold such a belief. Moreover, leaders with a CLI take that belief a step further. They are unwilling to conceive of failure in the long term. Setbacks along the way are rapidly turned into learning experiences that fuel advances toward future successes. As a result, these leaders are more likely to see projects through to completion, inspire others to high levels of performance, and commit to sustaining achievement for *all* students.

What are the elements of such a CLI, and how can they be developed? The next section addresses these questions.

Foundations for Success

The CLI was distilled from an extensive literature review on educational leadership and conversations with thousands of leaders over the past 20 years. Preliminary findings in the most recent study still under way show that the most successful leaders demonstrated characteristics that mirror those points listed above that are specific to highly reliable organizations. This type of leader does not consider failure to be an option. Specifically, leaders who turn failing schools around and keep successful schools moving forward exhibit characteristics that can be summarized in the following five axioms:

1. Begin With Your Core

This axiom refers to first clarifying the driving *internal* core of the leadership and the school community. "Authentic leaders build their practice inward from their core commitments rather than outward from a management text" (Evans, 1996). The core is defined here as the intersection of one's purpose, values, and intention. Determining one's core is a profound and intensive process that provides the enduring roots necessary to sustain efforts in the face of opposing forces. Elaine Wilmore (2007) defines our core values as

> the central part of our lives. They are what we stand for and what we are willing to put on the line for the sake of honor and integrity. They are established within us and are guiding principles of how we live our lives.

School leadership often requires balancing the interests of varying groups. For example, parents on the "right" may want to reduce access to certain reading texts for their children, whereas parents on the "left" may highly value those same texts as well as the concept of free access to information. How can leaders attend to the many disparate interests that tug at them without losing their own center? As one high school principal puts it,

> The non-negotiable that I come back to most often is being true to myself—heeding the call of my heart, *my core,* for better or worse. Sooner or later a great leader is going to stir the pot and, if great things happen as a result, is going to get splattered and slopped on. (Hallowell, 1997, p. 55; italics added)

Although mission statements address why schools exist (e.g., to assure that all students learn), the axiom of "beginning with your core" goes a level deeper. It answers the questions "Why do I care?" and "What am I willing to do about it?"

Clarifying one's core as a person and a leader is perhaps the most difficult and most fundamental of all acts. We should not be surprised that it is also rarely undertaken. In fact, one could find many understandable reasons for passing over this critical axiom, and there are many reasons why such practices are seen as unnecessary or impractical among modern-day educational leaders:

- There is too little time to do *anything*, much less "getting to one's core!" Donaldson (2001) refers to the "leadership-resistant architecture" of schools in which there is a "conspiracy of busyness" (p. 11) that leaves little time to convene people to plan, organize, and follow through. Although most leaders find this leaves them with little time for reflection, nonetheless the most effective among them make allocating their time properly a priority.
- There is an impression that "self-discovery" is "soft" or an otherwise unnecessary aspect of leadership. Our work with leaders indicates otherwise and more closely concurs with Warren Bennis' *Timeless* (1989) pioneering work in the field.

  "Know thyself" is the inscription over the oracle at Delphi. And it's still the most difficult task any of us faces. But until you truly know yourself, your strengths and weaknesses, know what you want to do and why you want to do it, you cannot succeed in any but the most superficial sense of the word. (p. 40)

- Acting on aspirations and ideals can be painful. Such actions expose leaders to what Ackerman and Maslin-Ostrowski (2002) refer to as the inevitable "wounding" experienced by true leaders. It becomes easier and less risky, therefore, to just do what is mandated by the district, state department, or province.
- Leadership is a lonely role to begin with. This isolation is compounded by the sense that many leaders feel that it is not safe to be themselves, even with their staff. They have an image to uphold and suffer what Mike Pedler (2011) refers to as "Leadership, risk, and the imposter Syndrome."
- In almost every society we researched there have been or still are mentors, spiritual guides, elders, and others who systematically assist people in self-development and self-discovery. Many African

societies we visited still use rites of passage with their young boys and girls. Several Native American societies use "vision quests" to help prospective leaders uncover their purpose in life. Such practices are seen as essential to leading a meaningful life, and especially important to leading others to do the same. This is no longer the case in most Western societies, and many people simply don't know where to begin such a search for self.

There are many ways that educational leaders can reach their core. Consider answering the following questions in pairs to get to "the heart of our life as a teacher":

- Why did I get into education in the first place?
- What are my core values as a professional??
- What special gifts and talents do I have to offer?
- What do I want my professional legacy to be?
- What can I do to remember my passion and stay true to my heart?

As Carolyn Powers, the director of elementary administration for the Fort Wayne Community School District in Indiana, reflects,

What do you want people to say about you once you leave? Are you here to make the adults in the building happy or to ensure that the children learn? It is difficult to stay focused on student learning when the pressure of status quo tugs at you from the existing culture. You have to look yourself in the mirror each day and say I will do what is right for the students under my watch.

Another way to get individuals to discover what lies at their core is through an activity that can be undertaken in groups of about 8 to 15. One group or several can do this activity at the same time within a room.

Ask everyone to begin by sitting in a circle while the activity is explained, and then break into groups of three. Each member of the triad recounts a story from his or her own life that captures the essence of the person in some way. For example: "When I was a young teenager, I saw a couple of other teenagers robbing an elderly woman, and I intervened."

The person telling the story then draws out the elements that describe some of his or her essential personal characteristics. In the above example, the storyteller might say: "This shows the essence of who I am and what I value because I protect those who need help, and I am not afraid of the consequences." Others in the triad may add to the list of characteristics and see if the storyteller agrees with them.

Someone else in the triad can write down each personal characteristic to share with the larger group. It is also possible to build an affinity diagram from everyone's notes in order to discover the "common core" of the group. This, in turn, can be used as part of the development of the school's mission or values (to be described in Chapter 5). The full group is reformed at the end of this sharing session, and everyone has the opportunity to briefly share their story and corresponding "essential" or "core" characteristics.

Educators can also get to their core by reflecting alone on these critical questions:

1. What do I *value* most? Another way to ask this might be: What behaviors can I *not* tolerate and why?

2. What do my past life patterns, strong interests, and passions tell me about my *purpose* in life?

3. How do my values and purpose in life overlap with what I am doing *here* in my current role? What are my *intentions* relative to the work I am now doing?

Defining the answers to questions 1 and 2, and ensuring alignment between this and the intentions of one's current work as a leader, helps to maximize the effectiveness of such an exercise. This process takes time, yet it builds a feeling of personal authenticity and therefore enhances trust within the organization (see Chapter 4 on trust).

"Leaders who are followed are authentic. Integrity is a fundamental consistency between personal beliefs, organizational aims, and working behavior" (Evans, 1996, p. 184). Defined in slightly different terms, leaders with the greatest credibility and moral sway know who they are. Their *purpose, values,* and *intentions* relative to their work are aligned. The next four axioms deal with leaders' *actions.*

2. Create Organizational Meaning

What's really important to being our best is concentration and focus on something that is meaningful to us.

—James M. Kouzes and Barry Z. Posner, 1999,
Encouraging the Heart

Victor Frankl (1959/2000) wrote persuasively about people's fundamental need for meaning in their lives. Despite the current focus on testing and standards, educators need more than incremental gains on their students' test scores to establish a motivating connection to their work. Similarly, students need to see the relevance of schoolwork in their lives. This is essential to gaining sustainable achievement or anything more than short-term results on tests. As one 14-year-old student shared with us, "What do I care about Romeo and Juliet? I ain't goin' to college . . . an' most of my friends ain't even made it to be 20 years old!" A statement like this catalyzed courageous actions by Erin Grunwell, whose English class was far more focused on their gang involvement than on Shakespeare. Erin threw the curriculum out and started where the students' concerns intersected. Eventually the class both made the connection to the gangs in Romeo and Juliet and started a movement named "Freedom Writers."

Uncovering the concerns of individuals begins the process of defining deeper meaning in the lives of *all* stakeholders, which in turn unleashes energy toward substantive school improvement. It also provides a sense of hope to those in despair. Such hope is a vitally important ingredient for success (Cooper, 2007; Evans, 1996; Fullan, 2001a, 2011).

One way to create organizational meaning is through reframing. Although a budget cut may demoralize a school community, for example, it can also be an impetus for change and an opportunity to rally the troops. It can be seen, therefore, as an opportunity to gather people together to discuss how the community can collectively make their current work more effective, drop things that are not working, and learn about how other schools are dealing with similar challenges. It can even be the impetus for a school community that was otherwise isolated to undertake action research on "best practices" for dealing with budgetary constraints.

Correspondingly, as we saw in Chapter 1, the Ysletta School District turned what many consider to be a liability—an 80% ELL student population—into a strength: "All students will leave here speaking at least two languages!" They then built a robust array of languages into their curriculum for students to access.

All leaders are faced with crises at some point. Leaders are also regularly faced with challenges. A leader's most productive reaction to such situations is to create positive meaning from them for themselves and for the people in their organizations.

3. Maintain Constancy and Clarity of Purpose

> Schools experiencing exceptionally rapid turnover are often reported to suffer from lack of shared purpose, cynicism among staff about principal commitment, and an inability to maintain a school improvement focus long enough to actually accomplish any meaningful change.
>
> —Seashore Louis, Leithwood, Wahlstron, & Anderson, 2010, pp. 165–166

Sometime in the 1970s, advertisers must have quietly signed a pact: *All products should now and henceforth be deemed "new and improved"!* Consumers gleefully bought the "latest" and most "improved" lawnmower, car, and soap. As a profession, we have also adopted this same regrettable concept—creating, consuming, and abandoning the latest educational fad every few years.

But the educator who purchases a quick and convenient "initiative du jour" is buying a mirage. Most of these new initiatives are later deemed ineffective and evaporate—or worse, they are kept indefinitely without further evaluation. In the latter case, the educational "bookshelf" is filled with a confusing array of possible ways to proceed. This approach is disjointed at best, and it is demoralizing for an already overburdened staff.

This axiom—to maintain consistency and clarity of purpose—moves us toward a disciplined approach to both clarifying and holding fast to organizational purpose. It saves time that would otherwise be spent changing directions and filling vacancies for departing, dispirited staff.

The "constancy of purpose" portion of this axiom (Deming, 1986) is made possible by first clarifying that purpose. In the Chilean mine collapse described in Chapter 1, the purpose was clear: Bring the 33 miners back alive. Had the purpose been vague (e.g., at one point there was question as to whether the government should get involved at all) or the constancy of that pursuit wavering (e.g., had the minister of mines, Laurence Golborne, given up after the first failed rescue attempt), the miners would not have survived.

Maintaining clarity and constancy of purpose accomplishes two major goals. First, it helps reduce stress among staff—stress that arises from multiple priorities coupled with insufficient time to accomplish them. A recent survey of California principals exemplifies the challenge. Their reduced budgets and turnover led to 60- to 70-hour workweeks and assumption of responsibilities as teachers, community liaisons, athletic directors, crisis managers, budget gurus, and nurses (Bland et al., 2011)!

Reports from Australia indicate that they share similar challenges as applications for school principalships continue to decline (Barty, Thomson, Blackmore, & Sachs, 2005). As one principal told us, "I feel like I need to be all things to all people. And district priorities shift like the desert sands. It can be overwhelming at times." Adhering to the axiom of clarity and constancy of purpose helps provide continuity and coherence in an otherwise ever-changing landscape, and it was the first reason named by Hillsborough, Florida's superintendent, Mary Ellen Elia, for the district's extraordinary successes: "I am only the fourth superintendent in over 45 years, and am in my 8th year. This stability is present in the board as well, where we even have had one member 20 years who is up for reelection! Whatever the purpose is, if there is constancy, you have a good chance of achieving it. You can move quicker with a level of trust from staff toward that purpose" (personal conversation, 2012).

Second, maintaining clarity and constancy of purpose leads to greater success within those areas of focus. Evans (1996) explains, "Studies of high-performing systems show that their leaders provide direction that is clear, strong, and unambivalent. . . . Clarity brings many advantages. The first is to foster trust" (p. 213). Evans goes on to advocate that any given team or individual considering a multifaceted project undertake "one thing at a time" (p. 218), which is consistent with research around the power of ensuring small wins early on to build momentum for the change effort (Fullan, 2011).

There are several ways to keep focus clear and constant:

- Be fanatical about the positives of a project. Continually point out the milestones that are being reached along the way. Celebrate success. Encourage experimentation and refinements where necessary. Empower people to continue the efforts on their own in order to build momentum.
- Systematically drop what should *not* be pursued. Involve stakeholders in creating a list of such activities or projects to determine "what needs to be done that is not being done now, and what can we quit doing so we can do what we need to do?" (Schlechty, 1992, p. 106).
- Provide a sense of urgency to the area of desired focus. In Chapter 1, we described a superintendent who determined that she and her staff were not teaching math and science, but saving lives! Such "reframing" in compelling and urgent terms helps to focus people on desired outcomes.

- Provide continuous feedback using data. Ensuring that pertinent data flow directly to those involved with a project (as opposed to being filtered through the leader) is even more powerful and focusing.
- When necessary, stretch out timelines to meet the goal. It is better to provide the time needed for success than it is to have several half-completed projects.

Effective leaders help their school community succeed by first personally defining their core, making meaning for their organization around core values and core purpose, and continually clarifying and focusing on priorities that are aligned with that purpose. Building in tight feedback loops to allow staff to see their own success is also critical. It turns out that the top motivator of performance is performance itself!

4. Confront the Data and Your Fears

In *Good to Great*, Jim Collins (2001) observes that successful companies consistently and accurately assess current performance with an eye toward improvement. "Facing the brutal facts" is often difficult and can be unflattering. In addition, educators tend to correlate certain types of assessment with personal and critical evaluation by administration. (For strategies on trust and assessment, see Chapter 4 and Case Story 4: Six Lessons Exemplified Across a Region in Chapter 7.) Naming and facing fears constructively can be the first step to overcoming them, thereby expanding the range of possible actions. Take these classic world events, for example:

1. The May 13, 2003, issue of the *New York Times* reported: "Scientists . . . said yesterday that the existing public health measures had been effective in containing the [SARS] disease in many countries and should work eventually in China and Taiwan, where the disease is now concentrated" (deLisle, p. 13). Ironically, SARS reportedly began in China but was contained in places as near as Hong Kong and as far away as Toronto, Canada, before it was under control in China. This is likely due to the Chinese government's initial denial of the problem. Unlike Hong Kong, China was initially unwilling to confront the data and face the fears associated with this epidemic. As this article indicated, "The New China News Agency reported that 31 officials in the capital were disciplined for poor performances in carrying out measures to combat the epidemic" (ibid., p. 13).

2. In February 2003, the space shuttle *Columbia* burst into flames on reentry into the earth's atmosphere, killing all seven astronauts aboard. The subsequent investigation revealed that a suitcase-sized chunk of foam smashed into the *Columbia*'s left wing and damaged a critical heat shield, causing the *Columbia* space shuttle disaster. According to the Associated Press (Test, 2003), "During *Columbia*'s flight, shuttle managers rejected engineers' request for spy satellite images to ascertain the extent of damage to the left wing" (para. 19).

Although it is impossible to know what the fate of this flight mission might have been had scientists confronted the data (and their fears) early on, it is clear that they did not take this approach. By contrast, confronting the data and facing fears were critical to saving the lives of the three men on *Apollo* 13 in 1970 (Blankstein, 2010) and 33 miners as described in Chapter 1.

As is true with other organizations, school communities tend to avoid certain facts and related fears. For example, we have entered many fine schools that pride themselves on an 85% passing rate on standardized tests, without examining who is in the 15% that are failing.

While addressing the Chilean crisis, the truly effective leaders and their teams worked with the same kind of sense of "calm impatience" Superintendent Mary Ellen Elia referred to in Chapter 1. This can be accomplished by practicing full engagement and dropping attachment. For example, if you were in the jungle forced to run for your life from a lion, the best chance of success would be to do so with total focus on the goal and total presence of mind (full engagement) versus running in a panic or feeling anger toward the lion (attachment). While people can push emotional "buttons" more successfully than can a lion, the reaction is still yours to choose, and one that combines calm with an urgent focus on the goal is most productive.

In sum, it is essential to develop the organizational norms and the personal "habits of mind" (Costa & Kallick, 2000) to dispassionately and regularly evaluate one's position relative to the ideal and to use data-based assessments as fuel for continued improvements, hope, optimism, and action.

5. Build Sustainable Relationships

In the prior "A Test of Courage" section of this chapter, we noted that each of the more than 5,000 leaders surveyed emphatically said "yes" when asked if they would enter a burning shopping mall if their child were in it. Although the "moral imperative" (Fullan, 2003a) of potentially saving children was the same in both questions 3 and 4 of this survey, the *relationship* was not. When the children in question were the *respondents'* children, there was no doubt as to whether they would risk their lives to save them.

Studies of courageous actions in war indicate that it is not so much moral purpose that lies behind putting your life on the line (although that can be a part of it), but the more tangible impact of loyalty to your buddies. "Quality relationships, in other words, are even more powerful than moral purpose" (Fullan, 2003b, p. 35).

Clearly, in this book we are not advocating that leaders or their staff put their lives on the line. The research is clear, however, that trusting relationships are a crucial element of student achievement and school success (Bryk & Schneider, 2002; Bryk et al., 2010; Goddard, Salloum, & Berebitsky, 2009).

It is important to understand that all of the preceding axioms interact with one another. Relationships serve to weave them together into a unified whole. Relationships support a leader in taking the risk to act from his or her *core* to create *organizational meaning*. Relationships allow leaders to maintain *clarity and constancy of purpose* and to *face the data and the fears*, though this might otherwise be too stressful, threatening, and disheartening.

In every district where we worked toward long-term school reform prior to 2005, we spent the first year on nonacademic items such as the development of mission and vision in ways that were collaborative and relationship enhancing (our work today expedites that process). It is interesting to note that although we did not focus on academics in the first year, in every instance academic achievement improved significantly during that same year. Even now, we spend considerable time on relationship building in order to more deeply and honestly address data-driven teaching practices. The Case Story in the next chapter on the Alton, Illinois, school district provides corroborating details.

Throughout this book, we share ways to enhance affinity among those in the school community. Chapter 4 advocates the creation of learning communities based on relational trust. These sections provide specific strategies for developing relationships critical to the success of schools.

Moving Forward

> This culture, and we as members of it, have yielded too easily to what is doable and practical. . . . We have sacrificed the pursuit of what is in our hearts. We find ourselves giving in to doubts

and settling for what we know how to do, or can learn to do, instead of pursuing what matters most to us and living with the adventure and anxiety that this requires.

—Peter Block, 2002, *The Answer to How Is Yes*

There is frequently a chasm between what we know to be the best action and what we do. The connecting tissue is often the courage to act.

Throughout this book, we appeal to the *heart* (as well as the mind) in order to find the courage to increase and sustain levels of student achievement. Given the challenges for staff, students, and the larger community in today's environment of accountability, there is much at stake.

As mentioned earlier, courage comes from the French word *coeur,* or "heart." Effective leaders act with heart. In the final analysis, their decisions are informed by judgment but this judgment emanates from their core purpose, values, and intention. Leaders who act in this manner transcend fears of failure that would otherwise impede them; they act with a courageous leadership imperative.

When courageous leadership permeates the school community, the *how to* questions of school improvement become easier to determine and implement. Where there's a will, there is indeed a way. When the will is lacking, questions about specific techniques and tools can become an obstacle to action or any real change. Developing the CLI goes a long way toward ensuring sustained student achievement. The next chapter looks in detail at 10 other common obstacles to school change and how to overcome each.

CHAPTER 3

10 Common Routes to Failure, and How to Avoid Each

Educational change is technically simple and socially complex.

—Michael Fullan, 2010a, *Leading in a Culture of Change*

Slow is smooth and smooth is fast.

—Jeff Pascal, Bicentennial East Coast
Weapons Champion, U.S. Martial Arts
Association Kung Fu Instructor of the Millennium

Every diaper-changing parent is likely to agree: Change is messy business. Chang*ing* is even messier! Although people may like the eventual *change*, they often don't like chang*ing* because the *process* can be uncomfortable. Installing new solar panels on your roof, for example, may be eco-friendly and cost-effective in the long run, but the disruption, chaos, and expense of the installation process are sure to give you major headaches in the short term.

Some of us are innovators and enthusiastic "early adopters" of change, but most of us take a cautious approach and have genuine concerns to work through.

Similarly, teachers are often less than enthusiastic about embracing change, especially when it is done *to* them instead of *with* them. Although they may agree with the overall *concepts* of new standards (e.g., learning walks, quality reviews, and differentiated instruction), getting accustomed to them can create feelings of insecurity and fear. This is especially true for practitioners who have experienced innovation overload. Questions emerge: "Why do *I* have to change?" "Haven't we done this before?" and "How exactly do you want me to find time for *this?*" If left unanswered, these inevitable questions can thwart any change initiative.

Educational Movements Come and Go, the Obstacles Remain the Same

In the late 1980s, the HOPE Foundation began working with quality guru W. Edwards Deming, whose work informed and became the basis for improving all Japanese manufacturing processes after World War II. At that time, it became clear that Deming's approach, often mistakenly titled total quality management (TQM), was more effective in creating high-performing organizations than what was then being used in most U.S. corporations (Blankstein, 1992). Most important for us, Deming's work shed light on a potentially powerful new paradigm for education.

Not long afterward, we introduced Deming and, later, Peter Senge to the top educational leadership of the era through a series of Shaping America's Future forums, and PBS-Adult Learning Satellite System (ALSS) programs. We proposed his concepts and those of total quality education (TQE) and learning communities for discussion in educational circles.

Lew Rhodes of the American Association of School Administrators asked to meet privately with Deming and a few months later began the Total Quality Network. At the same time, the Association for Supervision and Curriculum Development introduced *their* Total Quality Learning Network, with Jay Bonstingl leading the charge (Bonstingl, 2001). Powerful business groups, including the Business Roundtable, added "total quality" approaches to their current site-based management initiatives. Prominent educational authors like William Glasser (1992) began writing about total quality education. One could hear a swelling chant from the ranks of educational leaders: "TQE! TQE! TQE!"

By the end of the 1990s, however, the "movement" was dead. Only a few remnants of some of the more technical aspects of Deming's work remain. The leaders of the HOPE Foundation went on to help catalyze the next educational leadership wave—professional learning communities (PLCs)—through their publication of three works by DuFour and

Eaker (DuFour, 1991; DuFour & Eaker, 1992, 1998). Many publications furthered the movement (Blankstein, Houston, & Cole, 2008; Hord & Sommers, 2007). The cycle recommenced.

Creating substantive and sustainable change in education has been elusive. Figure 3.1, and the section that follows, explores some of the common obstacles to this goal and offers means and suggestions to overcome them.

Figure 3.1   Overview: Obstacles to Change and Possible Solutions

Obstacle	Possible Solutions
Obstacle 1: We Don't Want to Change	• Phase in sustainable change • Begin with the "willing few" • Create fail-safe environments for pioneers to operate • Provide forums for successes to be heard, celebrated, and emulated
Obstacle 2: You're the Leader, Tell Me What to Do	• Reevaluate the leadership style toward ensuring long-term commitment from staff to success of all students • Create teacher-led leadership teams • Endorse the changes teachers determine are beneficial for students
Obstacle 3: We Have No Time for This!	• Determine if time is the only issue • Ensure that the change process is seen as worth the time spent • Provide common planning time • Involve students in community-based service learning • Create banks of time • Explore the options discussed in Resource 2, Strategies for Making Time
Obstacle 4: Carrots and Sticks Don't Work	• Provide constructive alternatives to extrinsic rewards such as grades • Emphasize that the goal is to learn and grow continually
Obstacle 5: Students Must Be Tested and Graded	• Revise grading system • Use project-based learning alternatives
Obstacle 6: The Mandates Are in the Way	• Work with the school district toward acceptance of data on teacher performance based on the school's principles of learning • Use buffering strategies to protect staff

Obstacle	Possible Solutions
Obstacle 7: We Like Last Year's Silver Bullet Better	• Clarify intentions, beliefs, values, and mission to ensure alignment of new initiatives • Build internal capacity and direction versus external search for quick solutions • Show how new initiatives offer a well-planned and assessed means of reaching the school's smart goals
Obstacle 8: We Don't Know What We Want, What We Need, or the Difference Between the Two	• Ask school teams to take the quick self-assessment provided in Resource 3.
Obstacle 9: We Can't Agree	• Gain consensus on the definition of consensus • Confront behaviors that are inconsistent with the mutual agreement • Broadly tout and celebrate successes
Obstacle 10: We're Waiting for the Dream Team	• Recognize that taking leadership at any level—in the classroom or building—can still contribute to student success • Pursue the ideal response to a void in leadership: Fill it

Obstacle 1: We Don't Want to Change

People are often wary of new ideas, and in schools such resistance can present itself on many fronts. Teachers can tire of being asked to rethink their practice. Parents want their children's school days to be just like their own and are often reluctant to endorse new and different approaches to education.

It is possible to overcome this reluctance to change. Successful leaders begin with the "willing few" (Blankstein, 2011), create fail-safe environments in which they can operate, and provide forums for their successes to be heard, celebrated, and emulated. More suggestions appear in Resource 4: Strategies for Dealing With Resistance.

Obstacle 2: You're the Leader, Tell Me What to Do

Through our experiences as students and employees, many of us have learned that the leaders' role is to make decisions and control outcomes. In education, principals might fear that relinquishing control over every aspect of the school could hinder its effective functioning. Other members of the staff become comfortable in established roles as well and find it difficult to transcend years of experience as a "leader" or "follower."

True change requires that all individuals within an organization—administrators, teachers, staff members, parents, and students—work cooperatively for the benefit of the students. In the long run, monopolizing power inhibits individuals in these groups from viewing themselves as contributing to the overall success of the larger system.

The work at hand is often for leaders to reevaluate their own leadership style in order to ensure the path to long-term commitment from staff to success of all students. The processes described in Chapters 5 and 7 are designed to develop strong leadership teams. This systematically supports "diversifying the leadership portfolio" by giving teachers and parents the opportunity to lead as well (see Chapter 10 on distributed leadership).

Principals and district leaders increasingly promote change, for example, by acting as a participant, rather than leader, in meetings; encouraging teachers and parents to explore new ideas, instead of moving them toward a predetermined agenda; and endorsing the changes teachers determine are beneficial for students, versus asking their opinion and then following another path.

By playing a supportive role with staff, principals create a nurturing environment in which *teacher leaders* are unafraid to take risks in leadership roles. This shift in leadership style allows individuals throughout the school community to reevaluate both their roles and the concept of leadership itself.

Obstacle 3: We Have No Time for This!

This statement is, on its face, completely legitimate. There is simply no way of getting around it—the process of creating school improvement plans, completing needs assessments, collecting and analyzing data, and planning for change requires an investment of time. Successful schools also need to make time in the daily schedule for teacher collaboration and continued professional development.

At the same time, this statement can also be a smokescreen for staff that resist change. This ruse can be uncovered by asking, "Is time the only issue? If I were to assure you that you will have sufficient time to do this, would you become actively involved in the process?" The change process must be seen as *worth* the time spent. In fact, some cultures, communities, and educational systems may not value collaboration or in-depth professional development; others rarely receive it!

The National Staff Development Council (Learning Forward) status report, *Professional Learning in the Learning Profession* (Darling-Hammond, Wei, Andree, Richardson, & Orphanos, 2009), identified this:

> *Key Finding 15:* American teachers spend much more time teaching students and have significantly less time to plan and learn together, and to develop high quality curriculum and instruction than teachers in other nations. U.S. teachers spend about 80 percent of their total working time engaged in classroom instruction, as compared to about 60 percent for these other nations' teachers.

Rethinking the school culture and the importance of continual, embedded professional development is key for long-term success. Beyond this comes the practical issue of finding time. Here are some examples of how schools have addressed this issue:

- **Provide common planning time.** Schedule several classes for the same activity at the same time to free classroom teachers to work together (e.g., all third-grade art classes or seventh-grade PE classes meet simultaneously).
- **Involve students in community-based service learning.** At numerous schools where we work, high school students spend one half day of each week away from school, working in various community service programs. Teachers use the time for collaboration.
- **Create banks of time.** Add a few minutes of teaching time to each class in a particular period daily for four days. On the fifth day, the class is cancelled or shortened by the number of extra minutes accumulated. Students are provided with an alternative activity, and teachers use that time to meet in teams.

There are many ways to deal with the issue of time. An additional 12 ideas can be found in Resource 2: Strategies for Making Time. The ideas on this list are best used as starters to stimulate brainstorming within your own school. Each teaching staff must develop approaches that *they* believe will work and that they are invested in implementing.

Obstacle 4: Carrots and Sticks Don't Work (Pink, 2009)

For many years, the operation of American schools was modeled on the same assembly-line method that first permitted mass production of automobiles. In this system, which requires employees to meet quotas and product specifications, workers compete with one another for promotions and bonuses that are parceled out to a few "winners." The internal strife and long-term *de*motivation this system causes is well documented. Educators are increasingly being rated and ranked—often erroneously (Darling-Hammond, 2012)—and the addition of merit pay is now being foisted on them in the United States and United Kingdom (Darling-Hammond & Baratz-Snowden, 2005)—despite its proven deleterious effects (Ariely, 2010; Atkinson, Burgess, Croxson, Gregg, Propper, Slater, & Wilson, 2004; Darling-Hammond, Amrein-Beardsley, Haertel, & Rothstein, 2012; Fullan, 2006; Gabor, 2011; Irlenbusch & Ruchala, 2008; Marsh et al., 2011; Programme for International Student Assessment, 2012; Ravitch, 2011).

This extrinsic approach to motivation implies that if individuals are not rewarded, punished, or pitted against one another in competition, they will fail to "perform." In fact, in such a system, "performance" is the best possible outcome. Likewise, children learn to simply get the "right answer" instead of going on a road of discovery, which often leads to "wrong" answers, but enhances *true* learning.

In contrast with all major research on the topic for the past half century, pioneers like Deming based their philosophy on the opposite premise that individuals have an intrinsic drive to learn and do well and they do not want to fail. As summarized by Daniel Pink (2009), all major research on this topic for the past half century maintains that if allowed to pursue this natural drive, people will strive to reach their potential without any need for external motivators such as competition or fear. The role of the education system, given such an assumption, is one of guidance and formative assessments to enhance continual learning.

Obstacle 5: Students Must Be Tested and Graded

Accountability for teachers and school leaders has its analogue in grades and high-stakes test scores for students: both can crowd out innovation, student engagement, and profound learning. Legislators pressure schools to raise student test scores, and parents can be even more insistent on the need for grades because, unlike legislators, they have the added fear that their children's future in higher education or the job market will depend on grades. But as many educators now realize, grades and test scores do not reflect, for many reasons, what children are really learning, including but not limited to poorly constructed assessments. (See Chapter 8.)

It's interesting to note that if you have 10 teachers grade the same paper, you will get a wide variety of grades reflected in their assessment. So what do grades really mean?

The key is beginning with the *purpose* of grades. For example, if you had one student who began with 100% on his first test, and then coasted and did the minimal to make 80% on the next three, he would have an average score of 85. A second student got a 70 initially, but then he worked hard and got an 80, 90, and eventually a 100 on the last test for an average of 85. Both have the same average, but there are two very different stories behind it. Depending on the purpose of grades in the schools, there might be a decision to weight the latter grades more heavily. Moreover, if there are 10 grades in a semester and the student misses the first test and gets a 0, she would have to have a perfect 100 score on the next 9 grades to get an A in the course. Does giving a zero grade make sense? What does it signify? What about giving grades related to behavior? Homework? Should these be averaged into the overall grade? It depends on the purpose, and the answer would be "no," were the grade to reflect only student knowledge.

Instead of trying to definitively utilize a grading system (which is more difficult than it seems), what if schools moved toward a proficiency or a mastery scale in which the levels were 1 to 4, with 4 being the most complex of the tasks—say, reading several texts and then writing a piece comparing and contrasting them—while Level 1 was demonstrating use of correct grammar for that grade level? If students were also involved in developing the rubric, their understanding and interest level would rise. If they were able to tie the work to something personally relevant to them—as was the case with the class in Michigan that ultimately helped start a school in Haiti (see Chapter 1), then they would be less inclined to focus on grades at all. As Mike Reed, principal of the Columbus Signature Academy from New Tech High School in Columbus, Indiana, explained: "Kids who are invested in a project here are loathe to even leave the building. They are so focused on the work!" (Additional information about this is explored in Chapters 4 through 6.)

In sum, by focusing more on engaging, relevant pedagogy, and using precise and fewer ways to calibrate what is being learned, students and adults alike are better able to focus on what really counts: enhancing learning.

Obstacle 6: The Mandates Are in the Way

Even if a school successfully overcomes all of the internal barriers to change, external barriers still exist. State, provincial, and federal mandates dictate funding and often provide powerful stumbling blocks to truly transforming a school.

An effective and helpful strategy to overcome this obstacle is to "buffer" staff from distractions to teaching and learning. Referring to the government program No Child Left Behind, superintendent of the Mansfield School District Robert Morrison explained: "We don't even focus on NCLB and haven't for years. We focus on what is important for students to learn and how best to teach that, and NCLB takes care of itself" (personal communication, 2011). Although challenged by the most rapid growth in Texas, and with much of that growth coming from low (supplemental education services) SES students, this high-performing district was "Recognized" by the state. The leadership concerned itself with external mandates while providing "space" for teachers to become as good as possible using state-of-the-art teaching and assessment supported by strong leadership teams rooted in a common purpose, and a systemwide focus and framework for action. External mandates "took care of themselves."

Obstacle 7: We Like Last Year's Silver Bullet Better

Unquestioned belief in and adherence to PLCs, TQE, differentiated instruction, or this year's newest miracle cure will not significantly alter learning for students or improve the efficacy of the staff. Deploying mechanical techniques cannot become a substitute for understanding why we're doing what we're doing. Otherwise, the outcome is simply more of the same, but with an "exciting" new label.

In 1965, the United States had the No. 1 educational system in the world (Cohen & Moffitt, 2009) but has now declined in ranking to No. 17 (OECD, PISA rankings, 2010). According to Fullan, "The decline . . . is a function of superficial, silver-bullet solutions that actively disregard and disrespect practice" (Fullan, 2011).

When a school finds itself cycling through initiatives, it is important that the staff clarifies intentions, beliefs, values, and mission to assure alignment. (See Chapter 5 on Common Mission, Vision, Values, and Goals.) Any new initiative needs to clearly align with core beliefs, values, and the mission of the school in order to be effective. Moreover, it must become a well-planned and assessed means of reaching the school's SMART goals.

Obstacle 8: We Don't Know What We Want,
What We Need, or the Difference Between the Two

This list of 10 roads to failure does not apply equally to all schools—nor does *any* single approach to school improvement. For example, whereas some schools are "cruising" based on past successes and not yet willing to recognize and reveal their own areas for improvement, others have hit bottom and are desperate for *anything* that offers new hope (Stoll & Fink, 1996).

Without a clear picture of the *needs* of the school community, it is easy to be like a kid in the candy store when pursuing the appropriate means of enhancing and sustaining student achievement. Whichever speaker or program is the most enjoyable, interesting, or popular in the neighboring school district wins!

The quick self-assessment provided in Resource 3 allows school teams to get a clearer picture of where they stand. Completing this assessment helps to focus all school efforts, guide the school improvement process, and maximize the benefits of this book.

Obstacle 9: We Can't Agree

Understanding and empathizing with people's legitimate concerns and fears goes a long way in helping to overcome them. At the same time, in order to reach an overwhelming consensus for a particular schoolwide reform effort, often too much attention is paid to a few holdouts.

Gaining consensus on the definition of consensus is a critical first step. Here is one that may work for your school: (1) All points of view have been heard, and (2) the will of the group is evident, even to those who most oppose it (Eaker, DuFour, & Burnette, 2002). Once the school community has had ample time to reach consensus on an improvement initiative, it is better to spend time reinforcing those leading the change than on those trying to hold it back. "Water the flowers, not the rocks in your garden!" (See Resource 4 for more strategies for dealing with resistance.)

After there is general consensus, the leaders need to confront behaviors that are inconsistent with the mutual agreement while broadly touting and celebrating successes (see Chapter 5 on celebrating success).

Obstacle 10: We're Waiting for the Dream Team

The many nuances of creating meaningful change defy formulaic approaches. What works in a wealthy suburb may not work in an urban center or a region of rural poverty. Even if the change processes are equally applicable, the implementation is sure to vary. School staff members would likely lack commitment to any "imported" initiative. And becoming too attached to a given charismatic speaker, buzzword, or program is inherently contrary to developing ownership.

We have seen leaders *wait* to begin a new initiative until the sage of that particular program arrives to give a keynote speech or daylong workshop. Similarly, some school leaders, having had many of their past efforts thwarted by a new district leader, elect to wait before making changes so that their current superintendent can retire and the incoming leader can set the new direction!

While having districtwide alignment exponentially enhances outcomes for schools, taking leadership at any level—in the classroom or building—can still contribute to student success. The ideal response to a void in leadership is to fill it.

Case Story 2

Alton Overcomes Obstacles to Change

The following Case Story provides an example of how one school district grappled with fundamental changes and overcame many of the obstacles discussed in this chapter. It provides a picture of progress since the beginning, and at various points up to the present. Which solutions were most effective? Which are closest to your situation?

Part 1: Recognizing the Need for Change

James Baiter, Superintendent, Alton Community School District 11

In the spring of 2000, the board of education approved a plan to reconfigure the district to reduce operational costs. They closed four elementary schools, consolidated three middle schools into two buildings, and reassigned several employees. It became our goal for all schools to strive for continuous improvement of achievement levels for all students.

James Scaife, Principal, Lovejoy School

"We've heard a lot of this before." "This is the same old thing presented differently." Veteran staff members voiced these complaints when we started a new comprehensive school reform model now called Failure Is Not an Option (FNO). We had already been faced with an ultimatum from the state and the district to improve our low scores on state standardized tests (ISAT). Faculty had been required to meet almost weekly to come up with effective strategies to improve our scores—and they were not happy about another initiative that required additional time.

Debra Pitts, Former Teacher and
Assistant Principal, Alton High School

"How can this model help our students? Our school? Our community?" "How will our faculty react?" "How will we get the time?" My biggest challenge was getting my high school faculty to understand the new (FNO) model and to believe that it wouldn't be just another "here today, gone tomorrow" model. After 26 years in education, I had the same reservations myself.

Nancy Shin, Executive Director, HOPE Foundation

Alton was still recovering from the massive reorganization of the previous year. Leadership and faculty were all rearranged. People were very upset. People asked me: "How much time will FNO take? How will we get that time from the union? How will we convince others that *this* effort will work?" Within two years of beginning our change effort, we lost more than half of the entire group that began the process to retirement.

Mary Pat Venardos, Principal, Mark Twain School

When the HOPE Foundation team showed up to do their initial on-site evaluation, I thought, "Yes, this is what we have needed for a long time!" It was so exciting to work toward common goals throughout the district—to discuss similar topics concerning mission, vision, values, and goals with other administrators and to have central office support along the way. Still, I knew that getting the staff to buy into a model that included everyone in decision making would not be easy. My biggest challenge was helping the leaders of the previous reform model understand why we needed to look at something new.

Part 2: Responding to the Challenge

Mary Pat Venardos, Principal, Mark Twain School

I turned to the data and, before presenting them to the faculty, talked with a few key individuals about how the FNO process would incorporate elements of the prior model, include all our stakeholders in collaborative teaming, and lead to increased student achievement. I then presented the data to the entire faculty for discussion. It clearly showed that the previous model had not increased student achievement. We discussed the new process and how we would collaborate in grade-level teams, involve all faculties, and base all decisions on data.

The resisters initially declined to join the leadership team. I sought their advice on how to improve the process as we set up our teams and looked at learning issues in the building. As our leadership and grade-level teams experienced the process and realized how it would impact student achievement, building support began to grow.

James Scaife, Principal, Lovejoy School

I was concerned that bringing in a new approach would create a division between new and veteran teachers, so I recruited several veteran teachers to become a part of our leadership team. They were skeptical of "yet another program," so I set up a meeting for them with the HOPE Foundation representatives. When they recognized that their input was truly going to be valued, they became advocates for the process.

Part 3: What the Outcomes Looked Like in 2004

James Scaife, Principal, Lovejoy School

As we began our leadership team meetings and our grade-level team meetings, we called on teachers to collaborate and plan together. Collaboration became more commonplace and negative tension began to subside. The teachers started seeing some positive effects of this approach, and they began to share with each other.

When the results of the ISAT came back at the beginning of the following year, our work and collaboration had paid off. We went from 38% of our students meeting expectations on the test to nearly 50%. We easily surpassed the percentage needed to keep us off the Watch List. We still had a lot of work to do, but this type of collaboration put us on the right track.

Mary Pat Venardos, Principal, Mark Twain School

As the building leader, I was challenged to walk the walk. Terms like *data-driven, collaboration, research-based, mission, vision, values,* and *goals* became second nature to me. I learned to guide the leadership team in decision making by using data-driven processes. We began to support one another. I felt more like an instructional leader in the building than I had prior, and I liked that shift.

The lead team recognized that FNO was working because they saw that

- Language arts developmental reading assessment scores significantly increased;
- Discipline referrals dropped;
- Staff could be observed collaborating in grade-level and committee meetings;
- Minutes of grade-level meetings reflected the PDSA (the Shewhart cycle, also known as the Deming wheel—plan, do, study, act) plan (see also Chapter 8);
- They achieved their SMART (strategic and specific, measurable, attainable, results-oriented, and time-bound) goals for increasing student achievement at each grade level (see Chapter 5 on creating SMART goals);

- They observed that teachers' respect for one another was reflected in the ways students, in turn, respected each other; and
- They were proud to have a warm, family atmosphere at school that promotes this climate with students, staff, and visitors.

Debra Pitts, Former Teacher and Assistant Principal, Alton High School

This was the first time in my career that I witnessed teachers collaborating and looking at data to determine where students are achieving and systematically looking at ways to move them forward. I began to see change from the top down—our superintendent, assistant superintendent, and principals. We began talking the same language: *student achievement!*

Nancy Shin, Executive Director, HOPE Foundation

We created a closely knit group of principals and leadership teams early on. This group, along with our support team, enabled us to endure the many leadership transitions and move forward toward increased student achievement. At the end of the biggest year of transition for us (year one), the Alton schools performed better than the state average on 10 of 13 indicators on state standardized achievement tests (ISAT).

Part 4: What the Outcomes Looked Like Through 2012

Nancy Shin, Executive Director, HOPE Foundation

By 2004, the culture in the district, typified by Alton High School, had clearly become collaborative in significant ways, a noteworthy accomplishment in a school with more than 100 faculty and 2,000 students. When the high school received a Bill and Melinda Gates Planning Grant in 2004, their focus shifted away from collaborative learning communities toward building a freshman academy, followed by a three-year Gates grant for Career Academies. Barbara Gillian became Alton High School's assistant principal in 2006, and she was given the reins in spring 2008 by then principal Philip Trapani. Dr. Trapani had been heavily involved in the FNO process early on.

Barbara Gillian, Principal, Alton High School

By 2009, we realized that we had tried to do too much too quickly. We were in the process of once again reconfiguring the entire district, moving to a new high school building, consolidating the middle schools at the old high school, and restructuring the elementary schools. It became apparent that the curriculum development was not moving along because we weren't communicating—we needed to return to what we learned about PLCs to pull our improvement plans together.

Nancy Shin, Executive Director, HOPE Foundation

Data, including course rosters with race codes, showed that English I classes had been populated mostly by nonwhite students, while honors English classes were mostly white. The faculty teams and department chairs were appalled and set out to change the landscape. They began by eliminating English I and putting *all* students into CP (college prep) English I, the middle-of-the-road course. What they already knew but hadn't documented was that the freshmen coming from middle school were not prepared for ninth-grade reading. Consequently, for students at sixth-, seventh-, and eighth-grade reading levels, they implemented English lit and comp using Read 180 to focus on reading and writing for one hour a day, moving to a daily 90-minute block in year two. In one year, they advanced 18 students from that class to honors English.

Using this change as the seed for more growth, they eliminated science survey, the lower-level science course, and required *all* students to take biology. This was a struggle for teachers accustomed to working with only high achievers, but they focused on getting *everyone* to pass. The challenge is to retain rigor. Ongoing professional development oils the wheels of continuous improvement, supporting instructional improvement via professional learning communities.

Barbara Gillian, Principal, Alton High School

We have to be committed to ongoing learning ourselves, as leaders, to keep current with effective instructional strategies. We need to teach kids not just content but also how to learn.

Nancy Shin, Executive Director, HOPE Foundation

Alton has been looking at data for more than a decade now. They began with Positive Behavior Intervention and Support (PBIS), but recently, they've gone deeper into the data.

Over time, they came to realize as they studied their data more intensively that there is no correlation between the elementary standardized test (ISAT) and the Prairie Standard Achievement Examination (PSAE) and they needed additional tools to know how to prepare their students. By studying the data, they have gradually increased their standardized testing to follow each student for four full years with nationally normed assessments. Their American College Testing (ACT) scores went up consistently through 2008:

	2001	*2008*
Reading		
Illinois	58	53.3
Alton	55	66.9
Math		
Illinois	54	52.7
Alton	51	67.4
Science		
Illinois	50	51.2
Alton	49	59.0

Source: Used with permission of Nancy Shin, Mary Pat Venardos, Barbara Gillian, James Scaife, and Debra Pitts.

Snapshot of Alton in 2012

When everyone moved into the new building in 2008, the new motto posted at the door—"We are a community of learners"—brought many questions from students, staff, and parents alike. Today, no one questions what that means: They live it.

The hard work of 2000 to 2007 made it possible to return to the PLC constructs, including additional school improvement teams and book studies initiated by the principal. In math, for example, an Algebra Concepts team formed and began meeting biweekly to identify more specifically which skills and which students needed more attention. At the time of this writing, the team has evolved to the point where they flex their meeting schedule as needed to support their goal of serving every student, generally meeting once or twice a week. This math revision followed the path of the earlier revisions in English and Science prompted by new looks at data.

As they dug deeper into the issue of what students knew about math and when they learned it, it became clear that the middle school needed to be included in the plan. Looking at the curriculum as Grades 7 through 12 rather than Grades 9 through 12 led to teaming over the past two years with middle school math teachers from seventh and eighth grade. Having ALL qualified math teachers at the middle school was an improvement goal achieved this year. Likewise, the need to prepare all students for Algebra I prior to high school became apparent as they looked into the combined curriculum.

Only 50% of students were enrolling in this gateway course to college and the focus on getting more students into postsecondary education required a change. So, how is 2012 different?

1. The schedule. There is no more dedicated time for professional development from the district level. All teachers have their prep period from 7:45–8:25 a.m. daily, and they use this time for collaboration.

2. All courses now have a common midterm and a common final. In 2012, the school is looking to standardize unit tests. Tests are now analyzed by groups of teachers and administrators for what percentage of questions test for critical thinking skills in order to ensure rigor. Tests are revised to better prepare students for standardized tests and postsecondary education.

3. The admin team meets every Friday for PLC time. They do book studies and they look at pieces of data, D/F lists (grade lists), and lists of midterm/final comparisons to catch kids who may be falling through the cracks.

4. Staff members who did not embrace teamwork left through retirements or voluntary exits once it became clear that collaboration was a permanent part of the culture. In the words of Cathy Elliott, Assistant Principal, the push for change "just didn't go away. Now being part of the learning community is an expectation, not an option."

5. Teachers and administrators are commonly seen dropping in and out of classrooms to observe, not for evaluation, but for professional feedback and coaching. The new principal wants all administrators to be in 10–12 classrooms a week. People *believe* it is not a part of the evaluation—they do not feel they are being judged. There is ALWAYS more than one person observing at a time, so the observers can norm themselves against other observers.

6. A double classroom has been remodeled with one-way glass and sound so that teachers can use this room to have their lessons observed. The observers can discuss what they are seeing while the lesson is going on. This project was conceived by last year's teacher of the year, who leads it with a colleague. Teachers who volunteer to bring their classes to be observed can come in for 40 minutes and get specific feedback on their lesson.

7. PBIS data are now being used in conjunction with achievement data. Behavior influences academic performance and student engagement influences behavior. The two go hand in hand. For instance, Barbara Gillian felt that the number of fights was an important indicator of safety

and student respect for the school. By focusing on the top five indicators of discipline, and looking for ways to reengage the students who were misbehaving, the school has reduced all five. The number of fights has diminished to the point where the students feel safe, and in turn the staff feels safe. The number of suspensions leveled off last year, so they started to look at days suspended, focusing on keeping kids out of school for as short a time as possible.

8. They have new tools for evaluating PLCs. The Instructional Strategies Inventory developed by Dr. Jerry Valentine is used extensively in observations to assess engagement.

9. They developed their own PLC Fidelity Checklist (see Resource 5) that is reviewed periodically by all PLC teams. A few questions are also used in teacher preconferences for discussions prior to evaluations.

Looking toward the future, Alton High sees itself as ahead of the game. Cathy Elliott notes, "New teacher evaluations to be implemented statewide in 2016 started this year for us."

She also feels ahead in relation to Common Core. Last year they unpacked every standard, having every teacher in every course rate a yes or a no on *every* standard. In 2012, they started with an Excel sheet showing how many times every standard was covered in every course. Now they are looking for gaps and overlaps, concentrating on the A skills (essential), with B skills (supporting the A) given appropriate weight.

Cathy is also proud of the fact that in 2010, Alton High for the first time received a bronze award from *U.S. News & World Report's* best high schools in America. According to Cathy, this validated everything they had done. She notes, "Alton High was saved by NCLB," which forced them to look critically at how every student was doing. When they found that everything was disjointed and everyone was in their own little world, the journey with PLC began. She concludes, "Now you know what? We have happy students! And more than that, we have happy teachers. The results speak for themselves."

Moving Forward

This case study offers a decadelong review of change in one district that dealt with and overcame many of the "10 routes to failure" described in this chapter. Catalyzed initially by the need to turn around low performance, the district now boasts scores above state average, and includes an award-winning high school. In between they had to overcome fear and cynicism about "yet another" initiative. The nine building leaders supported their staffs individually and then collectively created lateral support and pressure for the change, and concurrently new norms. Eventually peer pressure and support across the district was the engine for a culture of continued improvement, fed by built-in feedback loops of hard data and stories of improved student performance. Each meeting of the schools and their leadership teams included celebrations of success, which ultimately trumped cynicism, and became the new norm.

The next chapter provides the research base for the rest of this book. It explores how relational trust provides a foundation for a true learning community: one that is likely to be sustained through many challenges, including change of leadership.

CHAPTER 4

Relational Trust as Foundation for the Learning Community

The relationship among the adults in the schoolhouse has more impact on the quality and the character of the schoolhouse— and on the accomplishments of youngsters—than any other factor.

—Roland Barth, 2001a, *Learning by Heart*

In the past, the technical aspects of a given model (such as total quality management) or the process for shaping cultures (such as professional learning communities) have gained widespread acceptance. The relationships and human side of change, however, are often left to chance (Bryant, 2009). The following section is focused on recent data that correlate "relational trust" with student success. In essence, every effective, sustainable, professional learning community (PLC) that we have worked with in the past 20 years was founded on a consensus of what it meant to be such a community and on relational trust. The next section addresses the meaning, importance, and development of *relational trust*.

Relational Trust

Relationships are at the core of successful learning communities as well as student success (Bryk, Sebring, Allensworth, Luppescu, & Easton, 2010; Bryk & Schneider, 2002; Ferguson, 2002; Haynes, Emmons, & Woodruff, 1998; Kruse, Seashore Louis, & Bryk, 1994; Meier, 1995; Wilcox & Angelis, 2009). This is particularly true for students who are "minorities" in their schools (Ferguson, 2002). A study of middle schools concluded: "One of the most striking features identified by teachers and administrators in higher-performing middle schools and credited as the primary reason for their success is 'respectful' and 'trusting' relations." As one administrator stated: "the single, most important thing . . . is to build trust with your faculty" (Wilcox & Angelis, 2009, p. 12). In its *Set for Success* report of 2002, the Ewing Marion Kauffman Foundation summarizes, "Stated simply, positive relationships are essential to a child's ability to grow up healthy and achieve later social, emotional, and academic success" (p. 2).

Those positive relationships begin with the adults in the school building and district. The personal rapport among teachers, students, and parents influences students' school attendance and their sustained efforts at difficult school tasks (Bryk & Driscoll, 1998; Bryk, Lee, & Holland, 1993; Bryk & Schneider, 2002; Bryk, Sebring, Allensworth, Luppescu, & Easton, 2010; Bryk & Thum, 1989; Fullan 1991; Porter, Murphy, Goldring, Elliott, Polikoff, & May, 2008). The history of relations between the principal and the teaching staff determines teachers' willingness to take on new initiatives, and the relationships among adults in the school greatly influence the extent to which students in that school will succeed academically (Barth, 2001b; Bryk & Schneider, 2002; Bryk et al., 2010; Goddard, Salloum, & Berebitsky, 2009; Kochanek, 2005; Marzano, Waters, & McNulty, 2005; Tschannen-Moran, 2004). In essence, if the adults in the building get along, so will the students.

The relationship among adults is an area for potential improvement in a great many schools. This is true of business as well; a 2009 international study reveals that "the majority of people trust a stranger more than they do their boss!" (Kouzes & Posner, 2010; Segalla, 2009). The corollary to schools in terms of performance in high-trust companies is similar as well: high-trust organizations outperform their low-trust peers by 286% total return to shareholders (Shockley-Zalabak, Morreale, & Hackman, 2010).

While it is relatively easy to install the technical aspects of a PLC—systems to collect data, time for teams to meet, and so on—the tough part is subtler, less scripted, and more interpersonal (Blankstein, 2007).

Building meaningful and productive relationships with people is complex; people are less predictable, and their emotions can be scary. How often are school leaders trained in the many nuances of dealing with an angry parent, a disgruntled staff member, or a crying teacher? Where is the how-to manual for these tasks? Moreover, who has time for these elements when the "real" work of increasing student achievement awaits?

As stated earlier (and throughout this book), relationships *are* the real work of school improvement! Without people and relationships, who will administrators lead and how far will followers follow?

Defining Relational Trust

The concept of "relational trust" came from a 5-year study of achievement in math and literacy in 12 Chicago public schools by the Center for School Improvement at the University of Chicago. As discussed in Bryk and Schneider (2002), these systematic case studies were augmented by researchers' clinical observations and field notes. The research results demonstrated that high-trust schools were three times more likely to improve in reading and math than those with very weak levels of trust; and those that remained low-trust over the course of the study had virtually no chance of improving in either reading or math.

The concept of *relational* trust in schools focuses on distinct role relationships and the obligations and expectations associated with each. When these expectations are met, trust is enhanced. When a person's expectations of another person are not met, trust is diminished.

There are four components of relational trust:

1. *Respect* for the importance of a person's role, as well as their viewpoint. Listening carefully augments a sense of respect and builds trust.

2. *Competence* to administer your role. This includes one's ability to act on commitments. On the building level, it is also associated with having respectful discipline, an orderly and safe school, and meaningful instruction and assessment.

3. *Personal regard for others* is highly associated with reducing a sense of vulnerability and with general caring. This is especially demonstrated by extending oneself beyond the requirement of one's role or normal duties—finding out about a staff member's personal challenges, helping teachers develop their careers, and so on.

4. *Integrity* in this context means alignment of words, actions, and ethics. Does this person keep his or her word, and are the intentions ethical? (Bryk & Schneider, 2002, pp. 23–26)

Communication is multifaceted and can be enhanced with an understanding of the framework shown in Figure 4.1. Thus, if the adults in the building cocreate a project with one another and/or with students (e.g., the anti-bullying day at Ridgewood Middle School discussed in Chapter 1), the shared reality is expanded, leading to more communication and greater affinity. If any side of the triangle is activated, then there is a greater chance to strengthen the other two sides.

Figure 4.1   Communication Framework to Enhance Affinity

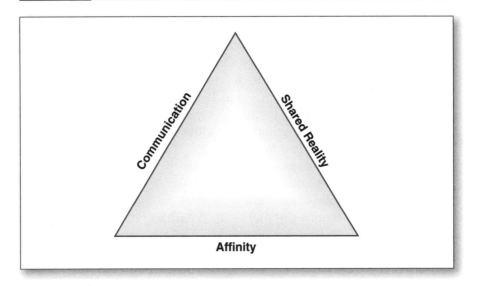

The challenge often comes in *listening* to others (respect) and their beliefs about your behavior (competence, personal regard, and integrity). For this reason, it is best to check in with people to determine their perspective of a given situation.

Building Trust Over Time

Here is how Carolyn Powers, an administrator, worked over time with her teams to build trust.

Each time I have taken a new administrative position, no matter how effective and successful I was at my last position, I started at the bottom on the trust scale and had to work my way up. The more informal information exchanged between individual staff members and me, the more I listened and took notes, the more I observed and confirmed the importance of each person at the school, the closer I came to a bit of trust. Time builds trust, walking the talk, and being visible and interacting with children builds trust. Calling parents to share the good news about their children builds trust. Without trust, complaints go directly to the superintendent, teachers call the union, and children do not feel anyone cares about them. With trust, parents call when they have an issue or stop me in the hallway; teachers know an open door means open, honest dialogue; and the union calls me in order to help my year be successful. Relationships are the key to success. Relationships build trust. Effective communication builds relationships. (personal communication, 2009)

Carolyn presented the following question to her staff: What can the new principal do in order to begin to fit into the culture of this school? The answer? Visit the classrooms, observe, and ask questions. This way, the principal gains understanding of the program and how the teachers view the children. Through dialogue, we move forward together.

In Chapter 1, we saw that Superintendent Marcus Newsome spent months listening to staff in order to help shape their focus as a "Committed Community of Learners." Likewise, O'Neill did the same before pronouncing ALCOA's strategic decision to make zero safety issues their No. 1 goal. In all these cases, the process was the strategy, and that process relied heavily on listening to and engaging the staff. Specific tools for consistently ensuring this kind of engagement follow in Chapter 5.

Strategies for Building Trust

Building relational trust with the staff is a precursor to sustainable success. In our work in thousands of schools and districts, this trust has been built by the leader using various approaches.

One-on-One Strategies

Listen First

It's essential to recognize that everyone wants to be heard. The new-leader syndrome, however, often entails changing things quickly to establish authority. Many veteran leaders, on the other hand, may feel they already know what is best and may move forward without building consensus. In both cases, the "slow" part—listening—of going "fast" is cut out of the process and initiatives are short-lived.

The "listen first" strategy has many components:

1. **Show appreciation via understanding the other point of view.** Surprisingly, effective communication has more to do with emotions than with logic, or intellectual "clarity" (Fisher & Shapiro, 2006). Most often problems arise when people don't *feel* understood. In addition to using simple paraphrasing and checking for understanding (e.g., "I am hearing you say X, Y, & Z"), the effective listener also taps into meta messages that are not directly spoken and then inquires further. For instance, "There are too many mandates!" may also mean "I don't feel capable of meeting new standards." Listening to "the music as well as the words" (Fisher & Shapiro, 2006) means tapping into the emotional tenor of the speaker: "I am *not upset*, thank you!" indicates a message that belies the words.

2. **Finding merit in what the person does, thinks, or feels is important in showing appreciation.** This is true even if you don't agree with the speaker's point of view. In Chapter 2, we saw a change process that involved getting naysayers engaged. In practice it looks something like this: "I know how hard you worked on the past initiative, only to see it abandoned. I appreciate that kind of effort, and understand how it might be difficult to see a new direction enter on the heels of all that work. I ask only that you consider this new approach for now, see how it unfolds, and advise me of your feelings and thoughts about it."

3. **Communicate understanding in words and actions.** In the example in Chapter 1, O'Neill built trust—not only by listening to, accurately identifying, and then voicing the predominant staff concerns about safety, but also by taking many actions. For instance, six months after O'Neill became CEO of Alcoa, he got a call in the middle of the night about the death of a young man who had died while making a repair. O'Neill and his executives reviewed the incident and found dozens of errors, mechanical and human, that led to this travesty. O'Neill then summed it up: "We killed this man. It's my failure of leadership. I caused his death. And it's the failure of all of you in the chain of command" (Duhigg, 2012, p. 116).

The executives were stunned. They had lost men before but, like the Chilean mine company owners, saw it as "part of the business." Now they saw that O'Neill was serious about this idea of zero safety issues.

Within a week, bright yellow safety railings went up at all Alcoa plants. New policies were written up. And O'Neill gave out his number for anyone to call him directly regarding safety concerns. Anyone who had expected that he would spend a couple of weeks on safety and move on got a big surprise: his actions told them another story.

4. **Show appreciation for yourself as well!** This can be done in a positive way that puts you and the listener on the same side: "Like you, I worked very hard on student achievement using the prior set of standards. I don't know how you feel about it, but on my worst day, I feel like I may have wasted a lot of time. It's not easy to move forward, but I feel good that I have made that decision . . ."

Find Common Ground

Finding areas of commonality may be the best way forward—even when they are few in number. Uncovering the underlying issues helps. In practice, one might say something like this: "The research indicates that holding students back in early grades does not work, but I can see your point about the need for there to be some 'rework' in the instruction before Johnny can advance . . ."

Overcommunicate

As Carolyn Powers' story indicates, it is best to do a lot of listening in the relationship-building process. Checking in with people to align their perceptions and your intentions as a leader is also critical. To that end, it helps to clearly communicate one's own perspective or point of view—and to do it often. If this is vague for people, or if there is a void of communication, it is often filled in with the fears, worst-case scenarios, and rumors of others.

Confront Inappropriate Behaviors

Chapter 1 conveys the benefits of using data in a neutral manner to confront behaviors that are not in keeping with the school's mission and values. There is little that will undermine a leader more than to ignore inappropriate behaviors. While it enables people to avoid a short-term conflict, it also erodes trust in the leader. The outcome is that respect for the leader and confidence in the school community's ability to succeed are diminished among those who *are* adhering to the agreed-on norms.

Organizational Strategies

Create Fail-Free Zones

While confronting behaviors is necessary, so is indicating in advance the rules by which people will be judged. Failing in a pilot project or doing poorly in a new instructional practice, for example, should be off-limits. However, by contrast, refusing to be coached, to collaborate, or to modify one's instruction when data reveal the need to do so may be among the areas that a learning community agrees would require intervention. Here are some specific ways to create fail-free zones:

- Adopt a "never finished" stance and expectation in which the new norm is that there is always a better way and continuous improvement is our job (Wilcox & Angelis, 2009, p. 13).
- Eliminate blame as a recourse or conversational option.
- Clarify expectations collaboratively with staff and ideally the students so that everyone is in agreement and fear of failure or fault is reduced.
- Engage staff on a voluntary basis initially to gain support and build capacity. The Case Story below demonstrates how one leadership team introduced learning walks in a nonthreatening manner, beginning with volunteers, calling it peer-to-peer, and initially avoiding any formal evaluations.

Peer-to-Peer Observations

As Duane Thurston and Reggie Rhines explain,

We have a staff that has always worked well together. As we discussed peer-to-peer observations, the benefits were numerous. We had the opportunity to learn from each other and become engaged in relevant conversations about instruction and learning. The challenge, at times, was making sure there was a desirable comfort level and trust as teachers came into classes to observe, learn, and begin conversations. We wanted to ensure that these observations were not seen as evaluative. This was not a situation where teachers were evaluating and "scoring" other teachers. To overcome this challenge, our first step was to simply ask each member of the staff to observe another teacher for a short time and e-mail the positive practices and strategies observed in the classroom. Not only did this let teachers share the good things occurring in classrooms, it also developed a high level of trust within the staff and let them know that this was a process designed to benefit staff and students. As the observations have evolved, we now spend more time in classrooms and take time to ask reflective questions that improve our practices. (personal communication, 2009)

Process Tools for Building Trust

Another example of going "slow" to later go "fast" is to develop the staff's capacity for making the change by creating a common language and knowledge base. This can be facilitated by teams working on a meaningful project together using a structured format. Consider, for example, the use of the guiding questions in Resource 1 to create a common rubric for defining excellent instruction.

Defining a True "Learning Community"

> Various definitions exist . . . but they all feature a common image of a professional community where teachers work collaboratively to reflect on their practice, examine evidence about the relationship between practice and student outcomes, and make changes that improve teaching and learning. . . .
>
> —McLaughlin & Talbert, 2006, pp. 3–4

For more than a decade, a growing confluence of research and practice has indicated that our best hope for success in schools is through the creation of PLCs (McLaughlin, 1993; Mullen & Schunk, 2011). This is very good news indeed. It seems to provide clear direction for educators who are contemplating substantive school change. At the same time, it invites as many questions as it answers.

- What is a learning community in practice?
- What are the key elements for making such a community succeed?
- How do I know if I have succeeded in creating such a community?
- What are my next steps in the process of creating and sustaining a learning community?

There are many definitions of a *professional learning community.* We include a summary of these, as well as a brief background on the rise of interest in this area, in the next section.

Trust and the Learning Community

How do you know if you are working in a professional learning community? Consider (with a smile) these possible indicators:

You know you are in a learning community when . . .

- You enter the school building and are warmly greeted by a parent volunteer.
- You see articles posted in the teacher lounge with highlights all over them.
- You are actually *happy* to see another teacher or an administrator visiting your classroom to observe instruction.
- Colleagues stop by your home on the weekend . . . to talk about work!
- Enhancing student learning is the primary focus of team meetings, and best practices for enhancing their achievement drive decisions.
- SMART goals (see Chapter 5) are set, regularly assessed, and achieved.
- Last year's worst-behaved fourth grader is tutoring a second grader this year.
- During professional development days, the *last* rows of seats are the ones left empty.
- The principal says, "I don't know. Let's research this together."
- When the final bell rings, the teachers and principal aren't the first ones out the door!

More important than the use of one definition or another, however, is the common understanding of what such a community looks and feels like, how one behaves in this context, what the mutual commitments are, and how all of this affects students in general and their academic achievement in particular. It is more common to find school professionals who say they are part of a "learning community" than it is to actually find a PLC in operation. In fact, a shadow version of true learning communities, "performance training sects" (Hargreaves, 2003, p. 176), provides intensive pressure and support for teachers in a limited number of instructional priority areas. While student performance is enhanced, it is rarely sustained and comes at the expense of other instructional areas (Hargreaves, 2003). Moreover, the research indicates that teachers dislike such highly prescriptive programs (Datnow & Castellano, 2000), which often diminish their long-term commitment to their work (Galton, 2000). There are many possible reasons for the disparity between the number of schools that *see* themselves as PLCs and those that actually are.

As we discussed in the previous chapter, making fundamental changes and shifts in assumptions, beliefs, and actions is difficult. It is far easier to make slight modifications to old behaviors and then give the effort a new name. Moreover, this can be reinforcing, because some of these modifications actually *do* bring about modest changes. For example, it is easier to create times when teams meet rather than to build a true collaborative culture in the school (see Chapter 7). One is structural, easily implemented, and *may* still have the benefits of creating a more motivated staff. The collaborative *culture,* however, requires more time, an effective school mission (as defined in Chapter 5), and deeper conversations about the meaning and focus of the collaboration. This collaborative culture also requires discipline to maintain a focus on student learning.

Clarifying terminology *alone* requires time and effort. W. Edwards Deming (1986) wisely called for developing "operational definitions" before undertaking a new project. He would say, for example, "Is this table clean? How could one answer the question without knowing for what purpose or use the table would need to be clean?" (i.e., defining *clean* in operational terms). "If this is to be used to eat on, it may well be clean. Yet this would not be clean enough to place a patient on for an operation" (personal communication, 1989).

Many schools striving to become PLCs, for example, are challenged to come to a common understanding of the word *community.* This is particularly true of both moderately high-performing "cruising schools" and low-performing "sinking schools" (to determine your school's profile, see Resource 1). In these schools, one is more likely to find changes occurring in *professional* structure (e.g., time for collaborative teaming) and even in a *learning* focus (focus on adult pedagogy and student learning). Richard Elmore (2002) describes the challenge:

> The schools that I have observed usually share a strong motivation to learn new teaching practices and a sense of urgency about improving learning for students and teachers. What they lack is a sense of individual and collective agency, or control, over the organizational conditions that affect the learning of students and adults in their schools. (p. 24)

This sense of *collective* agency and control over organizational *conditions* is embodied in the *community* of PLCs. Many schools—especially high schools—lack these qualities. These schools do not often benefit from the deeper meaning implied in the term *community*.

Cohesive Communities

There are several definitions of the word *community*. Here are two:

1. Common character, similarity, likeness, as, *community* of spirit.

2. The people living in the same district, city, and so on under the same laws.

The second definition is more commonly used. It is easier for a group of school professionals to achieve this definition since they generally work together, under the same rules, in the same location.

The first definition, however, is closer to how we would describe the ideal school community—one that leads to sustainable student achievement. "Community is concerned with the deep-structural fabric of interpersonal relations" (Gardner, 1991). "Soundly woven, this fabric permits a shared frame of reference and supports mutual expectations" (Rossi & Stringfield, 1997, p. 3).

Relationships and trust are the glue that holds this kind of community together. A professional community is built on more than a pay-for-service contract in which adults and children run for the exits when the final school bell rings. It is built on more than common geography. It goes beyond symbiosis, common rules, or policies that bind all to *minimum* behaviors. This kind of community is founded on mutual respect, concern, caring, reliability, and commitment to a common, larger cause. In short, it is founded on relational trust described in the previous section.

Creating common understandings, therefore, is hard work. Getting commitment from the school community is even more difficult. And changing fundamental assumptions or beliefs is harder still. Yet these are the challenges inherent in building a true learning community, and the payoff for doing so is enormous. The chapters on building a courageous leadership imperative and overcoming common pitfalls provide a foundation for beginning an enduring, sustainable learning community. The next sections of this chapter indicate the evolution of learning communities and more definitions of the terms used in defining such a community.

Origins and Definitions of the "Learning Community"

Peter Senge (1990) first used the term "learning organization" in his best-seller, *The Fifth Discipline,* and the term soon made its way into the education literature. Thomas Sergiovanni (1992) translated one of Senge's five principles—"team learning"—to an educational context: "The idea of school as a learning community suggests a kind of connectedness among members that resembles what is found in a family, a neighborhood, or some other closely knit group." This and "building shared vision" are two of Senge's original dimensions that have been embraced by the education community.

The concept of a "school-based learning community" was understood to include

- Reflective dialogue among teachers;
- Deprivatization of practice;
- Collective focus on student learning;
- Collaboration; and
- Shared norms and values (adapted from Kruse, Seashore Louis, & Bryk, 1994).

The terms continued to evolve as noted in Figure 4.2.

Synthesizing the research from the above sources, and factoring in research on effective schools, the U.S. Department of Education's criteria for excellent schools, and our own practice in the field, we have distilled the essence of PLCs into the following six principles:

Principle 1. Common mission, vision, values, and goals

Principle 2. Ensuring achievement for all students: creating systems for prevention and intervention

Principle 3. Collaborative teaming focused on teaching and learning

Principle 4. Using data to guide decision making and continuous improvement

Principle 5. Gaining active engagement from family and community

Principle 6. Building sustainable leadership capacity

These principles encompass the focus on student learning and collaboration emphasized in the above research. In addition, as with Shirley Hord's (1997b) definition, the ISLLC (2000–2008) standards, and the larger body of research of Newmann and Wehlage (1995), summarized earlier in this

Figure 4.2 Development of the *Learning Community* Concept

Date	Author	Terminology	Guiding Principles
1990	Peter M. Senge	Five disciplines	1. Systems thinking 2. Personal mastery 3. Mental models 4. Team learning 5. Shared vision
1994	Sharon D. Kruse and Karen Seashore Louis	School-based learning community	1. Reflective dialogue among teachers 2. Deprivatization of practice 3. Collective focus on student learning 4. Collaboration 5. Shared norms and values
1995	Fred M. Newmann and Gary G. Wehlage	Circles of support	1. Student learning 2. Authentic pedagogy 3. School organizational capacity 4. External support
1995	National Education Association Goals Panel	Keys to Excellence for Your School—KEYS 2.0	1. Shared understanding and commitment to high goals 2. Open communication and collaborative problem solving 3. Continuous assessment for teaching and learning 4. Personal and professional learning 5. Resources to support teaching and learning 6. Curriculum and instruction
1997	Shirley Hord	Professional learning community	1. Supportive and shared leadership 2. Shared values and vision 3. Collective learning and application 4. Shared personal practice 5. Supportive conditions

Date	Author	Terminology	Guiding Principles
1998	Richard DuFour and Robert Eaker	Professional learning community	1. Shared mission, vision, values, and goals 2. Collective inquiry 3. Collaborative teams 4. Action orientation and experimentation 5. Continuous improvement 6. Results-oriented
2004, 2010	Alan M. Blankstein	Failure Is Not an Option®	1. Shared mission, vision, values, and goals 2. Prevention and intervention 3. Collaborative teams 4. Data-based decisions 5. Family and community engagement 6. Sustainable leadership capacity
2000–2008	Interstate School Leaders Licensure Consortium (ISLLC)	Standards for educational administration	Promotes the success of all students by 1. Facilitating the development, articulation, implementation, and stewardship of a vision of learning that is shared and supported by the school community 2. Advocating, nurturing, and sustaining a school culture and instructional program conducive to student learning and staff professional growth 3. Ensuring management of the organization, operations, and resources for a safe, efficient, and effective learning environment 4. Collaborating with families and community members, responding to diverse community interests and needs, and mobilizing community resources 5. Acting with integrity, fairness, and in an ethical manner 6. Understanding, responding to, and influencing the larger political, social, economic, legal, and cultural context

Source: HOPE Foundation, *Failure Is Not an Option®* Success Series.

section, our sixth principle explicitly calls for the development of sustainable leadership capacity. Given the extraordinary rate of turnover in educational leadership and the tendency toward "launching" versus "sustaining" learning communities, we have found this principle to be critical to the success of our work with schools throughout North America.

Similarly, as cited in Newmann and Wehlage's (1995) "circles of support" research and the ISLLC standards (see Murphy, Jost, & Shipman, 2000), we have found that actively engaging family and communities (our fifth principle) is essential for long-term support and sustainability of school initiatives. This has been particularly true in times of great change, economic downturn, or intense media pressure on schools. Chapter 9 provides an abundance of research correlating enhanced student achievement and family support.

The prior synthesis of research and our own relevant experiences are presented as an explanation of how we arrived at these working principles for PLCs. Having "one best definition" for this or any other school improvement effort is counterproductive and defies all that we know about change efforts. In fact, there is danger in becoming too attached to one certain speaker, program, or set of principles. It is far more important that whatever is practiced is internally aligned, consistent with the research, and focused on student success. Taking a cue from the medical profession, it is advisable to continually scan for new best practices and to stay current with changes in the research:

> Here on our first day of med. school, we were presented with the short white coats that proclaim us part of the mystery and the discipline of medicine. During that ceremony, the dean said something that was repeated throughout my education: "Half of what we teach you here is wrong—unfortunately, we don't know which half." (Sanders, 2003, p. 29)

Moving Forward

This chapter was meant to serve as a final checkpoint. We have defined purpose as *sustaining student success because failure is not an option* (Chapter 1); developed a courageous leadership imperative for individuals and the entire team (Chapter 2); anticipated and sidestepped common obstacles to success (Chapter 3); and, in this chapter, determined the framework and system for moving forward with a foundation of trust. Now you are prepared to take action. The rest of this book emphasizes specific processes for building a sustainable learning community, beginning with the next chapter on creating common mission, vision, values, and goals.

CHAPTER 5

Principle 1

Common Mission, Vision, Values, and Goals

It takes more than toughness to keep going when the going gets tough. It's vital that you find purpose and significance in what you do.

—James M. Kouzes and Barry Z. Posner, 2010,
The Truth About Leadership

Leaders have the potential to unleash latent capacities in organizations.

—Seashore Louis, Leithwood, Wahlstrom, &
Anderson, 2010; Wallace Foundation, 2011

The research is conclusive and the results are in: teaching and leadership are the No. 1 and No. 2 factors, respectively, in affecting student achievement (National Staff Development Council [NSDC], 2010; Seashore Louis, Leithwood et al., 2010). And while teachers have more influence over student learning in their classrooms, it is only through a particular kind of building and district leadership that the pockets of excellence will spread and become the norm (Blankstein, 2011; Fullan, 2012; Portin et al., 2009). Teachers working collaboratively with the principal, therefore, lead to the greatest gains for students (Brown, Choi, &

Herman, 2011; Wallace Foundation, 2011), and the guiding force for effective collaboration is the leadership team.

Nothing advances the school and overall student achievement more than an effective leadership team:

> There is mounting evidence that if school leaders are to spread teaching and learning excellence beyond isolated classrooms, they need to create high-functioning instructional teams and distribute authority among staff members in the school building (including teacher leaders) to realize that vision and then provide support to help others exercise shared responsibility for improved learning. (Wallace Foundation, 2010b, p. 12)

This instructional team, supported by the district and composed of the building leader and lead teachers, shapes the school culture and enhances instruction both school- and systemwide (Portin et al., 2009; Wallace Foundation, 2011). There is only one problem: for more than a century, educational leaders have not been prepared to effectively play the role of facilitative team leader (Seashore Louis et al., 2010), and teachers as well have a long history of going into the classroom at the beginning of their careers and coming out at the end. Even among the most successful districts in North America, the biggest hole is in "facilitative leadership" (personal communication with Chris Kotowski, DE Department of Education; and Martin Creel, director of Enriched and Innovative Programs, Montgomery County Schools, 2012). This leadership is necessary to build the school culture in order to advance instruction systemwide.

The key insight that has emerged in recent years is that for leaders to be successful, leader*ship* is essential. Creating a high-performing team that is able to shape school culture and guide improvement in instruction is the key to sustainable student success (Hargreaves & Fullan, 2012; Leana, 2011; Wallace Foundation, 2010a, 2011). Moving leadership forward from the managerial role that has been expected for the past several decades (Seashore Louis et al., 2010) to the role of creator, convener, and leader of high-performing teams is the new challenge. It is worth the investment; the payoffs are enormous. Specifically, this approach

- builds collective teacher efficacy (Seashore Louis, Leithwood, Wahlstron, & Anderson, 2010) and closes teacher performance gaps (Leana, 2011, p. 34)
- enhances student performance in math and literacy (Wallace Foundation, 2010a)

- eliminates a sense of isolation and "brings out the energy that exists naturally within people" (Mintzberg, 2004, p. 214)
- fully engages staff and students who move from compliance to collective commitment
- spreads the responsibility of leadership to a team that is better able to lead the enterprise than any *one* person
- saves money on external, off-the-shelf "solutions," replacing them with solutions generated from the internal capacity to take on virtually *any* challenge

The four pillars forming the foundation of school success that are addressed in this chapter are core to defining the school culture. That culture reflects the collective commitment and values of those in the organization. These commitments and values, in turn, drive adult behaviors, which ultimately determine student outcomes. This chapter, therefore, begins with bringing some clarity to the word *culture* and then provides direction in formulating the leadership team that shapes the culture—beginning with the school and district mission, vision, values and goals.

Clarifying Culture

Some schools have productive cultures; others have problematic ones. But *every* school *has* a culture, whether one is aware of it or not. In essence, "culture" is best understood as "the way things are done around here." How would you categorize these three different approaches to introducing the idea of a four-day workweek and other cost-cutting measures?

How Decisions Are Made in Different Cultures

Scenario 1

In her excitement to save the district money and allow plenty of time for student learning, the superintendent studied the four-day workweek under way in other districts. She returned from visiting schools in Massachusetts to share the good data and announce district plans to make the switch, which would clearly be to everyone's advantage.

Later in the parking lot, one teacher shared with another:

Another change and less time to improve students' test scores! Look at these scores from my history class. They're just terrible. Quite a few Fs . . . most of them got Ds. We've been over and over this material, but they just don't seem to care. They don't do their homework, they don't participate in class. I have *no* family support. I'm overwhelmed and don't know what to do!

Scenario 2

In an effort to balance a shrinking budget, the district leadership decided to do a scan of best practices. They locked in on one that was neutral in every way except that it reduced costs—a four-day workweek. They hosted meetings and training of key staff to get their buy-in and to help deliver the message systemwide. If they could implement this the following academic year, no layoffs would have to occur.

Scenario 3

Leadership teams throughout the district had been meeting for more than a year to develop a common language and instructional focus and to strengthen processes for advancing improvements at their respective schools. Based on decisions made during their last meeting, they came to the present meeting with artifacts of their work around closing achievement gaps in several target areas.

There was news that derailed the scheduled agenda, however, and it involved cutting $15M out of the budget in this 50-school district. There were many ways to proceed, and most would likely be painful. The mood and the severity of the challenge did not allow for continuing with the scheduled agenda of that meeting as planned. The first order of business— for all stakeholders in the room—was now to tackle the challenge together. Several possible plans emerged, including a shortened week. In keeping with protocol, the leadership teams created a "reentry" plan so that all members of their school communities would be able to process the same information using identical techniques displayed by the facilitators of this meeting.

How would you categorize each of the above cultures based on the differing leaders' approaches to a similar problem? While the leader in scenario 1 is clearly enthusiastic and well-intentioned, there would likely be an ultimate disconnect between intent and impact. The enthusiastic, charismatic leader may move the organization forward almost single-handedly, but it is at best unsustainable in her absence, and at worst likely to alienate enough people to stall the effort at some point early on.

In scenario 2, there is a more "enlightened" approach to the change effort by enlisting one leadership team, researching the challenge, and attempting to get "buy in" through training and communication. The problem is that people rarely commit to someone else's solution by virtue of getting training, and "buy in" becomes acquiescence or compliance with the final outcome. Moreover, asking for people's input and then proceeding with the predetermined plan is a surefire way to diminish trust.

In the third scenario, the groundwork had been laid to deal with this and virtually any other crisis or opportunity. Lead teams were intact and had an infrastructure and the tools for problem solving. District leadership was transparent, and the challenge was *everyone's* to solve. Since everyone was using a common language and framework for analysis, conversation, and action, they were able to work through this effectively as a district and come to consensus in record time.

The more times that leaders include the staff in meaningful ways, the better the outcome for students. "If test scores are any indicator, the more willing the principals are to spread leadership around, the better for students . . ." (Wallace Foundation, 2011, p. 7).

Moreover, "Effective leadership from all sources—principals, influential teachers, staff teams, and others—is associated with better student performance on math and reading tests" (Wallace Foundation, 2010a).

By contrast, leaders who "go it alone," who fail to trust staff, or who neglect to develop the staff's collective efficacy foster cultures of blame and hopelessness. One high school staff was asked to analyze a situation in which 25% of their students were not passing state tests. After much deliberation, the staff reached a consensus: *It's that middle school! They were sending us students who were unprepared!*

A corollary to a culture of blame is a shift in responsibility for ensuring student learning. Consider the following often-heard statements:

- It's not *my* job to ensure that students *learned* the lesson—my job is to teach it!
- We believe all students can learn, but some learn better than others.

- In general, all students will learn, but *those* kids from *that* neighborhood aren't as smart or as motivated as the rest.
- If we had more_____ (fill in the blank: discipline, resources, time, parental support), *then* I would be successful!

What these statements have in common is that they shift accountability *away* from school professionals. What could be more demotivating for a school community than to believe that they have no power and that what they do makes no difference? As noted, expectations for oneself determine outcomes (Dweck, 2006); and collective teacher efficacy influences student outcomes (Seashore Louis, Leithwood, Wahlstron, & Anderson, 2010) as do beliefs in students (Porter et al., 2008, p. 13).

This chapter provides direction for shaping the school culture by a development of the four pillars of any organization: mission, vision, values, and goals (MVVG). Together they establish the common base on which all of our efforts will be built. The six principles of Failure Is Not an Option act as a system (see Chapter 1) and are not implemented in concrete sequential manner. Thus, the way in which the MVVG are created can also serve as a means of developing leadership capacity. Ideally, it will be the leadership team that leads the development of this foundational pillar. Thus the next section focuses on developing that team.

Developing the Leadership Team

Leadership teams are formed at the school level and ideally are networked with like teams throughout the district using a common framework and language for dialogue and action. The biggest gains come from district-wide use of the leadership team as defined in the list that follows. Yet individual schools can benefit as well. The elements of constituting such teams are outlined next and then reinforced throughout the rest of this book. Specifically, the team will

- **Represent the entire school building community.** The team should not be a reflection of the principal alone. While this would enhance an early and quick launch, it would be short-lived as those parties not represented slow the progress. While it can be onerous to include "naysayers," as long as they are not CAVE people (Citizens Against Virtually Everything), it is a good idea to have the "yeah buts" show up during the leadership team meetings rather than in the parking lot. Team members need to make the necessary time commitment and be open to the process that unfolds.

- **Constitute itself.** Using the guidelines of Principle 1 in this chapter, the team clarifies its purpose. This correlates with the actions of courageous leaders (Chapter 2) and with the school and districts' mission in the next section of this chapter.
- **Create meaningful protocols.** Again using the guidelines, the team determines its norms, how they will interact with one another, resolve conflicts, and so forth. This corresponds on an organizational level with the Values section of this chapter.
- **Align its focus with SMART goals for the organization and choose a starting point.**
- **Determine the process and framework for action.** Having a common language and the means to make cohesion out of the cacophony often found in schools is critical to coordinated action by the team. The previous chapter provided questions for leading teams to the creation of a specific and common rubric defining good instruction. Likewise, the team needs clarity, common language, and a well-researched system or framework for coordinating action in general.
- **Choose tools and align them with the focus and framework.** There are many such tools to draw on and they are selected based on what the team needs to get done and the manner in which the team operates (i.e., culture). The tools in this book provide this alignment.
- **Create engagement or reentry plans.** These help eliminate the inside-outside syndrome in which those not attending the team meetings feel left out. A plan to return and effectively engage others is needed at the end of each lead team meeting.
- **Return, report, and refine the new learning as it becomes the norm.** Ultimately, both the processes of change and the new changes themselves become embedded in the culture.

This infrastructure is an important assist to the development of high-performing leadership teams. Since 2001, this process along with specific tools to advance the dialogue have been continuously refined and field-tested in hundreds of schools. The team can now move forward on developing, or more likely refining, the organization's mission, vision, values, and goals.

The 21st Century Mission

The mission of an organization is essential to its success. A mission statement should be created and published as a means of giving those involved with the organization a clear understanding of its purpose for existence.

Mission statements are found everywhere—in schools, big businesses, small businesses, nonprofit organizations, organized religion, and at all levels of government. They are a popular management tool used by corporations to motivate stakeholders and keep everyone on the same page. A quick survey of mission statements reveals a common pattern: they use superlatives and absolutes. Such an approach leaves people feeling as though they had cotton candy for lunch: happy but still hungry for the real meal! Phrases like *world's best, premier, largest,* and *first choice of customers everywhere* abound. How "premier" status will be attained and how "best" will be measured are rarely clarified or discussed.

Schools and school districts also have mission statements—and they should. Unfortunately, education is not exempt from the tendency toward generic, vague, and meaningless mission statements. In their mission statements, *effective* schools move beyond simply stating generic hopes for their students.

The four critical questions to be addressed in the mission statement are, by and large, *not* new:

1. If we expect all students to learn, *what* is it we expect them to learn (Tyler, 1949)?

2. *How* will we know if they are learning it (Tyler, 1949)?

3. *How* will we ensure an engaging, relevant pedagogy (Blankstein, 2004)?

4. What will we do when they *don't* learn?

An effective mission statement must be specific enough to answer all four of these questions. If it does not, it will lack resonance for staff members, and it will quickly be forgotten or written off as meaningless. Because most schools already have a mission statement, it is best to review it in light of these criteria, and with the larger community defining 21st century educational needs. More expansive missions could involve creating the school as hub of the community (see Chapter 9) or ensuring successful student transitions from high school to careers and/or higher education. The P-16 and P-20 councils that are emerging in many states, including Kentucky, are breaking down walls across disciplines. This is leading to new preparation programs, better connections to meaningful work experiences for students, and opening the doors to exciting project-based learning opportunities (see Chapter 6).

Mission: Every Student Goes to College

Deborah Wortham, a district administrator, shared the following story about how she put the power of a school mission into action to reclaim a once successful school district that was heading south.

> As the central office administrator, I introduced myself by walking the halls and visiting classrooms to make sure everyone knew the former principal had been removed.
>
> Just one week prior, students had refused to go to class. They were in an uproar because their annual rally had been cancelled in response to poor behavior: roaming the halls, cutting class, leaving campus during closed lunch periods, and so on. Teachers and administrators enforced consequences, with the hopes of curbing the negative behaviors, by calling the city police, spraying students with mace, and giving them the ultimatum to go to class or go home.
>
> Parents were outraged by the consequences enforced by the teachers and administrators, and the students had put their anger into action. To encourage students to return to class, I asked them, "Where are you going to college?" They responded with the name of a college (true or not). My response was, "You can't get there from here [the hallway]!" This choice, and its outcomes, is a lesson in the value, power, and capacity for positive change that principals have when they choose to implement the mission of a school.
>
> I decided to devote the first professional development session with teachers to reviewing the mission statement. Did it respond to the four questions?
>
> 1. What should students learn?
>
> 2. How will we ensure engaging pedagogy?

(Continued)

(Continued)

3. How will we know if we are achieving it?

4. What will we do to guarantee success?

In that session, commitment was reignited! The teachers rallied around the mission statement, which stated that the reason the school existed was to get students into college. They rallied around the rich history of the school and the strong alumni. They rallied around the real responses to the questions and provided data to prove that they were achieving their goal. They spent time discussing ways to guarantee success. They knew that they could not continue in the manner in which they were headed. They had lost sight of their mission. They needed someone to navigate the course again.

The teachers left that session with a determination to stay focused on the mission of the school. They each were assigned a senior student to mentor. The goal was to work with each senior and support their quest for acceptance into college. At the end of the year, the school had the highest graduation rate of all 43 high schools in the district! They announced a total of $17 million in college scholarships and financial aid. Of the 350 graduates, 2 enrolled in the armed services, the rest in either a two-year or a four-year college or university! Oh, let's not forget the lone summer school graduate! (personal communication, 2009)

What Is Mission?

In effective schools, the mission statement goes far beyond an expression of "wishful thinking." The mission statement can serve as the bedrock of the school's daily activities and policies. It should be fundamental to every decision at every level. An effective mission statement expresses the school's purpose—its essential reason for educating in the first place. It expresses why a school *exists*.

The mission serves as a polestar, or guiding principle, for a school. Just as a ship sails toward but never actually reaches its guiding star, we too strive toward but never actually fulfill our mission. Why? Because as long as the world continues to change and evolve, our students' needs will change, and we will need to develop new ways to respond.

What *Good* Looks Like

The best mission statements are clear about why the organization exists and what will be done to ensure that the purpose is met. The mission statement serves the organization by providing specifics about

1. What do we want to do?

2. How will we know if we are succeeding?

3. What will we do to ensure success?

Given these three questions, which of the following mission statements would you consider effective? Mark each one with an E for effective or an I for ineffective, and note why you made the selection.

■■■

Mission 1 _____

The mission of this school district is to ensure that each and every student is prepared to succeed in life. This is accomplished in an environment of trust and respect that fosters positive attitudes toward self, others, work, and responsible citizenship. We are dedicated to maximizing individual potential and developing lifelong learners who will be contributing members in a global society.

Mission 2 _____

The mission of our school is to create and maintain an environment that ensures that every member of the school community reaches a high level of 21st century skills development and academic achievement as determined by state and national standards. Students will both graduate and go on to a career that pays a living wage or to an institution of higher learning. We commit to a comprehensive system of support to assure this outcome.

Mission 3 _____

It is our mission as a school district to educate students to be creative, responsible, self-sufficient citizens who have the capacity and motivation for continued individual growth and who will have the ability to make a positive contribution in our society.

Mission 4 _____

We are committed to the academic excellence of every student by empowering them with the means for the successful completion of high educational standards and by challenging them to become productive members of society.

■ ■ ■

What's your analysis? Consider the following.

The examples numbered 1 and 3 above do not attempt to clearly define *success* in measurable ways. "Success in life" would demand that we wait too long for feedback on how a school community is doing in fulfilling its mission. Similarly, terms like *creative* and *responsible* are vague and hard to measure.

Example number 4 provides more specificity on both the definition of students' success and how it will be measured (by "high educational standards"). However, it lacks the clarity to answer the third question ("What will we do to ensure success?"). Number 2 does answer this question.

Only the second example above addresses all the questions. But be aware: Photocopying this statement and hanging it underneath the office clock for all to see will not improve your school. It is the process of collaboratively creating a mission and spelling out all the specifics that are not provided in a generic mission statement that will lead to school improvements and cultural shifts. Figure 5.1 summarizes some of the differences between traditional and more effective mission statements. Here is another example of an effective mission statement:

Implementation Guidelines

Most schools have no problem creating a mission statement. A small number of people can sit down at a restaurant and hammer one out before the food arrives. The discussions leading to the final document, however, are as important as the final document itself. It is critical that the process involve representatives from all stakeholder groups—teachers, paraeducators (instructional assistants), administrators, community members, students, and parents. It is equally important that those involved reflect ethnic and socioeconomic diversity, as well as diverse learning styles. A statement of mission has little meaning or impact unless it reflects the thoughts of the school community and is collectively embraced by those whom it affects.

Figure 5.1 Effective Mission Statements

Traditional Mission Statements ...	Effective Mission Statements ...
Are vague or generic	Are clear
Say all kids can learn	Are specific (what exactly are students supposed to learn?)
Do not define learning	Are measurable (how do we know students have learned?)
Do not address the possibility of failure	Provide for failure (how do we respond when students don't learn?)

Source: Failure Is Not an Option® video series, HOPE Foundation, 2002.

There are various ways to collaboratively create a mission statement. The first step for any process should be to evaluate what already exists. Using the criteria that have been laid out, ask stakeholders to evaluate and revise the statement, using any of the following methods.

1. **Assemble a task force** made up of representatives from each stakeholder group. In this strategy, the representatives are responsible for soliciting feedback from and accurately representing the views of their constituencies. They are also responsible for sharing drafts of the evolving statements with their respective groups.

2. **Collect the views of each stakeholder group** in a more formal way, perhaps through a written survey instrument. Convene representative focus groups, then examine and discuss the views obtained through the survey. Ultimately, the focus groups report their findings to a task force, which is responsible for drafting the statement.

3. **Small-group work** is still another approach, used successfully in Alton, Illinois, that brings stakeholders together for small-group work around the four questions (see Chapter 3). In this approach, groups of representative stakeholders are first reminded of the four critical questions that their mission statement must answer. They then form small groups of five to seven people, and each group drafts a complete mission statement. The groups' statements are

posted on the walls around the room, and participants do a "gallery walk," reviewing each statement and offering feedback on sticky notes. At the end of the session, the school's leadership team collects all the drafts and sticky notes and uses them to write a statement—which then goes out for more feedback from all stakeholders.

4. **A "snowball" method** can also yield good results. In this approach, all stakeholders are paired into groups of two. After each initial pair drafts a statement, two pairs join together to share their thoughts and merge their statements into one. That group of four joins with another group of four, and the new group of eight then does the same. The process is repeated until there is one comprehensive statement that incorporates all stakeholder feedback. This statement is then reviewed by a representative group in light of the criteria for a good mission statement. The resulting statement is circulated for final approval.

In smaller schools, the above approaches can be, and ideally are, used with the entire school staff. Doing so takes longer, but it deepens the commitment to the outcome. In any case, it is vital to focus the discussion around the purpose and the three questions that ask for the necessary specifics. Collecting feedback from all stakeholder groups helps to ensure that the mission statement provides enough detail and is meaningful. Such an outcome requires plenty of time for thoughtful reflection and response—as well as time for writing, reviewing, and revising the statement through a step-by-step outline of the mission development process.

Sustaining Success

Once you have developed an effective mission, your next challenge is to establish it in action and keep it alive. In all schools, the entire student body is replaced every three to six years, and in a growing number of schools, staff turnover is even more frequent. How can you ensure that your mission statement remains a living, integral part of the school experience? Here are some strategies:

- Display your mission statement prominently within the school and in places where the school presents itself to the public, for instance, on your website, press releases, letterhead, and the like.

- Make sure the mission is cited as a guide whenever staff meets to set goals, plan programs, make decisions, or discuss problems. In Fort Wayne, Indiana, schoolwide plans and goals are regularly presented to other school, district, and board leaders for review and critical, friendly feedback to assure alignment of plans with MVVG.
- Coach teacher leaders in using the mission as a guiding force in their team meetings. Teachers' understanding of their role in maintaining the mission is critical for success.
- Frequently evaluate the school's policies and procedures to ensure their adherence to the mission.
- Schedule time to familiarize new staff and students with the mission. This should include in-depth discussions about the implications for how the school operates.
- Respond quickly and correctively to any and all failures to act in accordance with the school's mission.
- Formally review and update your mission every four to five years, or sooner in the case of fundamental shifts in educational demands. Examples include demands brought on by new standards, or requirements of fundamentally different learning outcomes (like 21C skills).

The Vision

> The capacity to imagine and articulate exciting future possibilities is the defining competence of leaders.
>
> —Kouzes & Posner, 2010, p. 46

Similar to creating a mission, creating a vision is another common part of the planning process in most organizations today. The word *vision* is used as an adjective (the visionary leader), a noun (a vision for the community), and even as a verb (visioning the future). But what exactly *is* this elusive vision—and where do you get one?

What Is Vision?

Whereas the mission statement reminds us of why we exist, a vision paints a picture of what we can become. Most of us employ vision in our personal lives. We strive toward a better, future version of ourselves that may be wealthier, smarter, better organized, healthier, and so forth. We use that vision to guide our behaviors on both a long-term and short-term basis.

A school's vision serves the same purpose—that is, it offers a realistic alternative for a better future. It says, "This is what we want to be." Just as our own vision guides the personal or professional course we follow, a school's vision should guide the collective direction of its stakeholders. It should provide a compelling sense of where the school is headed and, in broad terms, what must be accomplished in the future to fulfill the school's purpose. Every decision made, every program implemented, every policy instituted, and all goals should align with this vision.

Without a common vision, decisions are made randomly. At best, policies, procedures, and programs will lack unity and fail to adequately support one another. At worst, they will actually work at cross-purposes. Virtually no school lacks for new initiatives or programs; but *most* schools lack cohesion and a unified effort shared between those various programs and initiatives. Whereas the mission statement answers the question "Why do we exist?" the vision statement explains where the school is *headed*.

Vision as a Unifying Force for the District

Carolyn Powers, the director of elementary administration for the Fort Wayne Community School District in Indiana, reflects on how vision can provide a unifying force for the district.

Initially, many of the schools I worked with skipped over the vision statement when they engaged in the school improvement process. They felt they had spent time on a statement years ago and it still applied. They did not want to "waste time" rewriting the statement. They went ahead and created school improvement plans, but ultimately discovered that these plans did not raise student achievement. Consequently, when revisiting the planning process the next year, teams of teachers engaged in a shared vision process with the principal. The different vision statements from the schools related directly to the culture and needs of the individual buildings. From the shared vision, they crafted a statement of purpose for the entire district. With everyone onboard, the action plans for student achievement just fell into place for the teams. (personal communication, 2009)

What *Good* Looks Like

Like mission statements, a good vision statement should be detailed enough to carry meaning. The most successful vision statements are vivid and compelling; they motivate us to strive for an improved future. They provide a foundation for assessing the areas for improvement—and then a plan. Perhaps most important, an effective vision statement describes a *collective* vision and is shared by all stakeholders.

Figure 5.2 provides a comparison of traditional and more effective vision statements.

Figure 5.2   Effective Vision Statements

Traditional Vision Statements ...	Effective Vision Statements ...
Are vague or unimaginable	Are realistic, clear, and compelling
Are created by a select group	Have broad-based buy in
State hopes and wishes	Describe intended change
Are soon forgotten	Guide action

Source: *Failure Is Not an Option*® video series, HOPE Foundation, 2002.

Using these criteria, how would you rate the following vision statements? Mark each one with an E for effective or mark an I for ineffective, and note why you made the selection.

■ ■ ■

Vision 1 _____

As you enter Highland High School, the level of pride and accomplishment is evident. The school is well maintained and has a safe environment, with current technology appropriate to a wide range of curricular and extracurricular activities.

The learning atmosphere, which is exciting, stimulating, and success-oriented, also affords students the opportunity to learn from their mistakes. Since students are engaged in project-based learning and are often presenting their work to external partners, they learn traditional academics, 21st century skills, and character traits like perseverance, collaboration, and creative problem solving.

Students have access to a wide spectrum of academic and extracurricular experiences and are encouraged to widen their worldview by taking full advantage of diverse offerings. They possess a greater freedom of choice in decisions affecting their school community. The school climate engenders respect; students feel free to accept and express ideas without fear or prejudice. Adults are compassionate, competent, committed, consistent, considerate, and enabled.

Students at Highland accept their roles in education. This is evident by the way students accept responsibility for their learning, possess positive attitudes, and maintain well-rounded participation in academics and extracurriculars. Their communication is open, friendly, and caring, not only between students but also with staff. This exists because of respect among students and the adults in their lives. The students are self-motivated and excited about learning. Students have a true sense of direction, with goals and career paths clearly established.

Students possess a high sense of responsibility. Through their sense of good values, positive behavior, and high moral conscience, they hold themselves accountable for their actions. They accept the consequences of the choices they make.

Open communication exists between students and adults through mentoring; the mastering of all levels of communication, including oral and written; and the fostering of positive relationships.

Students come to school prepared, eager to participate, and devoted to their learning. They complete learning projects and assignments without hesitation and are successful because they believe in who they are.

Finally, all students work to become productive adults and contributing members of society. They aspire to be lifelong learners as they prepare and plan for the future.

The entire community embraces involvement in the educational development of all students. The parents and other members of the community demonstrate respect for education through their availability to and support for all members of the school population. Parents take an active role in their child's education by providing basic needs so their child is ready to learn. By learning values and good work ethics at home, the students are prepared to succeed at school. Mutually respectful and cooperative in school and community, parents and staff work together with the vision of helping students become productive members of Highland High School and society. Administrators and guidance counselors are visible and accessible to students.

Vision 2 _____

We envision a school where children and adults work productively toward success for all students. This would involve mutual respect, cooperation, and responsibility on everyone's part.

Vision 3 _____

Our vision is increasing reading skills by 6% in the next three years.

■ ■ ■

What is your analysis of these vision statements? Ours follows.

The second example fails to provide clarity. From our perspective, it is not compelling. The third example is very clear, understandable, and communicable. Yet it is not ambitious and likely won't galvanize the school community.

Although the first vision does not include any quantifiable data, it is very specific in describing a compelling future that is imaginable and feasible. This example, from Highland High School, is our preferred vision of the three.

Implementation Guidelines

Roland Barth (2001a) notes that there are eight ways for an organization to arrive at a vision. Following is an adaptation of his list of methods (pp. 197–204), along with associated advantages and disadvantages (see Figure 5.3).

Of the eight possible ways to come up with a vision, it is clearly the last one—growing a vision—that is most meaningful and effective. Just as with a mission, a vision is not something that can be handed down from on high. It must be cocreated by the entire learning community in order for it to have shared meaning.

Should the vision be developed at the school level or district level? Ideally, both the district leaders and the schools they oversee should have a role in the process.

Figure 5.3   Eight Ways for an Organization to Arrive at a Vision

Method	Definition	Advantage	Disadvantage
Inherit a Vision	Use what's already there.	There is no need to go through the periodic, introspective turmoil of crafting a vision.	The vision was engraved in the granite of the past, whereas faculty come from the present and the students must be prepared for the future.
Explicate a Vision	Make overt what has been covert by putting it in writing.	The vision is comfortable, genuine, and already existing.	This doesn't ask, "What would we like to be doing in the future?" Waking a sleeping baby often causes noise—we uncover what we don't want to hear.
Refine a Vision	Take inventory of past practice, present aspirations, and tune up for the 21st century.	The vision is pragmatic; it has something in it for everyone.	This can become an exercise in putting new patches on a defective tire.
Buy a Vision	Use one from a "model."	Most are rich, coherent, and fundamentally different from business as usual; those who don't like it can "shoot" at the creator rather than each other.	Looking outside reinforces the belief that those inside are unable to get their own house in order, perpetuating a sense of helplessness.
Inflict a Vision	A person or office outside the school supplies the vision.	It can come quickly and be uniformly and impressively portrayed throughout the district.	Teachers and principals are gifted and talented at offering superficial compliance to an imposed ideology while at the same time thwarting it.

Method	Definition	Advantage	Disadvantage
Hire a Vision	When things aren't going well, get a new principal with a better vision.	Change in leadership may bring a change in culture.	The principal's vision equals the school's vision, which sustains the paternalistic feeling that "This is the principal's vision, not ours."
Homogenize a Vision	Invite major constituencies to reveal their personal mission; common elements become the school's mission.	There is little in the final vision that is not in the vision of each contributor; little is unfamiliar or threatening.	People feel there is much in their personal vision that is not in the school vision and so lose interest; the least common denominator excludes out-of-the-box thinking (often the fresh, innovative, and most promising ideas of a few individuals).
Grow a Vision	Members of the school community devise a process for examining their school, and then create together a vision that provides a profound sense of purpose for each of its members. The collective vision emerges from the personal visions of each member.	It enlists and reflects not the common thinking, but the best thinking, beliefs, ideals, and ideas of the entire school community.	It is time-consuming; individuals must dig deep to come to grips with personal vision.

Source: Adapted from Barth, 2001a.

Should the development process involve only school personnel, or should it involve the larger community? Hargreaves' research (2001) calls for (1) developing (emotional) depth or connection to the effort, (2) breadth in terms of who is involved, and (3) sustainability in terms of leadership transition plans in order to achieve the best results. In light of this, school leaders gain the best long-term outcomes by deeply involving the broader school community in creating the vision.

The vision should also be rooted in research on best practices and reflect the school's history and existing culture. Ideally, the following information is gathered in preparation for creating a vision:

- Relevant information about the school or district, that is, data on parent and student perceptions and engagement, student success, and staff and faculty performance; copies of prior vision or values statements, internal and external factors affecting the school or district, findings of visitation teams who evaluated the school and district for accreditation purposes, longitudinal achievement data, and community survey results
- Research on school culture
- Research on characteristics of high-performing schools and districts
- Research on school change and reculturing
- An honest assessment of the current conditions in the school or district

Once stakeholders have had an opportunity to review the background information referenced above, they or a subset of the school leadership team can begin drafting the vision. Vision statements tend to be thoughtful, fairly lengthy documents that encompass many aspects of a school. For example, a school's vision might be divided into such sections as "curriculum," "attention to individual students," "personnel," "leadership," "students," "climate," and "community partnerships." The organization of the statement is not important, but the vision should include the ideas of all stakeholders and should touch on all aspects of the school deemed significant to realizing the ideal.

One method, used successfully by Linda Jonaitis, principal of Highland High School in Highland, Indiana, involves having all stakeholders make lists of the things that they think are important for a good school. The stakeholders then form groups of 8 to 10 people, combine their lists, and collaboratively agree on the top 10. The school improvement team takes the top 10 lists from all the groups and clusters the statements by common theme. The school improvement team divides into groups, with each group taking one of those common themes, and writes a paragraph that captures all the statements in that theme.

A similar approach requires participants to write their initial statements—as many as they wish—on sticky notes. Participants then work together to group the notes into clusters. Each cluster is assigned a name, which is used as a vision category. As with the previous method, small groups take the various categories and draft minivisions. Ultimately, all the minivisions are combined into a single statement and sent to stakeholders for feedback. A step-by-step process for developing the vision statement is found in this chapter.

The Values

Research indicates that in both business and education, an established set of shared values is a key factor in an organization's success (Kouzes & Posner, 2010). Echoing the actions taken in the Chilean disaster from Chapter 1 and the Courageous Leadership paradigm in Chapter 2, Kouzes and Posner write:

> **Video Connection**
>
>
>
> www.corwin.com/
> failureisnotan
> option3
>
> In Video 5.1, Principal Sandro Garcia from Timberview Elementary School leads a staff roundtable discussion about continuity of culture, including how to share the school's mission, vision, values, and goals with new teachers, administrators, and other staff members.
>
> Think It Through: The staff members discuss the need to show faculty and students that their mission is not just something that "sounds like a good thing to put on a website." Consider the framework that is currently in place at your school to help others invest in the mission, vision, values, and goals. Identify what further steps you might take to increase their investment.

"Before you can effectively lead others, you have to understand who you are, where you come from, and the values that guide you" (p. 31). Values represent the core of who you are individually and as an organization, and are particularly critical to clarify in turbulent times.

What Are Values?

Values are the attitudes and behaviors an organization embraces. They represent commitments we make regarding how we will behave on a daily basis in order to become the school we want to be. They are established and articulated guidelines we live by. "Values are best described in terms of behavior: If we operate as we should, what would an observer see us doing?" (Senge, Ross, Smith, Roberts, & Kleiner, 1994).

Values endure. They do not fluctuate with staffing changes, funding shifts, or trends in instructional methodology. They are never compromised for a short-term gain or a quick solution to a problem (see Two Approaches to High-Stakes Testing in Chapter 10). Values express a *shared* commitment to certain behaviors; they do not result from a top-down dictate—that is, they start with "*We* will," not "*You* will."

Ideally, values reflect the attitudes and beliefs of the school community. Ultimately, after they are created, value statements guide the behavior of everyone in the organization. School leaders cannot read minds or respond to perceptions of what people in the organization *believe.* Leaders can inquire as to staff members' beliefs on a given topic, but responses may or may not be forthcoming. At the very least, however, after having collectively created values, it is the leader's role to hold people to *behaviors* that mirror those values (as opposed to *beliefs*).

In high-performing schools, eventually the school *staff* will also help bring individuals' behaviors into line with stated values. Acting in accordance with these stated values becomes part of the culture. Lateral accountability for shared commitments and agreed behaviors becomes the province of the entire school community. In a "paired school" model we helped develop in one high-performing district, the entire staff of one school became responsible for and committed to the success of the staff of two other schools (Hargreaves, 2005; see also Chapter 1 on networks).

Without a shared commitment to a core base of values, schools fall into the "my belief versus your belief" pattern. These schools may have certain individuals or factions that operate as "rogue agents," taking actions that run counter to the school's mission and vision. For example, imagine a school with a mission that states that all children can achieve at a high level and that it will provide an environment to make that happen. Yet many classrooms in that same school have long lists of prerequisite criteria—many of which are quite subjective—that students must meet in order to access the more rigorous curricular offerings. Clearly, such behaviors do not support the school's mission. Therefore, it lacks a *functional* set of values—a schoolwide statement that dictates *all* behavior.

What *Good* Looks Like

A successful statement of values touches on the most pertinent, pervasive principles shared by a school's stakeholders. The statement goes to the core of our belief and the depth of our commitment. Note that this does not mean identifying what stakeholders *should* commit to; we cannot set values and insist that others embrace them. Core values do not come from a check-off menu of options or a list of values that people must "buy into." People must be predisposed to them.

A statement of values that captures only core beliefs should be relatively brief. It may contain as many as 10 values—but 5 or 6 is a more manageable number. Each value should be simply stated so that the general meaning is easy to grasp and remember. It should also relate directly to the vision statement.

The question to consider when articulating values is not just what values are appropriate for our school, but what values *specifically support* our vision statement and are aligned with our mission. For example, the value statement "We will give students multiple opportunities to learn and to demonstrate their accomplishments" is consistent with a mission that states "All students will learn at high levels, in accordance with state standards." If a teacher is failing half of the students in his or her classroom year after year, that behavior will not be in line with the school's values or mission.

The values of a school articulate what "we will" *do* and how "we will" *behave* (i.e., "We will model," "We will support," "We will provide")—not what we *believe.* Although a statement of beliefs might be useful in some circumstances, it lacks the critical element of prescribing action—of telling us what we need to *do* to make our vision a reality.

Effective values are

- few in number;
- direct and simply stated;
- focused on behaviors, not beliefs; and
- linked to the vision statement.

Implementation Guidelines

Some view the establishment of a set of values as the most challenging component of a school's foundation because it requires a commitment to changing behaviors. It can be difficult to convey the full significance of values to staff members and get them to truly grapple with their beliefs and their perceived roles in the teaching and learning process. We must all "live into" our values by evaluating our behaviors over time.

In order for serious discussions among stakeholders to be successful, schools must invest time. As with developing mission and vision, it is best to start the process by breaking up into small groups. This helps engage participants and fosters honest, genuine dialogue. One easy approach is simply to review the school's vision statement with participants and then ask, "How do we need to behave to make this happen?" Allow time to discuss and draft answers to such questions. Then continue to consolidate lists using the snowball technique described earlier, or have a task force collect the responses and use them to draft a statement of values.

Another approach is to have participants divide into pairs. Have the pairs ask each other, "What are some of the behaviors that we . . . or some . . . or all of us engage in that are not consistent with our mission and vision?" After they have identified what they would like to see changed, have them ask each other, "What will you commit to doing, starting today, to change that?" Have participants write down their list of commitments. The facilitator can then ask each person to report out as he or she consolidates the comments onto one sheet of paper. Or the facilitator might collect the lists and consolidate them into a master list. In either case, it is best to go back to the staff to ask for a collective commitment to the final list.

Whatever process you use, be sure participants know that it is not trivial. Although it may be easy to get a list of values that everyone says they agree to, it is far more difficult to arrive at a list of values everyone is actually willing to *live* by. One way to partially safeguard against abuses of the collective values is to go down the list and pose scenarios that might lead to someone bypassing a given value. Discuss the scenario and then ask participants to propose alternatives to behaving counter to the values.

The more energy and time you put into the process, the more effective your values will be at guiding day-to-day decision making.

The Goals

We must replace complex, long-term plans with simpler plans that focus on actual teaching lessons and units created in true "learning communities" that promote team-based, short-term thought and action.

—Mike Schmoker, 2004, *Tipping Point: From Feckless Reform to Substantive Instructional Improvement*

The three components of a successful school's foundation discussed thus far are meant for long-range planning. A school's vision, for example, may take several years to reach. Values are also ongoing; we commit to them for as long as we are part of the organization.

But we also need short-term successes to help us stay focused and motivated. In fact, little will energize and motivate staff more than success itself. Goals should be structured, therefore, to ensure quick wins as the team builds capacity for more complex action. And feedback loops that are self-sustaining and easy for teachers to regularly access—"feedback on demand"—are far better than hearing "good job" at the monthly meeting from the building or district leader.

It is very difficult to commit to and work toward something that has no definite "success point" or preidentified benchmark that will allow us to take a deep breath, pat ourselves on the back, and look with pride at a job well done. Most of us need to feel that we are making progress and getting things done. It is through the judicious use of well-written goals—the fourth component of our foundation—that this need can be met.

Clear attainable goals are particularly important in school cultures with little previous record of success. The process of setting, committing to, and accomplishing short-term goals builds credibility and trust. It can also serve as the beginning of positive momentum toward change.

What Are Goals?

If our vision is the grand target—a distant ideal that we are striving for—then our goals are the short-term minitargets that we aim for along the way. They break our long, winding journey toward school improvement into manageable, measurable steps. Goals provide intermittent reinforcement for our efforts and provide us with feedback on our progress toward the larger vision.

Goals also serve a more pragmatic purpose. They provide a detailed, short-term orientation for us in relation to our vision. They identify priorities and establish a timeline for our process of change. Equally important, goals establish accountability for stakeholders, ensuring that what needs to happen actually *does* happen.

What *Good* Looks Like

Goals, like the other foundational components we've discussed, are often too vague. A goal that is too vague to be measured is, essentially, worthless. After all, how will you ever know if you reach it? How will you know when to set a new goal?

Effective goals are both specific and measurable. They clearly identify the evidence that must be monitored to assess progress. They also set a time frame for completion. For example, "We will increase our students' average provincial test score by 20% this academic year" is a good, specific goal. "We will help all kids become lifelong learners," on the other hand, is too vague to be useful.

Goals should also focus on the results rather than on the process or the task. It's not uncommon for a school to have task-oriented goals, such as "We will adopt a new curriculum" or "We will have team meetings weekly." Although these are perfectly legitimate *inputs*, a SMART (criteria for SMART goals are listed in Figure 5.4) goal specifies the desired *results* of these actions in terms that are aligned with the school's mission and vision. To be SMART goals, these subgoals must go a step further, to answer the *so that* question: "We will adopt a new curriculum *so that we . . .*"

Ultimately, answering this additional question should get us to the *real* goal for student learning.

Implementation Guidelines

Developing goals for a school requires asking, "What steps do we need to take, in what order, to create our ideal school?" After identifying these steps, a time frame must be set or a deadline for completion. To be most effective, every stakeholder in the school or district should help to set the goals for their individual responsibilities. For example, third-grade teachers should set goals for the third-grade team.

Figure 5.4   SMART Goals

SMART goals are . . .

Specific and Strategic. In this sense, *specific* relates to clarity. *Strategic* relates to alignment with the confirmed mission and vision.

Measurable. In most cases, this means quantifiable.

Attainable. People must believe, based on past data and current capabilities, that success is realistic.

Results-Oriented. This means focusing on the outcome, not the process, for getting there. This refers to the desired end result, versus inputs to the process.

Time-Bound. When will the goal be accomplished?

Source: Failure Is Not an Option® video series, HOPE Foundation, 2002.

How do you choose a goal? How do you decide what will make it measurable, attainable, results-oriented, and time-bound? An earlier vision statement example cited a 6% increase in reading scores. One might ask, "Why 6%? Why not 10% or 20%? Are folks lazy? Are they overly ambitious?"

There are different ways to begin goal setting, and each should take into consideration the idea of initially breaking goals up into those that produce quick wins. Here are a few examples:

- A school may be in academic trouble and have a bottom line that must be achieved.
- A school may look at last year's outcomes and then estimate how much better the school or district can do this year, based on improved processes, technology, or pedagogy.
- A school may start with a long-term vision and determine what needs to be accomplished each year to reach it and then dedicate the resources necessary for the annual improvements.

Regardless of where you begin in the process, it is essential to look at past data, new circumstances, and processes that can be modified to improve results. What will be done *differently* this year from last? How and when will we evaluate whether we are on target? Heed the warning implied in the statement "If you do what you've always done, you'll get what you've always gotten!"

After SMART goals are defined and implemented, they should be monitored continuously and evaluated over time. If clear evidence emerges revealing that the goal or means of achieving it is not bringing about the desired results, then one or both of these should be amended or abandoned. If goals are well chosen, and the means of achieving them are effective, then a careful analysis of the outcome should be made to determine how

Video Connection

www.corwin.com/
failureisnotan
option3

Video 5.2 highlights a brainstorming session in which staff members from Timberview Elementary School identify with new staff specific ways that they can use SMART goals to sustain their mission, vision, values, and goals.

Think It Through: In this video, the teachers talk about how goals must be attainable or else teachers will start to feel "beat down." Look at three or four goals that your school has identified. Consider whether or not each goal is likely to be viewed by staff as attainable, and note any adjustments that you might need to make.

to continue and maintain the improvement over a longer period of time through the goal-setting and monitoring process.

Celebrating Successes

Many schools are reluctant to avail themselves of one of the best strategies for building positive school culture: celebrating success. In addition to concerns about lacking time, some school leaders are reluctant to single out individual achievements. Indeed, some school cultures are committed to mediocrity or egalitarianism to the point of hiding or ignoring successes!

But regular celebrations have the power to make the school's overall values increasingly positive. Moreover, celebrations help mark milestones and build motivation in the long journey of school improvement.

Here are some guidelines for celebrating success:

- Take steps that help assure the celebrations are deemed fair. This involves clarifying in advance exactly what constitutes success for all involved (see SMART goals in Figure 5.4 for additional guidelines).
- Tie celebrations explicitly to organizational vision, values, and goals. This provides an opportunity to reinforce these organizational pillars while providing more clarity, credibility, and rationale for the celebrations.
- Design celebrations that are attainable by all staff members. Having only one celebration with one winner per year can alienate a majority of your staff.
- For formal celebrations, communicate in advance the likely outcomes for success. This affirms the fairness of the approach.
- Make the celebration widely accessible. Involving more people heightens the impact of your school's values and goals for everybody.
- Arrange for both formal and informal celebrations. For example, simply using a staff meeting to congratulate a teacher on his or her excellent job in researching and recommending a new teaching methodology will go a long way toward encouraging others to do the same. Sometimes informal celebrations are needed to provide *timely* encouragement of people's efforts.
- Do not use celebrations to make direct or indirect comparisons between high- and low-achieving staff members. Focus on the positive results you are celebrating.

- Be specific about the nature of the success. "Eleanor actually took the time to visit the home of her most improved student, James," is far better than "Eleanor always helps her students."
- Use stories and be human.
- Build sustainability and community into the celebratory process by allowing staff and students to eventually take it over. Schools can begin early on by involving others in selection committees.

This chapter has outlined specific processes for building the foundation of a professional learning community. That foundation rests on four pillars: mission, vision, values, and goals. Creating a "product" for each of these pillars is technically simple. But the real gains in doing this come from the *process* and the *relationships* that are shaped along the way. Thus, creating common MVVG is an ideal way to effectively use data, build a collaborative team, and develop sustainable leadership capacity (see Principles 4, 3, and 6, respectively).

Challenges and Solutions

Challenge: "This has nothing to do with me and my classroom."
Getting faculty engaged in and supportive of the process can be difficult if they don't perceive it as directly meaningful to them.

Solution: Broad stakeholder involvement at the drafting stage. A top-down dictate will have little effect on the commitment of those on the front lines. The notion of assigning a purpose and a vision for others without obtaining their input is counterproductive. Every stakeholder group needs the opportunity to engage in thinking about a preferred future, to consider what the school stands for and what needs to be done. It is through ownership in the process and the creation of the guiding statements that the plan becomes truly meaningful.

Challenge: "I think we used to have a mission . . . or a vision . . . or something like that."
Too often, the excitement that is generated by a new MVVG statement is short-lived. School staffs become energized during the drafting and unveiling process but sometimes lose interest in the face of the challenges and pressures that are part of their daily routine.

Solution: Constant reinforcement. Keep your MVVG at the forefront of everyone's mind by constant reiteration and references to them in staff meetings, professional development days, and celebrations. Discuss them in orientations with new staff and in introducing the school to new stakeholders. Refer to them during group decision-making sessions. Create posters and hang them on the school walls. Use every opportunity to clarify and reinforce what the school stands for and where it is headed. Most important is confronting behaviors that are inconsistent with these agreed-upon statements of purpose.

Challenge: "I don't have time for more meetings. I have real work to do!"

Time is always at a premium—and it can be a real stumbling block for faculty and staff who are already overworked and exhausted.

Solution: Make the time, and uncover other reasons for resistance. This statement is, on its face, completely legitimate. There is simply no way of getting around it—the process of creating MVVG will require an investment of time. More important, schools will need to make time in the daily schedule for continual professional development. The issue of the necessary investment of time is covered in more detail in Chapter 2 and in Resources 2 and 6.

Moving Forward

In this chapter, you have learned the specific processes involved in building the leadership team that in turn lays the foundation of a professional learning community. Creating, or at least revisiting, MVVG is fundamental to all that follows. Chapter 6 poses and helps resolve one of the greatest challenges schools face: "What happens when children *don't* learn?"

CHAPTER 6

Principle 2

Ensuring Achievement for All Students— Systems for Prevention and Intervention

Not all of us are a mess, you know. [. . .] People often associate anyone who's been abused with "There's no hope for that child." [. . .] Tell people we can do it. That you can survive all that and be a fully functioning member of the community. Don't give up on that kid at age 7 and say, "Oh, he's been through so much; he's never going to amount to anything." [. . .] The abused are labeled. But you can change somebody around.

—G. Higgins, 1994, *Resilient Adults:*
Overcoming a Cruel Past

Get real. It's impossible to look at any classroom and pretend that all students are alike. Instead, focus on the differences that exist, value the diversity, and *allow each student the opportunity to shine.*

—NCTM (National Council
of Teachers of Mathematics), 2012

Consider this exchange between two teachers.

Ella: How are things going with your class, Jim?

Jim: Not well. I just gave my first test, and over half the class failed. I don't know how I'm supposed to teach these kids. They're all reading below grade level. They appear to have learned nothing in middle school. What am I supposed to do with them?

How do we ensure successful learning for all students? Most educators are trying very hard and bring to their work a genuine desire to succeed with each of their students. However, there are undeniably numerous significant obstacles to learning. These include, but are not limited to, differing learning styles, need for additional time and repetition, low socioeconomic status, a non-English-speaking home, and parent or family situations that interfere with the learning process.

In high-performing schools, these variables are addressed in a proactive manner so they do not become barriers to the successful achievement of all students. Proactive teachers engage in a continuous study of educational research to learn how to prevent failure and how to provide effective interventions for each student in need. They actively seek alternatives to failure, and the concept of "throw-away" students is itself discarded.

Since the landmark study by Werner and Smith (1977) more than a quarter of a century ago, research confirms that even many of the most abused and troubled children *self*-correct as they mature in age (Anthony, 1982, 1987; Comer, Joyner, & Ben-Avie, 2004; Garmezy, 1983, 1994; Kaiser & Rasminsky, 2004; Masten, 2001; Pianta & Walsh, 1998; Werner & Smith, 1977). Werner and Smith (1977) summarized one part of their 30-year longitudinal study on high-risk youth this way: "We could not help being deeply impressed by the resiliency of the overwhelming majority of children and by their potential for positive change and personal growth" (p. 210).

Teachers are among the most likely mentors and positive influences for underachieving students, and schools are often the only bastion of stability in a student's life. A committed school faculty, therefore, can do a great deal to enhance the life of every child. When acting in concert to create a reclaiming *environment* and to build *systems* to prevent failure, school communities dramatically enhance the likelihood for student success.

The challenge is getting all staff members to believe in the school's ability to intervene positively in a student's life and to act on this information in a sustained, concerted, systematic manner. That is the focus of this chapter. Here, we look at the research, the "end products" of successful schools, and the processes that high-performing schools undertake to succeed with even the toughest students.

Specifically, we look at three major aspects of ensuring success for all students through comprehensive systems for prevention and intervention:

1. The school community's belief system regarding low-performing students

2. The overarching philosophy that unifies staff behavior

3. Comprehensive systems for assuring success, including Response to Intervention (RtI)

What Does the School Community Believe?

In most schools, the answer to this question is, "It depends." Beliefs about low-performing students often vary among teachers. A small number of classroom teachers often account for the majority of those students who are referred to the principal's office. At the same time, other teachers are able to succeed with those same students. This is generally not a case of the student's becoming more intelligent or a better person once he or she reaches the classroom of the successful teacher. It has more to do with the varying belief systems and corresponding actions in operation within the school.

Consider how two different belief systems resulted in widely varying solutions to the same challenge faced by both schools: tardiness.

The first school created a new policy of locking the school doors after the 8:00 a.m. late bell rings. A few more students wound up coming on time, while many others became truant. The second school, D. R. Hill Middle School in Duncan, South Carolina, however, chose a more successful path.

Creative Scheduling

As Principal Steve Gambrell explains, D. R. Hill Middle School has found an effective way to both reduce tardiness and provide students with a "decompression" period between home and school. Every day at D. R. Hill starts with a designated period in which faculty advisors work with small groups

(Continued)

(Continued)

of students to teach life skills, such as cooperation and collaboration, through hands-on activities and exercises. Every student is involved, including those in special education, and students are grouped heterogeneously, with no segregation of any sort. According to Gambrell, the program has become an invaluable part of the day for both students and teachers:

> We feel like it's almost a sacred time. It's a time when those kids who bring baggage to school are able to get rid of that baggage so that when they go to their academic classes, they're ready to learn—and teachers are able to teach. (personal communication, 2009)

A side benefit is that this program has virtually eliminated tardiness to academic classes. Because of its experiential and active nature, students come early to ensure they can participate.

As indicated in Chapter 2, the links between student success or failure and teachers' and principals' expectations for those students are well documented. Moreover, the research in Chapter 3 indicates that one of the keys to success for highly reliable organizations (HROs) is both believing in and acting on this available information. The difficulty lies in the challenge of getting the entire school community to understand this connection and take appropriate action. Simply reading the research—absent belief and action—is not sufficient to bring about change.

Changing the belief systems of people is an extremely difficult and complex process. Most texts don't address this issue, focusing instead on changing behavior. In the previous chapter, we endorsed this approach as a practical way of addressing behaviors that are inconsistent with organizational values. In fact, changing individual beliefs more often than not begins with changes in behavior, leading to new and better outcomes, which in turn shifts that person's beliefs.

Ultimately, it is imperative that a school's entire staff holds high expectations for students, and this chapter addresses some of the practical complexities in this effort. Gaining staff *compliance* alone is not enough. It takes total staff *commitment* to succeed in the thorny work of reaching low-achieving and underserved students.

Addressing the core *beliefs* of the entire school community is a lengthy process. Along the way, it is essential to be sure to hold the line on *behaviors* and *language* that may conflict with organizational values and mission—otherwise, an environment in which "anything goes" is created. Without at *least* commitment to *behavior* that supports the school's values and mission, the fundamental aspect of almost any school's mission—that *"all students will learn"*—will become invalid. It is essential that the mission really means that *all* students—not *some* students—will learn.

Let's take a quick look at how a school principal confronts a science teacher whose behavior does not support the school's values and mission.

Confronting Behaviors

After numerous discussions with Bob regarding the poor grades his students consistently receive, the school principal meets with him again:

Principal: Hi, Bob. Did you get those grade distributions I sent you?

Bob: Yes, I did.

Principal: Great, let's just go over them. It's obvious from these numbers, Bob, that students in your class consistently underperform, semester after semester. Something is clearly happening in your class to cause this discrepancy, and I'd welcome any explanations you might have.

Bob: This is the way I teach, Mr. Martin. It's the way I've always taught. I teach responsibility. I'm very tough on them. I'm not going to enable them like these other teachers do.

Principal: It's not our mission to make courses difficult for students, Bob. It's our mission to help them succeed. We need assessments that accurately reflect what they know, and we need approaches that are consistent with our value statement—which you helped create. I'm going to ask you to work with the two other teachers in your division, and with your director, to develop some new assessments that are more in keeping with what we're trying to accomplish. If, at the end of the next grading period, your students' scores aren't in line with those of the other classes, I'll work with you directly to ensure the necessary improvements.

High-performing schools realize that (1) what they do matters to the learning of each of their students, and (2) all children can indeed perform at high levels. Many school communities do not take direct responsibility for the learning of each of their students. Here are three common reasons why this might be the case and some suggestions for addressing each:

1. The Teachers May Not Believe That a School Can Succeed With All Students

Some members of the school community have had experiences that, to them, confirm the worst: not all children can learn! Based on their own predispositions, initial bad experiences, or inabilities to reach all children themselves, some may understandably hold this view. In fact, it wasn't until relatively recently that schools were even considered a possible part of the solution to students' nonacademic life challenges.

Most educators have had minimal experience and training in dealing with the kinds of problems that today's children present. Dealing with students' problems ineffectively or misinterpreting a student's inability to learn is common. The teachers described in the next example, for instance, mistook one child's personal problems for an inability to learn.

Sidiki's Story

Several years ago, I was called to school for an appointment with the teachers of a 10-year-old boy, Sidiki, to whom I had become a "big brother." When I inquired into the purpose of our meeting, one teacher's analysis of Sidiki's performance was, "Sidiki is not performing at the skill level of his classmates. He has difficulty paying attention and refuses to participate in class. His reading comprehension is well below grade level and his scores on our standardized tests indicate that his math skills are only at third-grade level."

The team leader provided a more succinct analysis: "He just doesn't get it! I think he may be learning disabled."

I shared with Sidiki's teachers that he was an African immigrant who already spoke four languages, the last of which was English. I shared how enthusiastic and excited Sidiki could become once he was engaged in our evening tutoring sessions, remaining exclusively focused on his homework for hours at a time—often longer than I could! I also explained the tremendous tumult in his family life, and the pressure and abuse he received from his father.

> As I spoke, it was clear that neither teacher had been aware of Sidiki's impressive multilingual abilities, his enthusiasm for learning and capacity for intense concentration, his father's status as an international scholar, or the abuse—physical and otherwise—that Sidiki received from him. As I revealed these facts, a look of empathy began to play on one of the teachers' faces (Blankstein, 1997, pp. 2–3).

When Sidiki's teachers understood the situation, they redoubled their efforts and changed their approach, and Sidiki succeeded. If the challenge is one of school personnel truly questioning whether or not all students can learn at high levels, then this is more easily dealt with than the other challenges on this list. Teachers with a strong sense of self-efficacy can generally change their behaviors readily when faced with new information that calls for such a change. Similarly, professionals in a culture that focuses on continuous learning will be hungry to learn that there is a better way, and they will soon adopt that better approach.

If this is the situation, it is often possible to change behaviors (leading to changed beliefs) by introducing conclusions drawn from research. This generally creates cognitive dissonance for those questioning the possibility of creating a school in which low performers can turn around. The dissonance, for those with strong self-efficacy, can be resolved in favor of a pilot project testing the new theory, or wholesale change, depending on the school's culture.

Leaders can also create this dissonance, as well as pathways to change. Modeling alternative behaviors, demonstrating success, and forcefully challenging assumptions are all part of good leadership.

It is helpful, however, to check to see if "lack of information" is the only barrier to change. One can ask, "Do you really believe that you cannot educate all of your students to high levels of achievement? Does this mean that if you found out otherwise, you would try some new approaches and work with me and the team to assure all students' success?" If the answer to either of these questions is no, the real hesitation may be something else mentioned below.

Options for addressing a true information gap include reading and sharing research and best practices. Countless studies point out best practices and school successes in virtually any setting. (See the next chapter on maximizing research through collaboration.) You can also take a field trip to another school that succeeds or bring a speaker/practitioner from a school similar to your own. Most powerfully, discovering who within your own school succeeds with "low performers" opens up great possibilities for others to do the same. The network approach cited in Chapter 1 and again in Chapter 10 expedites the "see-feel-do" process for change within schools and across the entire district (Fullan, 2005).

2. The Teachers May Not Feel Personally Competent to Succeed With All Students

This is harder to uncover than the issue of teachers who do not believe a school can succeed with all students. The idea here is that the student's failure is actually the teacher's failure once the teacher admits that all students can in fact succeed. The response to this becomes one of support, on the one hand, and "creative tension," on the other. The idea is to build a sense of self-efficacy among staff members by challenging them to do things they *can* do, while making inertia uncomfortable.

One principal's story provides clarity.

Building Self- and Collective Efficacy

On June 6, 2006, the superintendent held a meeting with the staff of Jackie Robinson School in Brooklyn, New York, to introduce Marion Wilson, the new principal, who followed a string of departing principals. During the meeting, the district union leader stood and said, "No disrespect to you, but we don't want you here. We want the principal who was here before you." Then she walked out. One by one each teacher walked out of the auditorium. Marion didn't know what to do.

To address the situation, Marion decided she needed to do something different. That summer she formed a very small "cabinet" of four people in the school whom she trusted, and they planned a retreat that would involve the entire school. At first the budget office refused to provide the money she would need, but she insisted and prevailed. She also decided to use the first edition of *Failure Is Not an Option®* to help form cohesion and get everyone onboard quickly, so she ordered copies for each staff member. No one had ever taken the staff out; rarely had anyone bought them a book.

At the retreat, she began by forming jigsaw teams that coupled stronger and weaker staff, including support personnel and paraprofessionals. She assured them that moving forward, everything would be based on the six principles in the book, and they created a motto: "Excellence Is the Only Option." This tied in with the book and became their collective vision for every student.

Once back at school, Ms. Wilson's next job was bringing order and developing small wins toward developing that collective efficacy described in Chapter 1. She painted a line down the middle of the hallway to direct traffic flow. She also put in place other simple procedures, such as creating an orderly dismissal process to prevent all of the kids from running chaotically for the door and into the street to board a bus at the end of the day.

In the first year, she did not address instructional strategies, but she did work with her team to create a consistent curriculum and processes demonstrating how to use class time more effectively. Ms. Wilson also expanded her team to include both supporters and many who were on the fence initially. Teachers who once would not greet her had the courage and the humility to later become among Ms. Wilson's most ardent supporters once she established their trust.

Instructional improvements began with nonthreatening, informal walkthroughs done by her "cabinet." They started buddying teachers with one another through initiatives such as "lunch and learn." They also brought in consultants and held off-campus workshops for teachers as a way of building not only skills but affinity for one another and for the new principal who did things differently. When Marion Wilson took over the school in 2006, it was about to be closed down. Last year it was listed by the *New York Times* as one of the 5 top schools in the city (Blankstein 2011, p. 17).

By collectively generating the motto "Excellence Is the Only Option" and providing definition with some clear and specific goals, this principal and her staff created an inherent tension, then addressed a means of resolving that tension through small steps and successes. These baby steps in turn built a sense of efficacy among the staff, which enabled them to take on more difficult tasks, which in turn led to enhanced student achievement.

Another way to build creative tension is to bring staff members into closer contact and affinity with the students whom they feel are unlikely to succeed. As affinity increases, it becomes more difficult to dismiss an individual's academic potential.

In her 12-year study of 120 organizations in 35 cities, Milbrey McLaughlin (Lewis, 2000) found that building relationships with young people as well as holding relation-building events that "allow youth and adults to see each other in new ways" were two of six guiding principles for success (p. 643). Creating opportunities for shared experiences in the form of social events, field trips, or experiential learning activities deepens the affinity and the communication among participants. Figure 6.1 demonstrates this interaction among the elements.

Anytime one of the three sides of the triangle is enhanced, the other two sides are strengthened as well. This reality also applies to building support for students within the larger community. Having community members become mentors for students, for example, builds the communication, shared experience, and affinity for students and the school. Assigning students to research the history of community members has a similar effect while also providing an intellectual experience for the student.

This section presented a handful of ways to help educators overcome their fears of competency associated with committing to success for all students. The general principle is to provide both support and encouragement for the staff member while creating a cognitive dissonance or creative tension to spur movement.

Figure 6.1   Building Affinity

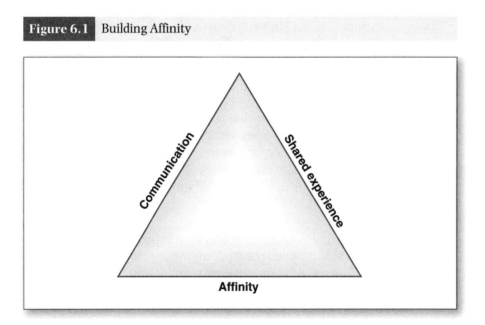

3. The Teachers May Believe
That New Reforms Aren't Worth Pursuing

Most veteran teachers have experienced disappointments at one time or another due to past waves of school reform. The idea of quickly embracing the next new reform seems foolish to some. Past failures may have been due to (1) a premature change of leadership; (2) a lack of political, financial, or other capital necessary to ride out the storms involved with the change effort; or (3) a superficial attempt to get teachers to simply "buy in" when committed engagement is actually required. Whatever the past experience, many teachers are understandably reluctant to jump with both feet into the waters of reform.

Understanding is required in such cases. It is also important to bring people's underlying assumptions to the surface so that they can be addressed: "Why do you feel this way? I'm interested in knowing what you have experienced in the past." (See Chapter 4 for multiple strategies.)

Shutting down people's inner concerns only leads to increased outside conversations or gossip. It is better to hear legitimate concerns firsthand in order to deal directly with the situation; for example, "I see, you have been burned in the past and don't want to dive in again before you know this is 'for real.' That's understandable, and I accept and respect that. Moreover, I will make sure that your concerns are addressed, as you will see over time. However, in the meantime, I would like to ask a favor. Could you withhold any negative commentary or judgment of this initiative until you have watched it unfold for a while? Then if you have any suggestions, can you see me directly?"

Another increasingly common reason for the "Why bother?" mentality, especially among new personnel, is the time and effort involved. The idea of succeeding with every student may indeed seem overwhelming. The latter part of this chapter discusses relieving *individuals* of this task, and instead instituting a collaboratively created, systemwide approach. The following section is a necessary precursor to that approach.

What Is the School Community's Unifying Philosophy?

One of the biggest challenges school leaders face is the tendency toward fragmentation of efforts and focus. Many demands are placed on educators, and those demands come from all directions. Often, the demands from the state, district, parents, staff, unions, and students are at odds with one another. Good leaders, therefore, are called on to make organizational meaning out of apparent chaos. In this section, we provide a framework and philosophy for how the entire school community can deal with one of the most difficult challenges: student failure to meet high academic standards.

Traditionally, when a student did not comply with school policies, he or she was punished. If this punishment didn't work, the student was suspended or expelled. Whether or not the student succeeded academically or grew from the experience was not generally thought to be the school's concern.

Although there may be a place for this cut-and-dried approach to student "misbehavior," there have been many advances in the behavioral sciences. This new information has the power to lead us to different understandings of the complex *interactions* between students and teachers, students and the school environment, and students and their home. We now know that there is more that the school community can do to positively influence behaviors and the development of young people.

Most of the traditional approaches to dealing with student behavior were based on the Skinnerian philosophy of reward and punishment. But students are more complex than rats, and the fact that these traditional approaches often lead to more misbehavior attests to that complexity.

The traditional philosophy regarding student behavior has led to a mismatch between how some schools deal with students who don't comply and what those students actually need in order to improve their behaviors. The behaviors worsen in such cases. This leads to frustration on the part of many teachers and administrators as they sense that "what we are doing isn't working!" Without an alternative to traditional approaches, there is a tendency to see the inefficacy of the "treatment" as the fault of the "patient."

Banishment becomes a popular response to the problem. Some schools where we work literally have hundreds of suspensions each year. The line to the principal's office looks like one for a rock concert! The only answer for some beleaguered teachers seems to be labeling and then referring these problem students to remedial programs, special education, and even alternative schools. This has become so widespread that entire mini-industries, as well as billion-dollar pharmaceutical treatments, have sprung up to treat the latest "disorders." So many of these diagnoses for children happen to begin with the letter *D* that the 10 Ds of Deviance were created to depict the label used and actions prescribed for each (Figure 6.2).

Figure 6.2	The 10 Ds of Deviance in Approaches to "Difficult" Youth

Perspective	*Problem Label*	*Typical Responses*
Primitive	Deviant	Blame, attack, ostracize
Folk Religion	Demonic	Chastise, exorcise, banish
Biophysical	Diseased	Diagnose, drug, hospitalize
Psychoanalytical	Disturbed	Analyze, treat, seclude
Behavioral	Disordered	Assess, condition, time out
Correctional	Delinquent	Adjudicate, punish, incarcerate
Sociological	Deprived	Study, resocialize, assimilate
Social Work	Dysfunctional	Intake, case manage, discharge
Educational	Disobedient	Reprimand, correct, expel
Special Education	Disabled	Label, remediate, segregate

Once there is a diagnosis for the disorder, the treatment becomes clear. Unfortunately, far less time has been spent creating diagnoses for young people's strengths.

A Better Way

What we want to achieve in our work with young people is to find and strengthen the positive and healthy elements, no matter how deeply they are hidden.

—Karl Wilker, 1983, *The Lindenhof*

Over the past 100 years, a relatively small but growing number of leading child psychologists and youth professionals have developed a strengths-based approach to viewing and "treating" young people. In fact, they have been surprisingly consistent in defining the basic needs that drive behavior (see Figure 6.3).

As shown in Figure 6.4, the Community Circle of Caring synthesizes this body of research to provide a common framework and core philosophy of action (Blankstein, 2004; Blankstein, DuFour, & Little, 1997).

Figure 6.3   The Basic Needs That Drive Behavior

Source	Basic Needs
William Glasser, MD *Control Theory in the Classroom* (1986)	1. Survival and reproduction 2. Belonging and love 3. Power 4. Freedom 5. Fun
Stanley Coopersmith *The Antecedents of Self-Esteem* (1967)	1. Significance to others 2. Competence 3. Power to control one's own behavior and gain respect 4. Virtue of worthiness in the eyes of others
Larry Brendtro, Martin Brokenleg, & Steve Van Bockern *Reclaiming Youth at Risk: Our Hope for the Future* (1990) Based on Sioux tradition	1. Belonging 2. Mastery 3. Independence 4. Generosity
Boys and Girls Clubs of America *Youth Development Strategy*	1. Belonging 2. Usefulness 3. Competence 4. Influence
Allen N. Mendler *What Do I Do When . . . ?* (1992)	1. Success and being capable 2. Acceptance, belonging 3. Influence over people, events 4. Generosity and helping others 5. Stimulation and fun
Alan M. Blankstein *Failure Is Not an Option*® (2004, 2010)	1. Contribution 2. Connection 3. Competence 4. Self-control

Figure 6.4   Community Circle of Caring

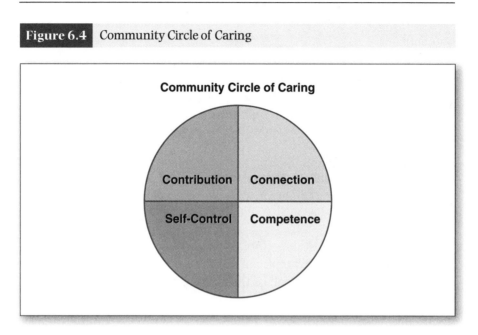

Young people naturally attempt to meet each of these four basic needs in either a prosocial or antisocial manner. One of the gangs we studied, the Latin Kings, uses a very similar framework, for example, to recruit and retain youth whose needs for connection are not being met prosocially. Young people whose need for competence is not being met in a positive manner may turn to auto theft, for example, to gain a sense of competence. The ultimate goal of the school, then, becomes one of creating an environment and culture that meets students' basic needs. Figure 6.5 shows examples of practices in such an environment, as well as contrary practices.

Building on Students' Strengths

Mike DiDonato, a school counselor, explains how his school started "The Bulldog Club" to provide fifth graders with leadership opportunities.

We chose the students who had a difficult time making positive choices but had leadership potential. We figured that other children in fifth grade were going to follow the "Bulldogs" no matter if it was in

(Continued)

(Continued)

a positive or negative direction, so we decided to make them a part of our "management team." By giving the Bulldogs responsibility and direction, they could make following the rules the cool thing to do at our school. In addition, through mentoring younger students and setting an example, the Bulldogs' personal behavior would change for the better as well.

Through the implementation of the Bulldog program, we have seen a distinct change in our students. The Bulldogs are well respected at Barth and have made a noticeable difference in student behavior at Barth. (personal communication, 2009)

Figure 6.5 provides examples of school practices that either enhance or impede development of each of the four Cs: *connection, competence, control, contribution.*

Figure 6.5   Four Cs: Practices That Promote Connection Versus Disconnection

Connection Occurs	*Disconnection* Occurs
Welcoming students even when they are late	Sending students to the principal's office, regardless of circumstances of late arrival
Greeting students warmly at classroom door	Working on paper at desk until all students are seated and the start bell rings
Systematically assuring every student is positively connected to an adult	Leaving personal connections to chance
Using extracurricular engagement data of all students as a measure of school success	Assuming most students are involved in extracurricular activities
Competence Develops	*Incompetence* Builds
Allowing make-up work	Having "one chance" policies
Demanding mastery of material	Averaging zeros into semester grades
Testing what is taught	"Surprise" tests and pop quizzes
Finding and emphasizing strengths	Focusing on weaknesses

(Self-) **Control** Is Encouraged	Compliance and Obedience Are Demanded
Allowing students to help create class rules	Telling students what the rules are
Eliciting input on class projects and readings	Recycling prior year's projects
Teaching empathy, self-awareness, and other emotional intelligences	Keeping emotional learning apart from academics
Contribution Results	Self-Centeredness Results
Allowing older students to teach younger ones	No student-led mentoring
Creating community service and project-based learning opportunities	Holding learning within the school
Encouraging cooperative learning	Teacher directs all learning

It is often the case that several of these Cs can be addressed at once. Consider how the following example simultaneously addresses the needs for connection, competence, and contribution.

Enriching Activities for Students

Icenhower Intermediate School in Mansfield, Texas, has implemented over 25 extracurricular clubs and activities. As Duane Thurston and Reggie Rhines explain,

> Most of the teachers involved in these clubs participate on a volunteer basis. These clubs may be athletic (basketball, volleyball, hockey), academic (Whiz Quiz, Academic University Interscholastic League [UIL]), or "real world" (cooking, green team). We believe that making connections outside of the four walls of the classroom is essential to ensuring success for our students. One particularly successful venture has been our Spanish Club, where some of our English Language Learner students actually become the teachers of this club and help other students learn Spanish. This provides an opportunity for students who do not have a second language to acquire skills in another language and also promotes leadership and

(Continued)

(Continued)

ownership by our (ELL) students as they become integral to the learning process. The Spanish Club along with the Cooking Club team up for a Cinco de Mayo fiesta at the end of the year for parents, where traditional music, the Spanish language, and a meal of Mexican food provide a vehicle to celebrate the success of our students and to engage parents in the entire school program. (personal communication, 2009)

The four Cs of the Community Circle of Caring provide a framework for rethinking and coordinating the actions of the entire school community. Once the beliefs and philosophy are agreed on, it is far easier to create a unifying system for action. The next section gives very specific examples of how two schools have done just that, as well as guidelines and steps to proceed on your own.

What Is the Comprehensive System for Ensuring Success?

Ensuring achievement for *all* students means having an overarching strategy that encompasses the majority of learners—and then having specific strategies aimed at those who need extra support. Essential components of a plan for all students' success include

- ensuring that pedagogy is engaging and relevant (see Chapter 5, "Mission");
- having an improvement plan for all students;
- having systems for quickly identifying those in need;
- providing a continuum of support and targeted strategies for low achievers;
- publishing results on closing the achievement gap; and
- using data-based decision making for continuous improvement.

The following sections discuss each of these components in detail. In addition, this section provides examples of intervention systems from two very different schools.

Ensuring That Pedagogy Is Engaging and Relevant

Engaging students around activities based on their own passions, interests, thoughts, and beliefs can lead to large gains in student achievement as well as reduce achievement gaps (Yeager & Walton, 2011). The concept has in fact been around for a very long time, and so have some of its modern-day pioneers.

Dennis Littky, cofounder and codirector of Big Picture Learning and the Met Center in Providence, Rhode Island, conveys that the "Big Picture School" has grown to 50 schools in the United States, 25 in Australia, and 25 in the Netherlands.

Focused on "real-world learning," the curriculum of Big Picture Schools is personalized and begins with the students' interests (e.g., "My mom has asthma—I want to cure it"). Every child has an individual learning plan. In addition, just as in the example cited earlier in this chapter regarding DR Middle School, Littky's schools make adaptations regularly. Littky explains, "When the sap runs it is sacred for this group of families in Lafayette School in New York, so students don't come to school during that time. Now the school community acknowledges it and lets them out of school but instead of penalizing the students, they have to write a paper about it" (personal communication, Aug. 14, 2012).

More than 100 "New Tech High Schools" have sprung up with a similar philosophy, as the next example shows.

Project Based Learning

Mike Reed, principal, New Tech High School in Columbus, Indiana, explains:

> Teachers are facilitators of Project Based Learning—where students take on real challenges of the community. Cook Medical Company came in to create a bio-degradable gelatin-based polymer and offered to patent it if the students developed one. It's no longer the teacher who asked them to do this—it is the scientist challenging them and giving them 4 weeks to present to a panel. Students come dressed in business attire and use all their 21st century presentation and "soft" 21st century skills, as well as interdisciplinary content.
>
> Students are graded 60% on content; 40% on learning outcomes: written; oral; collaboration and work ethic.

(Continued)

(Continued)

Students helped develop a rubric for the above. All is transparent. Then there are workshops on those skills: multiple chances to practice and be assessed toward mastery. For example, for "oral" it includes making eye contact; not using filler words; wearing professional dress; using proper grammar, and so forth. For "work ethic" it includes on-time work; quality of presentation; attendance; feedback from group members on efforts and follow-through on group agreements; and collaboration.

We use a consensus model—everyone impacted weighs in on the decision. The master schedule is determined by students and teachers. Adjustments are made systemically.

The staff, likewise, is fully engaged. The K–12 faculty meets monthly to work on subjects such as 21st century skills mapping; a collaboration rubric for different grade levels; Positive Behavior Intervention and Supports (PBIS); Universal Design for Learning—approaches to instruction with multiple means of media, engagement, demonstration of learning, and so forth. Facilitators create projects with help from colleagues and students. Every Monday after school they have "critical friends group" and project ideas are critiqued. They don't meet as departments but meet as an entire staff, and each discipline represented by that teacher gives feedback. Some projects bubble up from the students. (personal communication, July 30, 2012)

These are two models that begin inside out—with the students and their interests. There is little that yields greater success and more motivation than unleashing the power of combining one's interests and passions with an opportunity to learn and create something of significance. This approach also works exceptionally well with adults in the building. Keeping one's focus on these intrinsic drivers in the midst of a torrential downpour from external distractions and mandates is part of what this book—and acting from one's core and in concert with the lead team's defined interests— is about. Rooting in and keeping true to our core while adapting to significant changes externally is the challenge.

According to Tony Wagner, codirector of the Change Leadership Group at Harvard University, in response to growing inequities in the United States arising from major global and economic shifts of the 21st century: "We cannot spend our way out of this problem. We need a different answer" (Wagner, 2012, p. 2). His framework for developing students to be creative problem solvers starts—as in the examples above—with what he describes as three interrelated elements to intrinsic motivation: play, passion, and purpose. Tapping into these drivers provides the best chance for developing "essential qualities of a successful innovator": curiosity, collaboration, associative or integrative thinking, and a bias toward action and experimentation (pp. 15–16).

Having an Improvement Plan for All Students

The most effective schools provide a ladder of opportunities for struggling students, ranging from identification of students needing extra support before the school year begins to mandatory enrollment in remedial and/or skills classes. The effect of this range of interventions is to make clear to students that they may *not* fail. It tells students that the only choice is to learn and succeed. Resource 6 offers a worksheet for developing a school improvement plan.

> ### Video Connection
>
>
>
> www.corwin.com/failureisnotanoption3
>
> Too often, intervention immerses students into precisely the same situations that they already struggle with. For instance, students who have difficulty with math are given hours of math worksheets to complete. Videos 6.1 and 6.2 showcase creative steps to ensure that intervention goes beyond "more of the same."
>
> Think It Through: These videos showcase creative ways to offer students effective intervention. Brainstorm ideas for additional systems that can be put into place to help students. What steps would be involved in implementing these systems?

As prescribed in Response to Intervention (RtI), an effective improvement plan for all students includes components of both prevention and intervention. Some prevention strategies are targeted; others apply to the entire student population. The latter include

- building relationships with students;
- systematically identifying and building on students' strengths;
- meeting with students each day;
- having visible and available staff;
- involving students in the decision-making process (*Failure Is Not an Option*® video series, HOPE Foundation, 2002); and
- matching school structures to the real needs of students.

Often, school policies, schedules, or structures simply don't accommodate the young people they're supposed to serve. The following example shows how changing the overall structure or policies across the board can often provide the necessary support for preventing potential problems.

Aligning Structure With Philosophy to Reduce Suspensions

At Shambaugh Elementary, Principal Shawn Smiley emphasizes two methods for decreasing suspensions: (1) building and maintaining relationships, and (2) putting in place procedures that reduce behavior issues. He explains,

> The first thing I did when I got here was to look for patterns of behavior that were keeping students out of the classroom. I found, first, that students were going to lunch and then to recess, and second, that we lacked procedures to keep adults focused on the true task at hand, which was to ensure every minute of the day was devoted to learning.
>
> I changed the schedule for more than one reason. The referral rate was much higher in the afternoon. Students were being brought in from outside in an unruly manner. The teachers were not always there when the kids were returned, forcing the classroom assistants to maintain the "civility" at the beginning of the structured time.
>
> When the schedule changed to have recess precede lunch, the teachers then picked up the students from the cafeteria. Teachers were then on time from lunch and ready for their students to be returned to the rooms in an organized manner. Going from recess to the classroom doesn't make sense regardless of the behaviors that are shown by students. It is hard to believe we can get students from a high-energy, less-structured change of environment to the learning environment and expect them to be successful.
>
> A simple change in procedures changes the way people act and react to the same events. We can now go from 45 minutes of lunch and recess to the classroom ready to learn (and not in the principal's office because the students could not transition well). (personal communication, 2009)

Targeted Interventions

Intervention strategies target students who are not demonstrating learning at the level of expected performance. To be most effective, these strategies are graduated in their intensity. These types of graduated prevention and intervention systems take a pyramidal form; the prevention strategies at the bottom apply to all students, and the high-intensity interventions at the top apply to only a few. You will learn about how these exemplary "pyramid of interventions" (Noer, 1993) systems developed in a suburb north of Denver in Colorado and then eventually intertwined with a districtwide approach to RtI. They are in the "What *Good* Looks Like" section of this chapter.

Having Systems for Quickly Identifying Students in Need

Effective schools do not follow the sink-or-swim approach. Nor do they wade in to rescue students only when they have proven that they can't swim. Schools that are committed to success for all students systematically identify struggling students. They identify problems as early as possible—well before students have a chance to fail. The timely identification of problems is what distinguishes intervention strategies from remediation strategies.

When prevention systems are already in place for all students, it becomes easy to identify those who are at risk for academic difficulties. Mechanisms for identifying struggling students should ideally be built on the programs already in place for supporting all students. For example, a high school that monitors all incoming freshmen by having staff members submit frequent progress reports automatically has a net in place for catching struggling students. Here's an example of how an elementary school set up a similar net.

Identifying Students in Need

At Pelham Road Elementary, in Greenville, South Carolina, a special kindergarten class comes under the umbrella of the school's Special Education department. The children in the class are completely unaware that they are in a special program. The object of the class is to give children who have been identified as lacking necessary social or academic skills the boost that they need before starting first grade, without saddling them with the "special ed" label. The school chooses these students based on interviews with Head Start participants and places the identified students in a smaller-than-average class. The program's goal is to prepare participants for immediate mainstreaming into first-grade classrooms. In the great majority of cases, the program accomplishes that goal.

Providing a Continuum of Support and Targeted Strategies for Low Achievers

Students who are moving from one level of schooling to another—from elementary to middle school or from middle school into high school—need a continuum of support that sees them smoothly through the transition. Schools provide the resources necessary to ensure that new students can hit the ground running.

Schools use various mechanisms to facilitate a seamless transition for incoming students. One is collaboration between counselors in the feeder schools and in the receiving school. This allows counselors at the receiving school to become familiar with new students' needs and with what approaches in the past have been successful at meeting those needs. Another is "red-flagging" incoming students with the greatest needs and putting them in a "good buddy" program where an adult at the incoming school is assigned, unbeknownst to the student, to be a friend and advocate of that student serendipitously.

Other projects and programs include

- programs to prepare for the next school level (e.g., "Survival Skills for High School");
- reviews of student records before school starts in order to provide extra supports for children in need; and
- faculty mentor programs, in which every incoming student is closely monitored by an adult overseeing upperclassmen who gets to know him or her well.

Once high-performing schools have identified those students who are at risk of failure, they find ways to bolster their weak areas to ensure success. The types of strategies used vary depending on the grade levels served by the school and the needs of the students.

Video Connection

www.corwin.com/ failureisnotan option3

Video 6.3 discusses some of the ways students are identified for intervention and monitored for progress through the Pyramid of Intervention at the Roberta Tipp Elementary school.

Think It Through: This video introduces the Pyramid of Intervention used at Roberta Tipp Elementary in Texas and includes their use of data tracking sheets. What data are used to track students' progress in your district? How is this data currently shared with students and parents? How can you place intervention programs in a positive light so that students who are selected will feel "like they've won the lottery"?

Publishing Results

Making the achievement gaps an agenda item and publishing them for the stakeholder community to review adds focus to the staff's efforts. The schools in San Diego, California, used this strategy to help close their achievement gap. With so much media and public attention now on school and teacher "results," it's increasingly important to actually educate external stakeholders as to the *meaning* of grades and other data.

What *Good* Looks Like

Effective systems of prevention and intervention ensure that no student slips through the cracks. They are designed so that the majority of students benefit from careful, continuous monitoring and low-level support strategies. They have mechanisms in place to ensure the early identification of struggling students. And they follow a prescribed order so that higher-level strategies are implemented only after lower-level ones have failed to produce results.

The following Case Story, as shared by Kari Cocozzella (personal communication, 2009), highlights the comprehensive pyramid of intervention created over many years in her school outside of Denver, Colorado. The study integrates processes described throughout this book in the creation of a highly effective "pyramid of support" and response to interventions, which led to this elementary school in Colorado receiving an Accreditation With Distinction award. The case is then expanded to demonstrate how this school's pyramid becomes part of a larger, districtwide RtI initiative. (Also see Resource 7: Pyramid of Support at Coyote Ridge Elementary School.)

Case Story 3

RtI and Pyramid of Support at a Middle-Class Suburban Elementary School

At Coyote Ridge Elementary, the staff has been integrally involved in the implementation of a successful RtI. What is it that has caused the high level of achievement for all students?

1. The common mission and vision for the school is "all students can and will learn." There are no excuses.

2. All staff members are responsible for every student's success, both academically and behaviorally.

3. There is a clear, articulated pyramid of support for students needing additional assistance or for those already exceeding the standards. (This answers the question "What strategies should we use to support our learners?")

4. There is a comprehensive plan for the implementation of strategies, tracking of data, and design for whole-staff discussion and involvement in supporting students through vertical teams. (This answers the question "How do we ensure that we are meeting the specific needs of individual students based on data?")

5. The focus is on students' needs, not on curriculum, although best practices and strategies for high-quality instruction are integrated into the discussion.

6. Staff unfailingly revisit the pyramid and process for implementation two times per year in order to refine and improve strategies and teamwork. This review is focused on data and results of student achievement, as well as on the keys to effective teaming.

Common Mission and Vision

Creating and implementing the comprehensive plan of action was not easy, as the staff was embarking on unchartered territory in designing a schoolwide process for supporting all students. RtI was not a national or state expectation at the time Coyote Ridge began to discuss and initiate the model it currently utilizes. In fact, the original plan started in 2000 at Skyview Elementary, another suburban school in the same district. The principal, Kari Cocozzella, began the process at this school, and then transferred to Coyote Ridge in 2003. Both schools experienced a high level of growth using the model, even though the demographics of the two schools are vastly different. The initial idea for the model can be traced back to our attendance at a HOPE Institute in Denver in the fall of 2000. The concepts of a professional learning community at the high school level and the precepts of Failure Is Not an Option were the crux of the conference. However, the staff quickly realized that the ideas presented could just as easily apply at the elementary level.

At both schools, it became apparent that the mission and vision of Failure Is Not an Option, "all students are all our responsibility," and "all students can and will learn" must be clearly articulated and adhered to on a daily basis. Staff spent many hours creating clear language that would guide all decision making and programming at school. Leadership from the administration was and is crucial to the continued focus on the mission and vision. Because it is so important to have shared leadership and responsibilities, teacher leaders are identified and given a comprehensible job description, which includes required skills and required classes. These teacher leaders are critical to the success of the implementation of the model currently used.

Pyramid of Support: The Strategies

Purpose: "To identify additional support systems at varying levels of intensity in order for students to perform at their academic and/or behavioral potential."

Teacher leaders met to determine how to create a pyramid of support. They decided to have each grade level brainstorm every intervention or enrichment provided in individual classrooms, in the entire grade level, and included school-wide programs. After numerous lists were created, the entire staff met to discuss all of the interventions and support systems in place. They then put them in order of most intensive (individual) to least intensive (differentiated grouping within the classroom) to create the three-tiered, color-coded pyramid. Because it is essential to include all students needing additional support, even if they are identified as gifted and talented students, the title *Pyramid of Support* is much more inclusive than *Pyramid of Intervention*.

Vertical Teaming: The Structure and System

Purpose: "Vertical Teams are established to assist children who are not successful in the classroom due to issues of academics, attendance, behavior, family dynamics, and family financial issues. If a child is not showing academic growth or success in the classroom, the team will identify potential interventions/enrichment and monitor progress."

Many schools have created the tiered system of strategies for providing early intervention. They even have a focus on student outcomes rather than student deficits. The problem haunting most schools is not the issue of what to do, but *how* to do it in a systematic, comprehensible, and manageable method. Coyote Ridge created vertical teams, which are facilitated by the teacher leaders. These teams are made up of representatives from grade levels, special teachers (such as art, music, physical education, and technology), special education staff, ELL specialists, and gifted and talented coordinators. All staff members are expected to be an integral and active part of the identified team. The group makeup, process for meetings, timelines and purpose of each meeting, and tracking of information are all identified and clearly articulated. This eliminates fragmentation of efforts and creates a laserlike focus. Statements as to how vertical teams assist staff in becoming more cohesive and collaborative and why the teams help students to succeed are presented in writing at the beginning of the year.

In addition to supporting students, the teams end up contributing to a "pyramid of support" for teachers. Those new to the building or in their first years of teaching consistently hear of strategies and approaches veteran teachers have utilized in working with struggling or low-achieving students. Veteran teachers also learn from those just starting out. Ideas for how to support parents, instructional best practices, and strategies for creating affective behavior plans for students are provided during discussions. The entire process becomes a highly effective support system for students and teachers. No one feels as though he or she is "in it alone" or "the child is only my responsibility." The opposite foundation is now in place: We are all here to help and encourage you and provide additional strategies for the child in need of support. Consequently, the entire culture and climate of the building is enhanced, due to the increased efficacy of its staff.

Constant Improvement Through Revision

Because of constant change, whether it is student population, teacher expertise, or state and federal mandates, it is imperative to revisit the Pyramid of Support and vertical team process at least once, if not two times, per year. New initiatives or legal mandates must be shared, understood, and implemented, and suggestions for more efficient approaches for teamwork serve to increase the effectiveness of the model. The initial team meeting scheduled at the start of the school year is focused on the process and system in place, making sure all understand how to implement and utilize the pyramid. Team norms and expectations for participation are also reviewed. In January, the process is discussed again, just to ensure consistency and discuss any issues that may have occurred during the first semester of the year. Three times per year, each grade level meets with the principal to discuss the overall performance of all students based on required district performance assessments. Special attention is given to those students identified on the pyramid and discussed during vertical team meetings.

Student Success

Coyote Ridge has been recognized as a high-performing and high-growth school, acquiring the title of Accredited With Distinction in Colorado. In order to achieve this status, scores for all students (including English language learners and special education students) on state assessments were utilized to determine the level of student growth over time and a decrease in achievement gaps. Coyote Ridge earned 93.75% of the possible points. During the past five years, student achievement in reading, writing, math, and science has consistently increased even though the school has doubled in population and increased its English language learners by 300%. These numbers continue to rise. Conversely, the number of identified special education students has decreased. The school attributes this to their focus on early intervention—the focus is on excellent first instruction and the school philosophy that "all students are all our responsibility." This belief permeates the entire building and creates a positive energy focused on the success for all students.

RtI and Coyote Ridge Today

Five years ago, the district built on successes such as the one above, and introduced RtI districtwide. "It flopped," shared the administrative staff, "because it was uniformly rolled out. It was too standardized/generic, and lacked specificity of matching instruction to student needs. Instead it created a problem-solving team—there were 'experts' versus collective responsibility, and it was focused on 'fixing' students. Everyone was ready for an RtI checklist of what to do."

Now, instead, they have returned to the team-based approach to better understanding and implementing RtI, and they use it as a framework for success with ALL students. There is a standard district approach, including the overwhelming emphasis on engaging, relevant, and individualized instruction in the bottom two tiers of the pyramid. This comprises 95% of the situations, yet each school customizes the specifics.

Tina Hepp, principal of Cherry Drive Elementary in the same district, explains that they used a team approach to fleshing out their interventions, and more importantly defining and focusing on good instruction. "The best part is that this is all rooted in our belief about the capacity for every student to learn and succeed" (personal communication, 2012). Based on this belief, the trust built throughout the school, and the protocols staff created together, deep questioning of appropriate teaching strategies is the norm:

Teacher: Sammy isn't reading.

Principal: What are the formative assessments telling you?

Teacher: I did a PALS (Phonological Awareness Literacy Screening) and DRA (Developmental Reading Assessment) test and he doesn't know a third of the letters.

Principal: What has the instruction been so far? What about the other students. Do they have problems?

In this case, the principal may assign special education support staff to work with regular education teachers to get very detailed in their conversation and in synch on analysis and action rather than fit the child into a "program." The key is defining what exactly the student needs in terms of learning to read (chronological versus phonemic awareness, for example).

Grade-level planning sessions are filled with deep questioning:

- What should students learn? Why?
- Why do you use the daily lesson plans in this manner?
- What data will you use to determine success?
- How will you meet the needs of those who don't get it?
- How will your actions engage students?
- What is evidence of their engagement?
- Why do you do what you do?

This builds collective teacher efficacy and their own thinking skills. By approaching RtI in this manner, 80% of the students' needs are met in the regular classroom, and another 15% are met with additional reteach or preteach strategies based on daily formative assessments. Special support teams provide small-group work support for this 15% as well.

Implementation Guidelines

Developing a system of prevention and intervention is a major task. The approach you take will depend on both the culture of your school or district and the extent to which such strategies are already in place. As the above examples indicate, a successful approach includes:

1. Rooting the work in the schools' mission.

2. Getting engagement from the leadership team and ultimately the entire faculty around defining the goals of the intervention and the integral—versus separate—role it plays in the overall work of the school. In the previous chapter, for example, the critical questions around the schools' mission included ensuring relevant, engaging pedagogy; how will you know if students are learning; and how will you respond when they don't. All of this relates directly to this chapter.

3. Putting the emphasis on instruction minimizes the need for distracting interventions that take focus away from the core of the educational enterprise.

4. Slotting students into programs like special education should be a last resort. Deeper questioning, built on relational trust (Chapter 4); well-developed protocols (Chapter 5); meticulously developed

collective teacher efficacy (Chapters 7, 8, and 10); and rootedness in leadership's core purpose (Chapter 2) will likely address the needs of 95% of the school's students.

5. Agreeing on criteria for identifying students in need of assistance and ensuring they enter the appropriate programs. The referral of any student to a prevention or intervention program should be dependent on data that provide good evidence of his or her strengths, weaknesses, and root causes of learning difficulties. (Guidelines for the use of data are in Chapter 8.) In addition, make decisions in advance regarding what will be used as criteria for inclusion in each support program. Questions to ask include

   • What criteria, data, or information will be used to identify students who are eligible for each intervention program?
   • Who will help provide the information?
   • Who will be responsible for gathering and evaluating the data?

6. Surfacing objections and address resistance. Techniques for doing so are covered in detail in Chapter 3 and earlier in this chapter. Rolling out RtI in a major, systemwide effort was most effective on paper alone.

7. Piloting aspects of the new program. Start slowly, and implement just one easily implemented aspect of the pyramid. This allows for a more complete monitoring of the effectiveness of the programs, allows schools to work out any kinks, and allows for an early success to motivate further reform.

8. Building a culture of success. As soon as any strategy is implemented, a system for regularly monitoring its effectiveness should be established. As data come in that indicate a positive outcome, celebrate your success. In addition, be alert to any positive actions by staff or students that lead to better performance and an improved school climate. Be sure to acknowledge and praise these efforts publicly. Such public celebrations and "pats on the back" help to build a culture that believes in, values, and expects success.

9. Refining and adding to interventions. As you receive data on the results of your programs, use the information to refine existing strategies and to better develop new ones. Continue to phase in more intervention programs and strategies as outcome and disciplinary data suggest a need.

Getting Started

Work with your colleagues to sketch plans or procedures on separate sheets of paper for (1) identifying students in need of extra support and attention; (2) monitoring these students intensively; (3) providing mentors, "good friends," or other adult support to these students; and (4) establishing intervention programs. List programs that already exist; note whether they need to be modified or expanded and, if so, in what ways. For new programs, state the specific goal and then address questions that arise.

See Resource 8: Developing a System of Prevention and Intervention for more specific guiding questions for getting started.

Moving Forward

In this chapter, you have seen best practices in meeting the great challenge of providing for students who *don't* initially learn to standards. These practices included gaining staff commitment to the task, developing a unifying philosophy, assuring relevant and engaging approaches to teaching and learning, and creating systems of prevention and intervention. These are among the greatest challenges a school will face. How schools respond to the question "What do we do when students *don't* learn?" tells more about the values and collective commitment of that school than anything else. Although this chapter provided a clear picture of, and direction for, how high-performing schools tackle this challenge, the subsequent chapters help you develop the *capacity* to use these practices to address success for *all* students in your school.

CHAPTER 7

Principle 3

Collaborative Teaming Focused on Teaching for Learning

Central to the success of high-achieving schools is a collaborative culture focused on teaching and learning (Davis, Darling-Hammond, LaPointe, & Meyerson, 2005; Seashore Louis, Leithwood, Wahlstron, & Anderson, 2010; Wallace Foundation, 2011). This culture supports regular meetings of teachers who share responsibility for assessing needs and developing solutions that address all students' learning. Central to the success of these regular meetings of teachers is a common understanding of the purpose of the meeting, and protocols and tools for effective communication (see previous chapters and index tools). This chapter provides an overview of 10 possible areas for collaboration, examples of effective team meetings, a description of four types of school cultures, and a case study of a collaborative school culture that extends throughout the district and into other districts.

The Aim of Collaboration

Collaboration among colleagues is a means to an end: enhancing teaching for learning. In order to accomplish this, team members work *interdependently* toward a common goal (see SMART goals in Chapter 5). This goal, in turn, supports the larger school vision and is aligned with the school's mission and values. As a result, the school's mission, vision, values, and goals provide context and direction for all team members.

Teams invariably look at data (see Chapter 8) to assess how they are doing relative to their SMART goals. Members collectively brainstorm ways to improve, and they celebrate successes. Being committed to constant improvement, these teams will always find ways to raise the bar once their current goals have been accomplished. The high school that consistently graduates 99% of its students can, for example, determine to gauge their future success by readiness of those graduates for success in and after college, as well as by success in 21st century skills and character development, as noted in the previous chapter.

The Process for Successful Collaboration

While ultimately the purpose of collaboration is to influence the conditions, culture, and capacity for improved instructional practices in order to enhance student learning, different teams are formed to address one or another aspect of this overall goal. For example, in the previous chapter, the entire staff at New Tech High School in Columbus, Indiana, met to develop student projects that aligned with standards across the curriculum, while a different type of team convened in Coyote Ridge Elementary School to deepen instructional efficacy.

The *content* focus of these teams was different, yet the *process* for assuring productive teamwork is the same. (The opposite is also true: name the top 10 things you and your team dislike about meetings, and nine of them will be about dysfunctional *processes*, such as people having sidebar conversations or coming late to meetings.)

As indicated in Chapter 5, there are many tools to facilitate highly productive collaboration. The first order of business is for the team to constitute itself by clarifying its purpose. While this step is easily and often skipped, it is invariably done at the expense of the team's success. How many meetings begin with all thinking they are on the "same page" only to discover that one person thought the meeting was about ways to improve instruction, while another person thought it was about an evaluation of teachers' performance? Both get into similar content, but for very different purposes. The assumption is: "We already KNOW why we are here," but as is shown in prior chapters, if you ask 10 teachers to grade the same student work, you get 10 different grades. The corollary is that if you ask 10 people in the school to define the school's top three goals, or the strategy for attaining them, you normally get a wide variety of answers. Without defining both the purpose of the team and the desired outcome of each meeting, guess what you get when you ask10 team members why they are there?!

At the school level, defining and agreeing on purpose begins with the leadership team and continues throughout each school team. The same is true for the purpose of the team itself. Additional tools referenced in Chapter 5 help the teams develop for themselves how they will *behave* (protocols, techniques for providing critique, etc.) to reach their stated purpose.

Ironically, some of the tools and processes mentioned above are even more effective in developing productive teams when they are part of a larger community of such teams, representing schools from throughout the district or region. It is akin to inviting a friend from outside the family to a holiday meal, changing the family dynamics for the better! Yet in the network configuration, assuming continuous "meals" together, the advantages continue because the teams reconfigure their expectations based on the improved processes and enhanced facilitation of the conversations. (See Resource 9: FNO Tuning Protocols for further tools.) In other words, it may be even easier to configure highly functional teams across a network of schools provided the combination of (1) excellent tools, processes, and facilitation, (2) the right people in the bus, and (3) continuous consistent contact to reinforce the new norms.

The key to sustainable success both here and within the school is the culture created.

Four Types of School Cultures

As described in previous editions (Blankstein 2004, 2010) and drawing from the original work of Fullan and Hargreaves (Failure Is Not an Option®, DVD, 2002; Hargreaves & Fullan, 1998), when it comes to collaboration, there are four main types of school cultures.

1. Individualistic

In this type of learning environment, teachers are accustomed to developing their own practices and techniques for classroom management and may not consider the relevant experience of colleagues. In fact, in traditional school cultures, teachers often regard the intrusion of other adults into their classrooms as an invasion of privacy. In these cultures, one might hear, "Why do I have to collaborate? I'm a good teacher, and my students are doing fine!"

2. Balkanized

This culture is characterized by the presence of deep-rooted cliques within the staff. In a balkanized school environment, small groups of people align themselves with a particular technique or ideology, pitting themselves against other groups that hold opposing ideas.

Teachers may be intensely loyal to the members of their cliques and hold strongly to their ideologies, but they may have little loyalty for the school as a whole. The problem of exclusive cliques is particularly difficult to address because they can be deeply rooted in opposition to one another.

Inside a Balkanized Culture

In balkanized cultures, team members often spend their time taking sides and vying to achieve dominance, as in the following example.

Mr. Jones: Yesterday in my mailbox, I received the final state scores. Looking at them, it's easy to see which members of our team accomplished certain skills and which kids are lacking in certain areas. As a team, we should start talking about how to use these scores.

Ms. Rodriguez: Well, I was thinking of not necessarily putting students in small groups, because there's not enough time to do that in one class period. They need to be divided according to their ability and placed in a classroom with all similar abilities.

Mr. Hamilton: I agree—I think we should put them in separate classes.

Mr. Jones: Sounds like tracking to me.

Ms. Rodriguez: I don't think that's tracking, because they can always go into other classes depending on their level in that subject. We're not talking about every subject—we're only talking about instances in which students are struggling.

Mr. Hamilton: I agree. I think we should put them in different classrooms.

Mr. Jones: Sounds like another name for tracking to me.

3. Contrived Collegiality

In this culture, teachers appear to be collaborating. They may spend time on committees and in meetings, but they actually don't focus on deeper issues related to teaching and learning. In these cases, the structure of the school may have changed (e.g., meetings now occur), yet the deeper culture (represented by what happens in those meetings) has not. In this instance, teachers collaborate only on the surface without challenging one another's beliefs or approaches to teaching and learning. In this culture, one might hear, "How was your weekend?" or, "Ronnie has presented some behavioral challenges for me. How about you?" or, "Overall, our test scores are improving and that's good. What's next on the agenda?"

4. Collaborative

In a collaborative school culture, professionals are fully committed to and focused on helping students learn by becoming active learners themselves. They work continuously with their colleagues to improve their teaching strategies and better manage their classrooms. They recognize their crucial role in the educational process and know that they can meet the challenges confronting them only by solving problems in concert with their professional colleagues. Teachers in a collaborative culture make specific analyses of the data—by student, by area of challenge, and by teacher—to dig for areas of improvement and change teaching practices accordingly. For example, one might hear, "I noticed your students are scoring higher on problems that test for reading comprehension. Can I watch you teach a class? Would you watch me teach too and provide feedback?" Collaboration, in other words, extends beyond the meeting; it goes into the classroom. In the highly collaborative school (or network of schools), transparency of practice becomes the norm, and structures to support it—including brief periods away from classroom teaching in order to audit others' teaching—are directly supported by administrators and others on the team.

In sum, the collaboration in these schools is based on four elements:

1. Specific data regarding performance by individual students, individual teachers, and specific areas of instruction (e.g., decimals or syntax)

2. Trusting, structured, yet intensive conversations around these data

3. Commitment to action (e.g., structured and frequent instructional learning walks

4. Evaluation of outcomes from actions, continuous improvement of practice, and refinement of goals based on that evaluation

Schools with a successful culture of collaboration are aware that not all collaboration is necessarily good. Collaboration must take place with the overall success of the students in mind. The type of collaboration these schools foster is an open-ended inquiry that incorporates new ideas from both inside and outside the team. The team itself becomes a minilearning community, actively seeking literature on best practices from other members, as well as other schools.

Let's look at collaborative teaming in action.

Collaborative Teaming in Action

In order to demonstrate the power of a team, a principal in Fort Wayne, Indiana, used an activity called "Consultation" with the staff (Carolyn Powers, personal communication, 2009). The principal recruited a staff member who had a unique student issue that needed a solution. At the next staff meeting, this teacher sat at a table with six other volunteers from the teaching staff. The teacher shared her problem, and then the team asked clarifying questions for 10 minutes.

The teacher then had to remain quiet while the team discussed the situation with each other but not directly with the teacher herself. The teacher then was asked to respond to the discussion she had heard. As this process unfolded, everyone's engagement was very strong. At the end of the session, the staff was asked to comment. One member said, "If this is the power of collaboration and it could help me this way, I'm all for it."

Taking the above example to the next level, teams would then commit to specific actions. There should always be a "now what?" as part of concluding any meeting. As a matter of regular course, future meetings would include these agenda items:

1. What new techniques were tried?

2. What were the outcomes, and what is your evidence for them?

3. What worked? What did not work? What are your recommendations?

Areas of Collaboration

In setting up collaborative teams, it is important to choose the appropriate members. Team members should share common students or common problems, and the issues they deal with should be of concern to all members. Following are some areas that may lend themselves to collaboration.

Note how the work of each of these teams connects to the other five principles in *Failure Is Not an Option*®.

- **Professional practice forums.** Teachers who work with similar grade levels, or who teach related areas, should work together. They present colleagues with accounts of strategies that work for them, share concerns, describe challenges, research best practices, and plan new strategies.
- **Classroom observation.** Teachers observe classes of colleagues who are experimenting with new strategies or techniques. Through observation, they learn about new strategies and can help evaluate how well the innovation is working. Similarly, teachers can regularly observe classes of teachers having specific problems to provide constructive suggestions and support.
- **Curriculum planning.** Relevant groups or committees frequently meet to plan and monitor curriculum sequence and coordination. They may determine who teaches what subject area, what content will be covered, what skills they teach, which students they teach, and in what order. They synchronize knowledge and skills that students should have acquired at specific times and when they are supposed to have acquired them. They may also determine which assessments to use in order to gauge whether all students have successfully mastered core knowledge and skills in each academic area.
- **Vertical teams.** Vertical teams differ from grade-level teams by gathering representatives from different grade levels for collaboration (e.g., reading teachers from Grades 2–5 work together with English language learner specialists and library/media specialists). This eliminates fragmentation of efforts. (See Case Story 3 in Chapter 6.)
- **Professional study groups.** Teachers research and report to colleagues on articles and books containing matters of professional

interest, or they share the information gained at workshops or conferences. They may occasionally invite speakers or guests from outside the school with expertise on matters of interest to them.

- **Grade-level or subject-area teams.** These teams can identify curricular outcomes, determine methods of assessing student progress, select instructional materials, plan and present professional development programs in support of team-identified issues, and participate in observation and monitoring programs for mutual support.
- **Interdisciplinary teams.** Such teams deal with the same groups of students (e.g., all teachers of ninth graders) to focus on the curriculum and the needs of students. Case Story 1 in Chapter 1 provides an example of such a team focused on common reading strategies used in areas as diverse as PE and math.
- **Task forces.** These teams are drawn from all areas of the school to study and develop recommendations for dealing with a specific problem affecting the entire building, such as the best way to handle tardy students. Task forces dissolve when their task is completed.
- **Teaching strategy or professional interest teams.** Staff members who are interested in a specific approach or innovation (e.g., cooperative learning) form groups to research the approach, receive training, develop implementation strategies, and provide reciprocal observation, review, and evaluation. As with task forces, these teams are relatively short-lived.
- **Leadership teams.** As noted throughout the book, leadership teams serve as the engine driving the overall school improvement agenda.

What *Good* Looks Like

Schools where collaboration is the norm share some very distinct characteristics. They include the following:

- The staff members are committed to a shared mission, vision, values, and goals, and they recognize their responsibility to work together to accomplish them.
- Strong leaders engage teachers in meaningful collaboration and support their activities and decisions.

- The school is characterized by a culture of trust and respect that permits open and willing sharing of ideas and respect for different approaches and teaching styles.
- Decisions are data based and depersonalized.
- The staff has real authority to make decisions about teaching and learning.
- Meetings are well managed and truly democratic, following established protocols for setting an agenda and making decisions.
- The functioning of teams is frequently discussed and reassessed.
- A plan is developed to provide meaningful time for teams to meet (for strategies on making time to collaborate, see Chapter 3 and Resource 2: Strategies for Making Time).
- Each team has clear purposes and goals.
- Educators acquire and share training in effective teamwork strategies.

Let's take a quick look at cross-departmental teaming in action.

Video Connection

www.corwin.com/ failureisnotan option3

In Video 7.1, the teachers share ways they collaborate informally and formally through staff meetings and in-classroom modeling.

Think It Through: The teachers in this video discuss ways they model for and receive feedback from each other. Consider ways that modeling has worked successfully in your school. What obstacles currently exist? Brainstorm possible solutions you might implement to overcome them.

Cross-Departmental Teaming in Action

At the seventh-grade teachers' weekly meeting, one of the science teachers proposes a problem with science and social studies teachers. She explains that although science and social studies are tested on the state tests this year, the class schedule allows for less time for those subjects than for math and language arts. She presents her concern with getting her students ready for the tests, given the limited teaching time.

(Continued)

(Continued)

The team leader acknowledges the legitimacy of the problem and opens the floor for other teachers to propose solutions. Soon, a collaborative strategy is formed:

Language Arts Teacher 1: I realize that you have a lot of reading material in science and social studies that is difficult. And Mr. Evans and I would be glad to take some of that material and use it for our self-selected reading periods.

Language Arts Teacher 2: And maybe if you could get us information about what you were going to do during the following week, Ms. Shaw and I could collaborate to make sure that the questions we propose are similar to the kinds of questions asked on the state test. That way, you're not only reinforcing your science and social studies skills but also working on how to answer the questions.

Math Teacher: Regarding the mathematics aspect, Mrs. Atterman and I could help to teach measuring skills. I know that in science one does a lot of measuring—and I know from my student-teaching experience last year that a lot of students really need help with that. Also, if you had a set of data, we could use graphing calculators and let them do a presentation on that data.

Science Teacher: Okay . . . well, let's sit down and bounce these ideas off some other people in our department and see what we can come up with in the way of a schedule. We'll also want to determine what a "success" will look like in terms of student learning and how we'll know if this effort is successful. Let's get input on these questions and discuss this again next Friday.

The preceding scenario shows one aspect of true collaboration. The teachers jointly accept responsibility for student learning—*across* subjects, not just in their own classrooms—and work together to overcome an obstacle. They also commit to defining *success* before trying this new approach and assessing their efforts toward that success. While in this meeting, they are addressing structural—and not pedagogical—issues; the spirit of collaboration and jointly solving the problem is clear.

In the next example, the collaboration extends across networked schools in a region of 8 districts in Michigan. Case Story 4 includes many key elements for success described earlier, beginning with a foundation of trust, focus on MVVG, and implementation practices that include transparency of instruction and collaboration within and across schools in the network.

Video Connection

www.corwin.com/ failureisnotan option3

In Video 7.2, a group of teachers across subject areas meet to establish objectives prior to a learning walk and then discuss what observations they can share with their department.

Think It Through: The teachers meet before and after the classroom observation. How are classroom observations organized in your district? Do meetings take place before and after? Consider whether or not you think that step is important, and why.

Case Story 4

Six Lessons Exemplified Across a Region

The goals of education have been and will continue to be debated and redefined in the context of history. Whether by carrot or stick, each method seeks to raise the bar and close the gaps.

Setting achievement goals for standardized tests has never been a problem. However, the proverbial devil is in the details of how to get from here to there—a question that has challenged educators from the boardroom to the classroom. For decades, the research has been clear that effective collaborative learning communities are the key to continuous improvement. Consequently, schools and districts have proudly proclaimed themselves "professional learning communities" (PLCs) as their technical pieces are put into place: teams, time for collaboration, data, goals, mission, and values. Yet the results have fallen short of the promise as the more difficult and complex human side of the equation has been marginalized amidst the clamor for quick results. To be successful, PLCs must have a firm foundation that includes relational trust, a belief that the job can really be done (and MUST be done), time, and the climate for teams to learn how to connect the dots through trial and error.

This Case Story was shared by Principal Christine Sernak (personal communication, 2009). It comes from Williamston Middle School, which is about an hour outside of Detroit and is part of the Williamston Community School District within the Ingham County, Michigan, regional service center area. Under the leadership of Cindy Anderson, seven districts in the region became a part of the same network of schools called the Courageous Leadership Academy (CLA), facilitating a regionwide sharing of knowledge and resources. The systems approach as well as all the other lessons of this chapter are exemplified in this Case Story.

At the start of this multiyear project, Principal Christine Sermak shared her concerns with the Regional Educational Center Coordinator, Nancy Fahner. "Our building is working on relational trust," she explained. "However, we still need an outside group or someone to help get us to the next level." They decided that their next step would involve attending conferences and building the school improvement team. As Christine explains, "That helped us move in the same direction."

Teacher team members Tania Dupuis, Anne McKinney, Laura Hill, and others had already begun the trust building with students in various ways. For example, to get students to form new bonds in the cafeteria, teachers asked them to pull numbers from a jar to determine where they would sit. Students then learned more about one another by answering questions placed at their tables. The adult trust building began with a self-assessment. Christine notes:

> Just giving the leadership team the chance to really review what great things we're already doing in our school was a refreshing change! We then looked at the many activities we have going on: which ones we want to stop or continue, and other activities we want to start.

Relational trust was intentionally *deepened.* She continues:

> We did mix-it-ups by seating people at meetings with others not from their content area (e.g., a PE teacher, ELA (English Language Arts) eighth-grade teacher, and a sixth-grade science teacher) and tackling issues like building cross-curricular activities or how to tear down the walls of cliques. When all the ideas were collected and presented for us to choose from, it was powerful.

This was the foundation for more intensive, professional relations to come, focused on teaching and learning.

The Answer Is Down the Road

Relations were also *expanded* districtwide. Christine explains:

> During this period, we had time to build relations with other schools in and outside of our district. So we sent a team to Okemos, which is in another

district, since they were also creating their values. After a general discussion of values, we gave everyone two stickers to vote on up to five and ultimately reached consensus around what ours would be.

Learning across districts became the norm as well. We sent a team to Haslett Middle School, just 15 minutes away, to see how they were handling academic labs for their students struggling with literacy and numeracy; and we did the same thing with a high school in the Holt district that developed a skills-based report card.

Year One Actions

"We began building sustainable leadership from the start by bringing everyone into the process," Christine continues. The leadership team was diverse and open to anyone who would commit to making all sessions. It included one parent and one board member as well. The school staff developed two subgoals that aligned with our larger SMART goals (strategic and specific, measurable, attainable, results-oriented, and time-bound) around reducing student behavioral incidents and advancing academic proficiency.

Subgoal 1. By the end of the year, all teachers will incorporate writing using a common graphic organizer, editing tool, and rubric.

Subgoal 2. We will develop the whole child (physical, emotional, and behavioral aspects included).

(For more on creating SMART goals, see Chapter 3.)

To address these goals, we created professional development and assessed accordingly. After the professional development (PD) for Goal 1, for example, everyone took a survey based on Ken O'Connor's (2007) book *A Repair Kit for Grading: 15 Fixes for Broken Grades.* The survey asked questions ranging from their understanding of the session to their intended use of what they had learned. The data-based determination of instructional planning followed, as did alignment of our Professional Development (PD), which was designed to embed training and ensure changed practice.

The next step was to encourage teachers to share their work with one another using tuning protocols (see Resource 9). This allowed everyone to get to know one another on a professional basis while building trust.

Teachers also shared their skills with classroom walkthroughs. Initially, the walkthroughs were presented by lead team members, not the principal. They were done on a voluntary basis, in a nonjudgmental and nonevaluative manner, and the successful outcomes were trumpeted. Here is an example of an e-mail sent out following a class observation in year one:

I "walked through" Shelley Kranz's room on Thursday, 11 December. She taught a lesson on push/pull factors that influenced Irish and German immigration to the United States in the mid-1800s. Shelley had set up her room and technology in a way that made much better use of the space available than the layout in my room. Shelley seemed to have a very informal relationship at times with her students, lots of smiles, but also was able to rein them back in when needed.

To further refine the common tools outlined in the first subgoal, Principal Christine Sermak and a small group of teachers decided to pilot the writing across the curriculum with two science teachers, an art teacher, a PE teacher, and a Spanish teacher. Christine explains,

> We partnered them with a language arts teacher who helped walk them through a writing assignment using the common graphic organizer and rubric that we had developed prior.

One of the teachers summed up their success in this way:

> The first year success was manifest in part by our taking ownership and finding our own answers. Everything wasn't coming from Christine anymore . . . we were the ones kind of leading the school and it had a different feel than having an administrator always giving direction from the top. Everyone was investing in the whole system.

Year Two Outcomes

Classroom observations continued to flourish during the second year. Christine notes,

> An e-mail goes out now if a teacher is going to teach using the graphic organizer, for example. Others will sign up to watch that, and someone from central office will cover their classroom. It is now the expectation that everyone will see someone's classroom, and have his or her class opened for viewing as well. We were able to do this due to the relational trust built in year one.

To support consistency, staff meetings often focused on a particular student's work. Teachers used the common rubric to collectively view and analyze the work and then strategized around how to improve teaching accordingly. This led to more embedded PD and more walkthroughs around what the team determined they would do in the grade-level or crosscurricular meeting.

"Collaboration has increased and intensified," says math teacher Laura Hill. "I've been working with a teacher who teaches an academic lab but is really strong in writing and literacy. We'll get together over lunch and I'll pick her brain about using the editing tool in my math class. She'll give me a good idea, and I'll say 'how about if we do that as partners!' Then we'll send out an e-mail for others to watch and give us feedback."

Teachers and other staff also began taking the formal lead in continuous learning and improvement. Christine says, "They talked about their experience in front of the whole staff. It worked extremely well, which led to everyone signing up to see another teacher teach writing."

Growing the leadership capacity to collaborate, with a focus on teaching for learning, and a basis and foundation of trust have all been the keys to this school's success. The results include reducing referrals from 1,152 to 368; and reducing detention by almost 25% in less than four years. Incidences of absence and tardiness went from 119 to 11 in the same time period.

The numbers continued to improve as the team moved forward. As Narda Murphy, the superintendent of Williamston Schools, celebrates:

> The state just released a list of focus schools—schools that have too large a gap between the successful students and the not so successful students. Williamston is NOT on the list and I attribute that to the work we started with Failure Is Not an Option!! It has been one of the best journeys I have taken as an educator. Focused, purposeful, and morally right!!!! And believe you me . . . I have been on some real journeys. (personal communication, 2012)

Implementation Guidelines

After forming teams to work on different aspects of teaching and learning in your school, teams establish protocols. Ideally, decisions should be written down and signed by each team member. Some of the questions may appear to impose an unnatural formality on friends and colleagues who have long worked casually together, but deciding these issues in advance helps to avoid future problems. (Note: See the implementation guidelines in Chapter 5 before proceeding. This section assumes an understanding of the material presented there.)

1. Team Organization

- What should the team organization be?
- Is there a chair? If so, who? What responsibilities does he or she have?

- If there is no chair, how are operational decisions made? Consider such details as time and place of successive meetings, responsibility for minutes or other team records, and so on.
- Who is responsible for acting as spokesperson for the team?

2. Decision Making

- Are the team's decisions made by democratic vote? By consensus? How are conflicts resolved?
- What commitment can be made to team members who may end up on the losing side of a debate or in a minority position?

3. Managing Meetings

- How are discussions and debates managed or led?
- In what way can the team ensure that each member has a turn to speak but that no one is permitted to dominate or divert the members from the task at hand?

4. Sharing the Workload

- How can the team ensure that all members share the workload equally so that no member is overburdened in comparison to the rest?

5. Commitment of Team Members

- Develop an agreement (preferably written, but at least a clearly articulated verbal statement) in which each member commits to (1) attending all team meetings, (2) working toward consensus on each matter of difference, (3) speaking openly and candidly with each other while respecting different opinions, (4) ensuring that each team member's input and views are sought and heard, and (5) supporting the team's decisions when a consensus is reached.

6. Communication Protocols

- As team members work on different tasks, how do they alert other members of problems, situations, events, results, or other matters?

- If a developing problem requires discussion by the entire team, what is the protocol for calling a meeting?
- Who is responsible for keeping and disseminating minutes of each meeting, copies of information gathered, reports of task forces, survey or focus group results, worksheets and planning forms completed jointly, and any other pertinent documents? These are the basis for the team's communications with the rest of the learning community, and they must be accurately maintained.

7. Monitoring Team Progress

- At what point and in what way, as a team, do you evaluate your effectiveness in carrying out your mandate?
- What steps do you contemplate if it appears you are not working very effectively?

When the previous issues are settled, begin to address your assigned task:

a. Establish Goals

- Articulate short-term or intermediate goals within the larger purpose assigned to you.

b. Prioritize and Assign Tasks

- Decide whether you work on the short-term goals in sequence or simultaneously.
- If the latter, who works on each?

c. Decide on a Sequence and Timetable of Tasks

- What are the first steps to take toward achieving the first goals?
- What is the timeline for taking these steps?
- How soon should the team (or a subgroup of the team) meet again to discuss progress, findings, or results?
- What task does each member complete before the next meeting?

8. Implement and Institutionalize the Successes

- How are successes spread and then institutionalized beyond the team?
- How do you systematically close the "implementation gap"?

- There are high-performing teams and individuals in every school and district. How can one person's successes with low-performing students, for example, become the *norm*, even long after that person has retired?

Other agreements around the eight items just mentioned should also be regularly reviewed and easily accessible. Some 80% to 90% of the challenges in meetings are structural or procedural (sidebar conversations, people coming unprepared, etc.) and are not about content. To eliminate these issues, it helps to standardize meeting formats, posting the "desired outcomes (dos) for the meeting at the top of the agenda, and listing the agenda and protocols for all to see and refer to during the meeting.

Challenges and Solutions

Collaboration is not natural or common in the traditional school environment. For generations, teachers characteristically closed the classroom door behind them and acted as independent agents of their own domains, expecting neither oversight nor support from colleagues. One principal commented that he had to use a crowbar to get one of his teachers out for knee surgery. Teachers with problems may frequently feel ashamed to ask for help, believing that their plea will be interpreted as confusion or a confession of failure. Such feelings and the traditional school culture have given rise to several identified challenges to collaboration.

Challenge: "Sure, I'll collaborate . . . whatever."
Collaboration is an ideal that is often articulated by the administration and staff of a school but, in fact, is not optimized. When teamwork is undertaken, the goal is often not seen as serious or as drawing on the pooled experience and knowledge of team members. Without a shared commitment to work together to address a common concern and a shared responsibility for developing a solution, collaboration becomes an empty gesture.

Solution: This requires changes in the school culture. Making a structural change is not enough to truly foster collaboration among teachers. The culture needs to shift to one in which collaborative teaming is valued as the most effective way to help students learn. Information about making culture shifts is found in Chapter 3.

Challenge: "I'll go to the meetings, but I really can't take on any responsibilities beyond that."

Members who assume that their presence at meetings suffices as a gesture toward collaboration can undermine the improvement process. Meetings are actually only the visible part of collaboration; every successful team requires members to think, read, discuss, write, phone, or do any of a number of other tasks between meetings. If nothing of this sort is done, successive meetings simply retread old ground.

Solution: Clarify expectations at the outset. Make certain team members understand what collaborative teaming is really all about—and what role they are expected to play in it. Don't sugarcoat the process or lead them to believe that it consists only of meetings that take place from 9:00 to 9:50 a.m. Also, be sure that each team has enough members so that assigned tasks, when shared equitably, are not too burdensome for any one member.

Challenge: "I'll go to the meetings, but I'm not going to get sucked into the discussion."

Silent resistance is a common challenge among teams, with certain members simply refusing to become engaged in the group's conversations or efforts.

Solution: Break into smaller groups. Break the larger team into several subteams, so each member has the responsibility for collecting information or ideas and then reporting back to the larger group. It may also be possible to ward off fatigue or complacency with groups by encouraging physical activity in a meeting. These moments can prevent disaffected members from retreating into passivity. Consider also a regular and well-facilitated book study to develop a common knowledge base and group cohesion. If there are holdouts to participation after using these and other such techniques, there may be other concerns that need to be addressed. See Chapter 3 and Resource 4 on dealing with resistance.

Challenge: "I'm willing to collaborate . . . but exactly what are we trying to accomplish?"

Collaboration must have the goal of improving student achievement if it is to pay off. Team members can lack focus and direction, ultimately accomplishing little.

Solution: Set and clarify the desired outcome of the meeting in keeping with the larger context or purpose of the team's overall work. When teachers understand that the end goal of their collaborative efforts—and of every meeting—is to boost student success, they tend to be much more focused and productive. Providing feedback and data on "quick wins" and short-term goals is also motivating.

Challenge: "Why are we always tinkering with the way things work? I'm happy with the way my classes are run, and my students are doing just fine."

In Chapter 3, we stated that people may like a given change, but often don't like changing. Ironic as this may sound, it is a common problem—people often resist change, especially when it means that *they* have to change.

Solution: Let people see the possible outcomes. Before launching the change process, make certain that faculty members understand what the change is designed to accomplish. If you have developed a compelling vision statement and clear measurable goals, use these tools to paint a picture of where you are headed, and why. (Additional strategies are in Chapter 3.)

Challenge: "There's no way I'm doing this. I'm completely opposed to it."

Occasionally, a team member resists a team decision, no matter how much consensus building may have taken place within the team.

Solution: Confront dissenters in a respectful and positive way. Confront team members who seem to be holding back, listen to their reservations or negative response to a team decision, and then insist that the team's consensus decision must be enacted in spite of the individual member's opposition. Then lay out a plan that combines support for the teacher who must change as well as oversight to make sure the change occurs.

Often, as pointed out in Chapter 3, real challenges to collaboration, such as lack of time, become reasons for abandoning the effort altogether.

Moving Forward

Building truly collaborative teams is a difficult but necessary component of school success. This chapter illuminated four types of cultures relative to collaboration. Brief examples of productive collaboration in schools throughout North America were also provided.

The next chapter addresses gathering and using the essential fuel for productive collaboration: meaningful data tied to results for all students. Chapter 8 goes into detail on how to collect, analyze, discuss, and put such data into action on behalf of student achievement.

CHAPTER 8

Principle 4

Data-Based Decision Making for Continuous Improvement

Educational institutions are awash with data, and much of it is not well used.

—Lorna Earl and Steven Katz, 2010,
*Creating a Culture of Inquiry: Harnessing
Data for Professional Learning*

I fear that data-based decision making and research-based practice can stand in for careful thought . . .

—Rick Hess, 2008, "The New Stupid"

Even in the "hard" area of data, it is the "soft" skills that determine its successful use. As the opening remarks indicate, the past decade has seen an explosion of new ways to collect, sort, and distribute every type of data imaginable to schools. Test data alone is now a multibillion-dollar industry. Yet the real challenge in the successful use of data toward continuous improvement lies not in the technical side of the equation but, rather, in the human side. Consider these four Cs of using data for improvement:

- Collecting, sorting, and distributing data in the form of reports
- Creating the climate and culture of trust for effective data use

- Capacity building for analysis of data
- Committing to and achieving consistent implementation of data-based decisions

While there are still some important things to consider in terms of collecting, sorting, and distributing data, which are taken up later in this chapter, the major challenges facing schools concern the productive, data-based conversations that lead to consistent implementation. Next, each of the "soft Cs" is discussed individually.

Creating the Climate and Culture of Trust for Effective Data Use

> What has been discovered is that first, people will not voluntarily share information—especially if it is unflattering—unless they feel some moral commitment to do so and trust that the data will not be used against them. . . . Data without relationships merely causes more information glut. Put another way, turning information into knowledge is a social process and for that you need good relationships.
>
> —Michael Fullan, 2001a,
> *Leading in a Culture of Change*, p. 6

In a recent conference that included top data and assessment experts in North America, both Tom Guskey and Ken O'Connor shared their list of the major issues to address in successful assessment. For both, their No. 1 priority was for school communities to start with the "purpose" of the data. For individuals, beginning with "purpose" is advocated in this book in Chapters 1 and 2, and for the organization and teams in Chapters 5 through 7. Combining the essential nature of purpose for both leaders and data use, Lorna Earl advises that "Data-literate leaders are those who . . . think about purpose(s)" (Blankstein, Houston, & Cole, 2010, p. 24).

Peter Hill (2010), whose work led him to the top ranks of educational assessment in Australia and Hong Kong, makes the link between purpose and trust for us:

Openness, transparency, and frank discussion of any accountability program are essential so that both declared and perceived purposes can be aligned. There needs to be a climate of trust rather than of misunderstanding and fear. (p. 45)

Let's bring this statement full circle to the components of relational trust discussed in Chapter 4:

- Clarifying and declaring the "purpose" provides the *ethical* alignment between actions and intention.
- "Transparency" addresses the same and also builds confidence in leaders' *competence*.
- The "openness" and "frank discussions" provide for the *professional respect* that builds trust.

Building a climate of trust requires openly explaining who is evaluating whom, and to what end.

In the example below, consider the role that trust played at Shambaugh Elementary School where they successfully made public what might have been very threatening and very personal performance data.

The Data Wall for All

To emphasize data-based instructional practice, Principal Shawn Smiley set up a data wall in the faculty lounge at Shambaugh Elementary School. "It's a ginormous piece of butcher paper about 10 feet tall and about 15 feet wide," says Smiley. Set up as a grid, the data wall shows Grades K–5 as column headings and achievement levels down the rows: *Above Grade Level* is the top row, followed by *At Grade Level, 0–6 Months Below Grade Level,* and *6 Months + Below Grade Level.*

Each student's first name, last initial, and reading score are then listed on a sticky note and positioned in the appropriate grid on the data wall. "Although we had general consensus about this approach, some teachers didn't initially like it, I'll be honest with you," says Smiley. "At the beginning of the year, they were offended to see students' names showing that they were reading below grade level. But we wanted everyone to know the data,

(Continued)

(Continued)

including the students." When those who held reservations saw that this public display of data wasn't used punitively, they generally came onboard. Smiley reports that students understand the data too:

If you ask students in the hallway what their reading levels are, they're going to know it. They also know where they're supposed to be. So if a student is at 450 and supposed to be at 480, they know where they are, the goals they're supposed to have, and how we're going to get there.

The data wall is paying off with real results. "If I talk to somebody about numbers, it's just numbers," says Smiley, "but if they walk into the lounge and see this giant green butcher paper on the wall with 441 sticky notes on it representing 441 students, that's real. As time passes and students who were reading below grade level begin to shift to the middle or upper part of the grid, that's rewarding for teachers to see" (personal communication, 2009).

Capacity Building for Analysis of Data

One of the big challenges around effective use of data is the staff's capacity to interpret it. In fact, so often school teams seek easy off-the-shelf solutions—and there are plenty of corporations ready and willing to sell them! As Superintendent Jeane Claude Brizzard indicated, technology salesmen "try to shoehorn in" their products to your situation. Yet these approaches reduce rather than expand the staff's capacity. In addition, externally provided professional development "typically represent others' ideas about needed skills and knowledge, but seldom reflect teachers' thoughts about what they need to learn or how to learn it" (McLaughlin & Talbert, 2006, p. 2).

The better (and far less expensive) investment is in a highly trained and experienced facilitator of the collaborative change process (Fullan, 2009; McLaughlin & Talbert, 2006). In her extensive school study around building school-based teacher learning communities, McLaughlin noted, "Schools that made significant progress did so with expert guidance . . . they achieved significantly greater student learning gains than schools where this strategy was not well implemented" (McLaughlin & Talbert, 2006, p. 46).

One aspect of building internal capacity relates to developing one's ability to reframe or redefine the problem in order to solve it. This generally takes a deeper analysis on the part of the learning community and highly skilled guidance from the leader or leadership team. Consider this:

> We have the community define the big issue they are facing and then solve one smaller (high-leverage) aspect of it. In Clairton, Pennsylvania, outside of Pittsburgh, the highway and the streets bypass the town. There are economic problems, and a high incidence of violence among teens. We are still in the inquiry phase now, but when we first asked school personnel about the nature of the problems youth are facing, they identified it as violence. If you ask the students, 50% of them give another answer: being suspended for tardiness. Those suspensions lead to a lot of angry young people being on the street with nothing to do. (personal communication, Monique Sternin, 2011; Blankstein, 2011, p. 37)

As with O'Neill from Alcoa (an example from Chapter 1), it often takes multiple sources of data—and considerable time, focus, and depth of understanding and dialogue—to determine the high-leverage action that will have the greatest impact on addressing the challenge. In the conversation outlined above, while the initial analysis by the staff defined the "problem" as youth violence, those closer to the "action" (the students) had another insight that gave clear direction for the intervention: Change the policies leading to truancy and out-of-school suspensions. This appears to be the lever for changing the outcome of youth violence in this case.

As this example indicates, effective analysis of data, therefore, requires several elements:

- **Clarifying accuracy of the data.**
- **Using multisourced data and soft, "perceptual" data.**
- **Understanding what the data are telling you.** In the above case, there is an interpretation linking truancy to violence among teens. The data alone do not provide this interpretation; people do!
- **Understanding what the data mean.** This step is critical. For example, many schools use percentages at or above "proficiency," as represented by test cutoff scores. Yet as Peter Hill (2010) notes, it turns out that "For many small schools, the degree of uncertainty or measurement error around the school's performance (typically expressed as the percentage of students meeting a given standard)

turns out to be greater than the amount of change that the system has declared to be necessary to meet adequate progress" (p. 44).

- **Tapping well-established, high-performing teams in open and frank dialogue** (see Chapter 5). This approach normally develops better analysis than a discussion with any one individual. (This is not true of teams where trust or well-facilitated exchanges are an issue.)

Commitment to Implementation

If the purpose for data collection is defined by those who use it, and a trusting, collaborative culture composed of capable staff allows for honest and incisive dialogue about the meaning of the data and actions that should be taken, then the chances of consistent implementation are great. The more depth and breadth of involvement of the stakeholder within the learning community, the more likely and widespread the implementation.

Principal Kristen Peltzer offers an example of how the use of data prompted her to create a program to address missing assignments.

Using Data to Move Students Beyond Failure

As Kristen notes, when she began as assistant principal at Ridgewood Middle School, "the school was a dumping ground for staff within the other 18 schools of the district. Police officers were there regularly. Graffiti and racial slurs were everywhere. And only 7% of the students were proficient in math."

She and the principal created a vision: Make Ridgewood Middle School a place where everyone loved to be, with a character and service learning base, and with top performances academically. They had a long way to go.

When Kristen looked at the data, there were 600 Fs entered reflecting a total of 500 students. None of the teachers said it was because students were incapable; rather, it was due to the norm of putting a 0 in the grade book for various offenses. Kristen recognized that once a student received a 0 for any purpose, statistically speaking, if there were only 10 grades in a semester, it required 9 grades of 100% for a student to climb out of that F hole back to an A. In reality, most students would simply give up trying, resulting in even more disciplinary and academic problems.

She guided the staff into dropping zeros altogether. Now, when students miss an assignment, the teacher fills out a form and the students work on the missing assignments during lunchtime with her. The program takes place during a ZAP lunch; this stands for Zeros Aren't Permitted.

Most days, Kristen oversees the program personally; another adult steps in when she is not available. So now she knows immediately if she has a student in ZAP for multiple days; she doesn't need to wait until first quarter to see who is failing. She is able to connect with these students individually and find out specifically why they are struggling; for example, issues may involve a home life situation that is not conducive to homework. In response, she can set them up with a mentor, keep them after school to allow them time to work in a quiet place, provide food if they don't have any, and so forth. The school also has a crisis closet for kids who need clothes.

As a result of this program and approaches exemplified in the case below, Kristen has no failing students in school. All students are passing classes. The proficiency has risen to 70% in math; it has soared from 30% to 70% in language arts (personal communication, 2012).

Kristen was also able to use data to develop schoolwide norms while at the same time building full engagement and collective capacity for action. Although she admits that during the first three years she ran a "dictatorship" to keep order and create new norms, she explains that "Now the staff and students run the school." Let's see how that translates into action.

Using Data From Multiple Sources to Identify and Solve Problems

Kristen has an open-door policy, and she offers many forums for student interaction. One day, students came to her with concerns about cheating. To check another source, she asked the staff if they thought there was widespread cheating. When they replied that they did not think it was a big problem, she turned the power over to the students to work with their faculty advisors to determine the next steps.

The student-led Character Council then conducted a wider survey of all students. Data showed that there was a widespread belief among students that cheating was rampant, so the Council utilized internal meeting structures and advisories to write and refine what became a unanimously codified Code of Honor.

(Continued)

(Continued)

The Character Council then had an idea. They asked, "What about a code for the teachers as well? How will we all be in synch around, for example, the difference between 'helping understand the test question' and 'providing too much direction'?" Further discussions ensued, and then the council collectively created an Integrity Pledge, which was endorsed by the staff and students.

This example depicts how key elements discussed here and in prior chapters come together. Kristen supported the shared vision by encouraging staff and students to engage in an "inside-out" process in which they defined their own core purpose. They used multisource data that was openly and incisively analyzed by a variety of teams in order to bring about collective, systemwide implementation with agreed outcomes.

The latter part of this chapter is dedicated primarily to some advanced work recently completed with Jay McTighe, based on his and Ken O'Connor's seven assessment and grading practices to enhance learning and teaching (HOPE Foundation, Video, 2009b; McTighe & O'Connor, 2005). First, some groundwork about the technical issues of data collection and use is helpful.

Possible Uses of Data

Good data used appropriately offer a multitude of benefits for schools and their stakeholders:

- To advance student achievement
- To address "whole-child" needs
- To provide feedback to students on academic progress
- To screen students for special programs
- To inform parents of student performance and inform the larger community of school and district gains
- To inform teacher judgments about improving classroom instruction
- To organize schoolwide learning support programs to ensure that no student falls through the cracks
- To validate student and teacher efforts to improve
- To guide professional development activities

- To gauge program strengths and identify opportunities for program improvements
- To promote public accountability
- To monitor continuous progress

To successfully use data to drive continuous improvement, schools need to answer three important questions:

- What data should be collected?
- How should data be used? (includes determining the recipient(s) of the ensuing report)
- Who should be involved?

Each of these points is discussed in the sections that follow.

What Data Should Be Collected?

Many schools rely on state or provincial and national standardized test scores as the primary indicator of student learning. These scores can provide evidence of systemwide, schoolwide, and classroom-level achievement and, when properly disaggregated, can help identify students in need of additional support and intervention (as outlined in Chapter 6). Increasingly, schools are tracking a broader set of data types to more fully assess their progress.

One of the most powerful and effective ways of working with data is for vertical or grade-level teams to analyze student work together based on common assessments or assignments. This process encourages all faculty members to share in the responsibility for success of *all* students.

Results-oriented data analysis should include such questions as

- What criteria are used to determine proficiency?
- Does this piece of work show proficiency?
- In what areas are students doing particularly well?
- What are patterns of weakness?
- What can be done to address the weak areas?

Teachers who are accustomed to using data strictly as an evaluative or summative device—to determine whether students did or did not learn what was required—may need training and encouragement to add formative assessment to their instructional practice. As trust among teachers grows (see Chapter 4) and as team-meeting protocols become well established (see Chapters 5 and 7), data sharing among teachers becomes easier. This is always done with the intent of collegial sharing of internal best practices. It is never used to rank or blame individual teachers for poor performance.

Other data sources include the following:

Academic Outcomes

- Outcomes on nationally normed tests
- Student performance on district- or school-level common assessments
- Student work on assignments, especially those common to the grade level throughout the school
- Grade spread on unit tests or semester exams, compared with previous results
- Course and curriculum analysis to measure alignment with state and national standards
- Graduation rates for high schools
- Continuing education levels, such as the percentages of graduating students pursuing higher education or the percentage of students entering regular or honors high school classes (after junior high or middle school)
- Outcomes on state or provincial achievement tests compared with previous years and with other schools of similar demographics

Correlates to Student Achievement

- Engagement levels of students in extracurricular activities
- Character, social, and emotional learning
- Attendance numbers, including enrollments and dropouts during the course of a year and hour-by-hour or class-by-class attendance figures
- Discipline actions, such as the number of in-school or out-of-school suspensions, the number of repeat cases, and times and places of their occurrence

Descriptive Data

- Census, enrollment, and lunch subsidy applications, to profile the demographics of the whole school

- Observations of daily activities, occurrences, and situations that do not appear in any type of formal record keeping
- Surveys of students, staff, and parents to gauge satisfaction and attitudes toward the school

Data overload is common, and narrowing what is needed and how to best use it is a challenge. The next example demonstrates how one school is taking a hard approach to soft data.

A Hard Approach to Soft Data

At Icenhower Intermediate School in Mansfield, Texas, grade-level Student Success Teams (SSTs) piece together a comprehensive picture of each student using shared spreadsheets to track student behavior, office referrals, academics, engagement, attendance, and other data. "You may think a student is excelling in your classroom," commented one teacher,

> but when you look at the data on the spreadsheet, you realize there are extreme deficits somewhere else. And even though you see those kids all day long, you may not know to what extent they are struggling in another class.

Sixth-grade counselor Reggie Rhines notes that SST members consider themselves to be facilitators:

> We track what they're doing and what they've done in the past at their different schools. So, if they come to us already struggling and at risk, we refer to a rich array of data to diagnose the situation. We look to and talk with the parents, we try to put in modifications to help them be more successful, whether it be adding constant mastery to their day or reducing the amount of work they have to get done because they struggle so much. And then, of course, we place them into tutoring groups and other realms where they can get extra help as well. (personal communication, 2009)

Combining hard demographic and formal assessments with soft data about engagement and behavior—while protecting student confidentiality—is a complex task. Principal Duane Thurston comments, "You can't boil it all down to get one answer; it is much more complex than that. Yet having a group of professionals looking at the same expansive set of data helps" (personal communication, 2009).

Using multisourced data and good root analysis is essential to solving a given problem or better understanding a child's needs. The same elements are true for determining a school's effectiveness, as outlined below.

Guidelines for Data Quality

A school's ability to make improvement plans is directly tied to the quality of its data. Without clear, quantifiable information about the school's current status, leaders will find it very difficult to create focused improvement plans. Data from diverse sources guide each step of planning and implementing initiatives for academic improvement. At a minimum, useful data should be multisourced, relevant, timely, consistent, and disaggregated.

Multisourced Data

The data collected should be drawn from a variety of sources in order to give a complete picture of a school's progress. Data should include demographic and socioeconomic information, absentee rates, dropout rates, suspension and disciplinary rates, report card grades, and, of course, scores on state and nationally normed tests.

However, a school is more than a set of numbers, and student, teacher, and parent perceptions of their learning community are an essential part of its achievement. Uncovering and recording these perceptions is a fundamental part of the improvement process. This requires a variety of "soft" data and the use of information-gathering strategies such as surveys, questionnaires, interviews, focus groups, brainstorming, or roundtable discussions.

Relevant Data

To be useful, data must be relevant to the school's goals. Schools revamping their curriculum to align more closely with new standards, for example, will want to look closely at the results on related tests. Schools that have adopted a goal of improving writing skills through a program of writing across the curriculum may find that samples of current student work provide the best indicators of progress.

Relevant assessment data

- align with the curriculum and the overarching SMART goals of the school;

- are sufficiently specific to show achievement and progress of all groups of students and to drive targeted interventions; and
- reveal problem areas and areas of strength to build on.

Timely Data

Since large proportions of student populations turn over annually, outcomes of last year's tests may not reflect the strengths and weaknesses of this year's enrollment. Curricular goals and emphases also change, and they do not always correspond to state test standards. The most useful data for teachers and students, therefore, are the more immediate feedback from formative assessments.

In many schools, the timeliest data are generated by internal assessments and measurements. Teachers cannot rely solely on test results to guide their daily decision making. The data on which they base their day-to-day instructional decisions must be more immediately derived from classroom tests, homework, class work, and observations. Another important data source for teachers is administrator feedback.

Consistent Data

In order for assessments to indicate trend lines, outcomes from the same assessment instruments are viewed at different points in time. Data from this year—whether test scores, absentee rates, or average numbers of writing exercises completed per student—need to be compared with similarly collected data from previous years to be meaningful. Only a comparison of results from several years indicates the trend line of the school.

Disaggregating Data

All data should be analyzed in terms of the identifiable ethnic and socioeconomic groups in the school.

Video Connection

www.corwin.com/ failureisnotan option3

Video 8.1 explores how the use of data has changed over time in the Fort Wayne School District. It emphasizes the importance of using "fresh" data and making weekly adjustments to classroom instruction.

Think It Through: Video 8.1 emphasizes the importance of using "fresh" data and making weekly adjustments. How often is data gathered and reviewed in your school? Discuss some situations where instructional adjustments based on data have lead to greater success in the classroom.

Although district-level enrollment information available from the central office may not reveal a child's cultural, ethnic, linguistic, or socio-economic status, creative improvement teams can develop the information by correlating test results, grades, and other outcomes with subsidized lunch lists, English language learner (ELL) class enrollments, residential addresses, and other recorded information.

They can also require teachers to correlate the children in their classes with preestablished categories (e.g., limited English proficient, newcomer to the community, and living in public housing), then compare the scores of these groups with those of the school as a whole. Such analysis allows schools to set goals and prioritize prevention and intervention strategies for the children who need them most.

Guidelines for Using Data

Once data have been collected and analyzed, teachers and administrators can find ways to apply the results of their data explorations to their day-to-day efforts with students. Following are some ways in which data can be effectively used.

Using Data to Drive Decisions and Set Goals

The selection of goals, instructional practices, materials, programs, and policies in a school should be directed by good information from good data. For example, if a school's data reveal a strong correlation between discipline problems and a particular time of day or place in the school, staff schedules and assignments can be adjusted accordingly.

Data can be used first to determine where the needs are, what kinds of goals need to be established, and whether a goal is achieved. A measurement (or rubric) must be chosen to indicate whether progress has occurred. For example, a school that is determined to raise students' math performance needs to decide how to measure improved performance: What test or observable performance demonstrates how well students are doing? How will the school know when the goal and milestones along the way are attained? The selection of the measures and target scores are best established at the outset and articulated as part of the goal.

Using Data to Target Interventions

The more current the data, the better it can be used to create on-the-spot interventions for struggling groups of students. Teachers can now get real-time data on student performance using whiteboards and other monitoring devices. It is no longer necessary to wait until the grading period to identify and assist struggling students. Interventions can be immediate.

Using Data to Support Change Initiatives

Change is hard (see Chapter 3). It is in the interest of school leaders to use relevant and credible data to support their calls for change to teachers and other stakeholders. A bar graph showing declining student success over time, for example, can be a powerful motivator for action.

Using Data to Guide Continuous Improvement and Redefine Success

Although it may seem that data can most effectively be used to identify problem areas within a school, it can also be used to discover areas of strength that could be made even stronger (see Figure 8.1).

Continuous improvement can play out at the school level in various ways. One way to improve is through periodic evaluation of teaching plans, lessons, unit designs, and assessments by using a set of design standards. Such an approach compels administrators and teachers to apply these same standards to their own work.

Using Data to Monitor Progress

The value of any instructional practice should be judged according to its results. When implementing a new instructional strategy such as differentiated instruction or response to intervention (RtI), teachers must use data to monitor outcomes regularly and frequently to determine how well the new practices work.

Using Data to Guide Professional Development

In Grand Island, Nebraska, the school district has developed a curriculum-based assessment system that includes various performance assessments, common rubrics, and high school exams based on district and state standards. In addition to providing assessment results to teacher teams, the district uses the results to target staff development efforts.

| Figure 8.1 | Collecting and Examining Data in Your School |

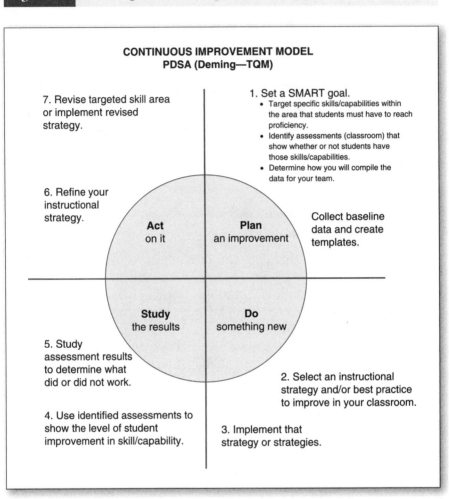

CONTINUOUS IMPROVEMENT MODEL
PDSA (Deming—TQM)

7. Revise targeted skill area or implement revised strategy.

1. Set a SMART goal.
- Target specific skills/capabilities within the area that students must have to reach proficiency.
- Identify assessments (classroom) that show whether or not students have those skills/capabilities.
- Determine how you will compile the data for your team.

6. Refine your instructional strategy.

Act on it

Plan an improvement

Collect baseline data and create templates.

Study the results

Do something new

5. Study assessment results to determine what did or did not work.

2. Select an instructional strategy and/or best practice to improve in your classroom.

4. Use identified assessments to show the level of student improvement in skill/capability.

3. Implement that strategy or strategies.

Source: Used with permission from Linda D'Acquisto, Pat King, and the HOPE Foundation.

"Rather than having the flavor of the year, the programs are much more data-driven," says Jay McTighe (quoted in HOPE Foundation, Video, 2009b), an author and consultant who has worked with the Nebraska district. "If the scores indicate that students are better at creative writing than persuasive writing, then that suggests the need for a professional development focus on strategies for teaching persuasive writing." Such a curriculum-based system provides several assessment points throughout the year, enabling schools and teachers to monitor ongoing progress and make necessary adjustments along the way.

McTighe goes on to note that this approach is compatible with a sports coaching model. "We don't wait until the game to see how we're doing," he says. "We run scrimmages and look for the problem areas, and that's what we work on in our practices" (HOPE Foundation, Video, 2009b).

What *Good* Looks Like

Leaders and teachers in high-performing schools don't view "data" as abstract, out-of-context information that shows whether they're meeting their goals; they interact with data in a much more personal way, using data of various kinds to make daily decisions about teaching.

Consider the following example.

Overcoming Fear of Data

Principal John E. McKenna (2009b) of Mullen Elementary School in Tonawanda, New York, and 2012 New York State Administrator of the Year, reports that his school relies on "data, data, and more data . . . to ensure that we maintain an absolute focus on student achievement." Grade-level teams and vertical teams in language arts, math, science, social studies, and technology integration use running records, Qualitative Reading Inventories (QRIs), and daily anecdotal notes from guided reading sessions. Teams meet for data reviews at frequent intervals:

- **Daily**—For a 30-minute common planning period before school
- **Weekly**—To assess progress against benchmarks
- **Monthly**—To discuss instructional goals and data
- **Quarterly**—To assess data from the prior quarter and to set benchmarks and action plans for the quarter to come (McKenna, 2009b).

(Continued)

(Continued)

An essential first step in implementing the new protocol was McKenna's realization that he had to build relational trust to help teachers move past their fear that data might show they weren't good teachers or that data might be used against them by school administrators. "I had to stop using top-down, judgmental methods and move to a nonjudgmental, bottom-up approach where we worked together and assumed mutual responsibility for our students' success," says McKenna (personal communication, 2009).

Specific methods and strategies recommended by McKenna for principals who want to help teachers learn to trust data include

- **Direct involvement.** Principals who administer assessments to students and correct them with teachers are "getting in the trenches." This changes data dialogue from top-down and the directive to affiliating and collaborative.
- **Be proactive.** Developing an assessment map or schedule outlining all of the year's formative and summative assessments helps teachers know what to expect and how to prepare with no surprises.
- **Periodic review.** Align team meetings to analyze and discuss data with the year's assessment schedule. The more dialogue about data, the more comfortable teachers feel about it.
- **Set specific and realistic goals.** Measure goals in small, incremental steps, building on success.
- **Develop a long-range plan.** Identify data goals for three to five years in advance. Each time that teachers achieve incremental goals, principals can remind them that they are one step closer to the long-range goal.
- **Shift responsibility of analysis to teachers.** Principals who begin with direct involvement—modeling data analysis and leading conversations in data review meetings—can scaffold the transfer of responsibility to staff as competencies increase.
- **Empower teacher leaders.** Some teachers will grasp the data better than others. In fact, many will surpass the principal's knowledge because they apply it daily. It is important to empower these teachers to lead data meetings and present at faculty meetings. They can serve as turnkey trainers and mentors for other teachers and new staff.

"I know I've been successful in working with teachers when I say very little in a meeting," McKenna explains. "The teachers know where their strengths and weaknesses are. They feel comfortable with the data and feel proud of their accomplishments. That's when data actually become the teachers' friend."

A Closer Look at Student Assessment

Jay McTighe and Ken O'Connor recommend that teachers focus on seven assessment and grading practices to enhance learning and teaching (HOPE Foundation, Video, 2009b; McTighe & O'Connor, 2005):

1. Use summative assessments to frame meaningful performance goals.

2. Show criteria and models in advance.

3. Assess before teaching.

4. Offer appropriate choices.

5. Provide feedback early and often.

6. Encourage self-assessment and goal setting.

7. Allow new evidence of achievement to replace old evidence.

Applying these practices before (diagnostic assessment), during (formative assessment), and after (summative assessment) instruction ensures a continuous flow of timely, relevant, and multisourced data that empowers learners and teachers throughout the school year (see Figure 8.2).

Diagnostic Assessment

Diagnostic assessment tools are used before teaching to plan appropriate instruction (HOPE Foundation, Video, 2009b; McTighe & O'Connor, 2005). They allow teachers to

- find out what students know and what they don't know;
- learn about student misconceptions;
- understand student interests, learning styles, learning preferences, and multiple intelligences; and
- inform students of learning goals and performance assessment criteria.

Ideally, diagnostic assessments are short and nongraded. Students can enjoy them and they should not diminish students in the eyes of their peers. Preassessment strategies could include concept maps, Know-Want to Know-Learned (K-W-L) charts, true-false quizzes, drawings, surveys, brain drains, and so forth (HOPE Foundation, Video, 2009b).

Figure 8.2   Summary: Diagnostic, Formative, and Summative Assessment

Diagnostic Assessment (Preassessment)	Formative Assessment (Feedback)	Summative Assessment (Review)
"Diagnostic assessment is as important to teaching as a physical exam is to prescribing an appropriate medical regimen." (Jay McTighe & Ken O'Connor)	"Formative assessment is probably the most important assessment . . . assessment that happens while the learning is going on. . . . It provides information that enables teachers and students to make adjustments in their learning." (Ken O'Connor)	"Educators should frame the standards and benchmarks in terms of desired performances and ensure that the performances are as authentic as possible. . . . Then present the summative performance assessment tasks to students at the beginning of a new unit or course." (Jay McTighe & Ken O'Connor)
Characteristics • Used before teaching • Based on short, nongraded instruments • Helps to find out what students know, what they don't know • May reveal misconceptions • May inform about student interests and learning styles **Cautions** • Inform students of learning goals, performance assessment criteria (offer models) • Preassessment strategies should not diminish students in the eyes of their peers	**Characteristics** • Ongoing and continuous • Uses formal and informal, nongraded techniques • Provides teachers with information about students' learning progress • Guides teachers in modifying lesson plans • Helps students see progress and improve work • Teaches students to self-assess work **Guidelines: Good Feedback Must Be . . .** • Timely • Specific • Understandable • Allowing for self-adjustment	**Characteristics** • Aligned with learning goals • Authentic (knowledge and skills can be transferred) • Offers options to students to display learning • Evaluated against clear criteria **Cautions** • Options should address and demonstrate students' mastery of learning goals • Tasks should be worth students' time and energy—no busy work!

Diagnostic Assessment (Preassessment)	Formative Assessment (Feedback)	Summative Assessment (Review)
A Few Strategies • Concept maps • Know-Want to Know-Learned (K-W-L) charts • True-false quizzes • Drawings • Surveys • Brain drains	**A Few Strategies** • Quizzes • Observation • Skills checklists • Oral questioning • Individual whiteboards • Personal communication • Hand signals • Exit cards • Graphic organizers **Prompts for Self-Assessment** • What part of your work was most effective? What is the evidence? • What part of your work was least effective? Why? • What actions will improve your product or performance? • What will you do differently?	• Be realistic about your own time and energy—no need to offer a great variety of options

Source: Reprinted with permission from *Failure Is Not an Option® 3: Effective Assessment for Effective Learning* [Video series]. Bloomington, IN: HOPE Foundation, 2009b.

Resource 10: Checklist for Using Diagnostic (Preteaching) Assessments offers a checklist for using diagnostic assessments.

Formative Assessment

Formative assessments provide continuous feedback to teachers and learners about progress. They focus on assessment *for* learning (Black, Harrison, Lee, Marshall, & Wiliam, 2003, 2004; Stiggins, 2004; Stiggins, Arter, Chappuis, & Chappuis, 2007) rather than assessment *of* learning (summative assessment). Formative assessment strategies may be formal or informal, graded or nongraded, daily, weekly, or as needed. Tools may include quizzes, skills checklists, individual whiteboards, personal communication/conferences, oral questioning, observation, hand signals, clickers, exit cards, graphic organizers, rubrics, and so forth (HOPE Foundation, Video, 2009b).

Rubrics for Learning

Jay McTighe recommends the use of rubrics throughout the learning process:

> Rubrics are valuable in helping students to see their levels of performance across several criteria so that they can make appropriate decisions about what they need to work on to achieve greater success. When students can set personal learning goals, they're more likely to set forth the effort to achieve them.

McTighe also emphasizes that rubrics allow students to understand what is most important for them to learn and how teachers will evaluate their work. "They need to know in advance the characteristics of a quality performance and the criteria that will be used to judge their work," says McTighe. "A scoring rubric identifies the key elements of the product or performance being evaluated and the criteria that describe varied levels of quality for each of those key elements" (HOPE Foundation, Video, 2009b).

Video Connection

www.corwin.com/
failureisnotan
option3

We often think of data as information just for teachers and administrators, but giving students ownership of their own data can have a very powerful effect on their educational experiences. In Video 8.2, two elementary students from Scott Academy share their data and their folders and discuss how this helps them achieve success.

Think It Through: In Video 8.2, the elementary students discuss how the data is used to help them get where they're "supposed to be." In your experience, how do students perceive data in your school? What additional steps might you take to help them use data to become more empowered and take ownership of their own learning?

Teachers can use the data from formative assessments to differentiate instruction, modify lesson plans, and choose appropriate interventions. Carol Tomlinson (HOPE Foundation, Video, 2009b) comments, "The formative assessment allows me to see where students are in relation to what really matters. And then, the most important piece is to say, What do I do tomorrow? What adjustments do I need to make?"

Jay McTighe (in HOPE Foundation, Video, 2009b) emphasizes the benefits for learners: "Formative assessments help students to see their learning progress and to see the importance of taking an active role as learners by monitoring their own growth. Effective

learners use habits of mind that include goal setting and self-assessment."
Good feedback for students must be timely, specific, understandable, and
allow for self-adjustment by the learner (McTighe & O'Connor, 2005;
Wiggins, 1998). Some effective self-assessment prompts for learners are

- What part of your work was most effective? What is the evidence?
- What part of your work was least effective? Why?
- What specific action or actions will improve your product or
  performance?
- What will you do differently next time?

Readers can refer to Resource 11, which offers a checklist for using
formative assessments.

Summative Assessment

Jay McTighe and Ken O'Connor (2005) advise educators to use summative assessments to frame meaningful performance goals and to allow new
evidence of achievement to replace old evidence. When teachers have successfully used diagnostic assessments before teaching and formative
assessments during teaching, the results of summative assessments
should be evidence of student mastery and cause for celebration.

Effective summative assessment should be aligned with learning
goals and evaluated against clear criteria. Ideally, it is authentic—meaning
that students can demonstrate transfer of knowledge and skills to real-
world problems—and it should offer options to students to display their
learning not only through tests but also with portfolios, essays, videos,
performance, and so forth. "Effective summative assessment," says Ken
O'Connor (in HOPE Foundation, Video, 2009b), "provides opportunities
for students to demonstrate that they know, understand, and can do
whatever are the learning goals. . . . Ideally, it involves some transfer
from general knowledge, understanding, and skill concepts to specific,
authentic tasks."

Readers can refer to Resource 12, which offers a checklist for using
summative assessments.

Challenges and Solutions

Challenge: "Our test scores are great. Why mess with success?"

In high-performing schools, the staff can be challenged to "add value"
to the student learning experience.

Solution: Develop more authentic performance tasks that assess for understanding and transfer. Such contextualized assessments are often more challenging, but also more relevant to students than typical state and national standardized tests. Their development and use can help a school or district move from good to great. Consider adding new goals and benchmarks for measuring student success such as social-emotional growth, wellness and whole-child initiatives, and career success.

Challenge: "Testing data are great for periodically making sure you're on track, but I don't use them to make day-to-day decisions."

Solution: Help teachers understand how to analyze relevant and timely classroom data by providing appropriate staff development to team leaders. Once teams are established, they can watch and learn from one another by visiting other team meetings.

Challenge: "Data analysis is just a fancy name for a witch hunt. What the administrators really want is to find out which teachers aren't getting their kids ready for the state tests."

The idea of slicing data by classroom puts some teachers on the defensive. They may feel that if their students' scores are low, they will be unfairly blamed.

Solution: Use one of the following approaches:

1. Have teachers collaborate to look at data that have been "depersonalized" in such a fashion that teachers aren't able to focus on students' specific classroom, level, or teachers. For example, an administrator might draw a team together to look at students' tests or assignments, using codes in order to avoid connecting the work under evaluation to a specific teacher. Teachers can score anonymous student results, then spend the rest of the meeting looking for patterns and designing appropriate intervention strategies.

2. Get teachers together in vertical (cross-grade-level) teams to discuss what students are expected to know and be able to do, how to determine if they have achieved proficiency, and what must be done to ensure success for all students.

3. Build general trust among teachers, and back it with specific actions. It is critical that teachers know that administrators will

never use student achievement data to rank teachers against one another. Nor should this information be used in any public forum until a high degree of trust allows for that. (In several schools where we work, the staff has decided to use data walls to publicly share both student and teacher performance—all to the end of the entire community working on behalf of success for 100% of the students.) Without making this commitment, it is very difficult to collect accurate data. Alternatively is the use of formative teacher assessments (for coaching purposes only) to assist in better outcomes on final summative assessment(s) that are used for evaluation.

Moving Forward

This chapter featured guidelines for the productive use of data by instructional teams focused on ensuring student success. Additional tools and strategies were also covered that focused on diagnostic, formative, and summative assessments. The next chapter shows how successful schools grapple with bringing about meaningful student, family, and community engagement.

CHAPTER 9

Principle 5

Gaining Active Engagement From Family and Community

Alan M. Blankstein and Pedro A. Noguera

There is a major difference between involving parents in schooling and engaging parents in learning. While involving parents in school activities has an important social and community function, it is only the engagement of parents in learning in the home that is most likely to result in a positive difference to learning outcomes.

—Alma Harris and Janet Goodall, 2008,
"Do Parents Know They Matter?"

The research is abundantly clear: Nothing motivates a child more than when learning is valued by schools and families/community working together in partnership. . . . These forms of involvement do not happen by accident or even by invitation. They happen by explicit strategic intervention.

—Michael Fullan, 1997, *What's Worth Fighting for in the Principalship?*

Does the following exchange sound familiar?

Teacher 1: How's it going?

Teacher 2: Not good. My kids don't seem to care about learning at all. They're not motivated, they don't study, and some of them don't even seem to care if they fail.

Teacher 1: It's such a shame, but it all starts in the home, you know.

Teacher 2: What can we do if the parents don't care?

The common corollary to the above scenario is often found in wealthy districts where "helicopter parents" seem to want to run the school. Regardless of the circumstance, it is clear that the proper support and involvement of students' families and the community at large is fundamental to student achievement in schools. Joyce Epstein at Johns Hopkins University, James Comer and Ed Zigler at Yale, and Maurice Elias at Rutgers University all speak eloquently on the topic of parental/guardian involvement in schools. Their research concludes that greater parental involvement leads to higher levels of student achievement and improved student behavior, irrespective of such factors as socioeconomic status or ethnic background. That same research shows that the most accurate predictor of student academic achievement is the ability of the student's family to create a home environment that encourages learning; to communicate high, yet reasonable, expectations for achievement; and to stay involved in the student's education in meaningful ways (Comer, Joyner, & Ben-Avie, 2004; Elias & Arnold, 2006; Epstein et al., 2009).

Moreover, most educators know that their highest-performing students come from families where the parents are involved. This doesn't necessarily mean that they are present at the school for meetings and events. Rather, it means they play an active role in the home reinforcing the importance of learning and the value of education for their child. Given the clear importance of this kind of involvement to child development and student achievement, how do we get more parents to play an active and supportive role in the education of their children?

In some schools, bringing about a meaningful increase in the quality of parental involvement presents a significant set of challenges. In communities where student achievement is consistently low or where wide disparities exist in patterns of student achievement, relations between school, family, and community can often be strained—a recipe for misunderstandings, misinterpretations, and disagreements. Moreover, it is often the children who are performing least well whose parents are the least involved. This is one of the reasons why several researchers have suggested that closing the gap between parents and schools must be seen as a critical part of the effort to closing the gap in student achievement (Boykin & Noguera, 2011).

In schools where parental involvement is minimal, educators sometimes assume that parents simply don't care about their children's education. However, a vast body of research shows that most parents want to see their children succeed academically, and many have a genuine interest in being involved in the schools their children attend (Marx, 1996). This raises an important paradox: If both parents and teachers want the same thing—student success—why is it that strong partnerships between parents and schools can be so hard to create?

When we look closely at schools that have succeeded in forging strong partnerships between parents and the schools their children attend, it is clear that ties with parents are based on mutual interests and an understanding that there is a common goal: student success, both academically and in life. While this might seem obvious, in many cases it isn't. In schools where parents have not been involved, educators often develop assumptions based on the notion that parents don't care. Similarly, parents who have had negative experiences in school themselves frequently assume that the educators don't care about their children. This is why creating strong relationships takes a lot of understanding, a bit of work to make time for the partnership, and a willingness on the part of educators to communicate effectively with the parents they serve and assure parents that, as educators, they are indeed invested in the success of the children.

Unfortunately, in some schools, it is common to hear educators blame parents for low student achievement and to complain that parents are not doing their part. As we observed in the opening vignette, it is common to hear educators complain that parents send children to school late, unfed, and unprepared for their classes. Certainly there are parents who are not doing enough to support their children or to address behavior problems when they occur at school. However, even when these complaints are legitimate, it is a mistake to conclude that parents don't care or that they don't want their children to succeed.

The fact is many parents are struggling to make ends meet and are overwhelmed in their efforts to raise their children. After a long day of work, some parents are too tired to supervise homework, much less attend a meeting at their child's school. Furthermore, parents who lack college degrees and formal education may simply not know what to do to support their child's education. This is why empathy, based on a recognition that most parents are doing their best to raise their children and rooted in an understanding of the challenges that parents face and respect, is so critical. While we never want to make excuses for those who may be negligent, empathy and respect are essential if we are going to create partnerships rooted in trust that reinforce the importance of learning and make it possible to have difficult conversations about student behavior when these are necessary.

There is no consensus on where the responsibility rests for ensuring parental involvement in schools (Harris & Goodall, 2008). According to a 1994 survey (Center on Families, Communities, Schools, and Children's Learning), 90% of teachers surveyed felt that parental involvement was needed in schools and they supported the idea of parent volunteers. However, only 32% felt that it was their responsibility to initiate such involvement, and 50% indicated that they did not have enough time to do so. Given such statistics, it is perhaps unsurprising that many parents do not feel welcome at their children's schools, and 70% of parents surveyed said they had never been invited to volunteer in their children's schools.

The trends shown in these studies and others, many more than a decade old, are still relevant today. At a time when the pressures on parents are greater than ever, what can schools do to create welcoming and supportive environments so that parents want to be involved? Particularly in so-called "failing schools" where poverty is often concentrated, what can educators do to ensure that parents are able to play a supportive role in the educational process? Parents of children in such schools often develop distrust and even hostility toward educators they may believe are not serving their children well. Disaffection often results in low levels of parental involvement and hostile relations between parents and teachers. In turn, this creates a cycle of negative reinforcement, blame, and distrust.

Schools that are not performing need strong partnerships with parents, and they must find ways to overcome distrust and suspicion to develop positive relationships with the families they serve. Given the importance of parental support at home in producing higher levels of student achievement, it is essential that schools find ways to enlist parents as genuine partners in the educational process.

As challenging as this work may seem, the fact is that a number of schools have found ways to get parents involved and to sustain partnerships over time. Successful schools devise a variety of plans and activities

Video Connection

www.corwin.com/ failureisnotan option3

In Video 9.1, Dan Bickle, Area Administrator of the Fort Wayne School District, and Mike Morris, instructional coach, talk about the need to give parents ownership of their child's education.

Think It Through: How would you characterize your school's relationships with parents and guardians? Which parents are least likely to be involved? How can you prove to parents that "this isn't the same school you went to, or the same experience you had"? How can you help parents and teachers feel more like a team?

throughout the academic year for involving families. They make sure that the first communication between parent and school is not a call about bad behavior or poor academic performance, and they build trust with parents so that when difficult conversations about student conduct are necessary, communication without incrimination is possible. In such schools there is an overriding recognition that relationships with parents are too important to school and student performance to be treated as a low priority.

Some schools surmount the many obstacles in their way and succeed in forging close and productive relationships with parents and community members alike. In the following pages, we look at some of the approaches and principles that these schools have in common.

Building Positive Family and Community Relationships

Schools that have become true professional learning communities have addressed the gap between parents and schools by employing three key principles to build positive family relationships:

1. Mutual understanding based on empathy and recognition of shared interests

2. Meaningful involvement of family and community in a variety of school activities

3. Regular outreach and communication to family and community

Mutual Understanding and Empathy

The first step toward building or repairing home-school relationships is to gain a common understanding, with empathy for students' families. This means that the school staff becomes aware of the specific challenges that affect many families and thus make it difficult for them to support their children's learning. This includes the recognition that many parents have had negative experiences with school and are afraid to become involved. Parents may be intimidated by feelings of ignorance and uncertainty, and they may assume that their children will experience the same kinds of difficulties that they encountered while in school. Additionally, many parents are struggling to make ends meet. Some are working more than one job and have little time to supervise homework. Others are grappling with layoffs, housing foreclosures, and lack of health benefits. Instead of penalizing children and criticizing their parents for lapses and failures in attendance or preparation, teachers in high-performing schools work with families to help them overcome problems and barriers.

Schools that are committed to student success devise creative ways to respond to the difficulties that students face. Some areas in which schools can extend understanding and support include

- Creating afterschool homework centers so that children who don't have someone at home to help them are not penalized because they have not completed assignments;
- Creating schedules, policies, and programs that take into account students' home-life challenges;
- Providing translators who can communicate with non-English-speaking families and produce versions of important school announcements and communications in the languages spoken by the families that are served;
- Creating waiting areas (with coffee and tea) at school for parents and other visitors so that they don't have to stand at the counter while waiting to speak to a member of the staff;
- Arranging for transportation of students to afterschool activities, and for families to school events;
- Setting up alternatives to telephone communication for families who lack telephones; and
- Holding meetings for parents at public libraries and community centers when transportation to school is a problem.

Empathetic Decision Making

Nancy Brantley, principal of Pelham Road Elementary School in Greenville, South Carolina, tells a story that illustrates how the challenges of a child's home life can spill over into life at school. On the first day of state testing at Pelham Road, school buses were late arriving from an outlying neighborhood. When the buses finally arrived, the students on them were visibly upset and agitated; there had been a shooting in the neighborhood the night before.

One little girl, in particular, was extremely upset, so Brantley took her aside for a private talk. The student explained that the shooting had occurred in her apartment building. Without a phone to call the police, she and her family were powerless to do anything other than "hide and cry."

The little girl wanted to know if she had to take the test that day. Recognizing that the student faced personal issues that superseded the academic ones, Brantley excused her from the testing. "While testing is important, on that particular day, that child was lucky to even get to school," Brantley said. "Children should never ever have to live in situations like that—something that we hope we'll never have to experience."

Brantley's decision in this case was very much in keeping with other Pelham Road policies, such as its policy on tardiness. When a student arrives late to school, he or she is not penalized. In most cases, the child simply receives a pass and is sent on to class. Even with a chronically tardy student, the school does not seek to punish or reprimand. Rather, it looks for ways to help parents resolve the problem even as it also stresses the importance of punctuality. Brantley says,

> If it's a real big problem, although it rarely is, we call the parents in to see if we can help. Because sometimes they simply cannot get an old car started, they don't have a way to school, they've missed the bus— so that's where we step in as a community school to help. (personal communication, 2009)

Effective Involvement of Families in the School

According to Barbara Eason-Watkins, the best way to ensure parental and community involvement in a school is to welcome people into the school. Although this may seem obvious, it is actually a common stumbling block in community-school relationships. Eason-Watkins says, "In many conversations I've had with parents and members of the community, they felt that most schools didn't want them to participate, didn't want them to be part of the school" (HOPE Foundation, Video, 2002). This feeling of being unwelcome and shut out sometimes stems from parents' own experiences in school. Those parents who struggled during their own academic careers may feel distrust or even anxiety about interacting with school authorities.

Connecting the School and Community

When Deborah Wortham accepted a new position as superintendent in a small district, she decided to connect the school and community by making home visits. She explains:

> The visits, which occurred over five Saturdays and included several community leaders, enabled me to meet students, parents, and taxpayers (who were initially shocked to see the superintendent on their front porch early on a Saturday morning!). I also obtained information from assessment data and interviews with board members, administrators, teacher leaders, central office staff, and selected support staff (including paraprofessionals, secretaries, and cafeteria and facilities staff). Questions sent out in advance allowed the conversations to proceed with ease. Some participants wrote detailed responses to the questions. Here are a few of the questions I used for discussion with parents, businesspeople, and community members:
>
> - Please give me a very brief autobiographical sketch of yourself.
> - What are your general impressions of the school system?
> - What are the top three (3) issues that the district must face?
>
> I also used these questions for discussion with the board of education, along with several others, including
>
> - Describe the kind of leadership you wish to see in the future.
> - As you think about how the board functions as a group, what works well, frustrates you, or would you like to see changed?
> - How can I help you be a better board member?
>
> By the end of the summer, I had interviewed more than 400 stakeholders. The information I received was invaluable, and I was able to use this data as the framework for school improvement throughout the district. (personal communication, 2012)

In other cases, language and cultural differences create a barrier to parental involvement in schools. In some districts, many parents speak and read English imperfectly or not at all, making meaningful involvement in the school difficult, if not impossible. Parents who don't speak English may be hesitant to contact schools and unsure of how best to communicate with school personnel about their student's needs. In many cultures, educators are treated with deference as authority figures. The perception of their elevated status makes families less willing to ask questions or voice complaints. For undocumented immigrants, the barriers may be even more significant. Fear of being identified may make parents reluctant to participate in school activities and less likely to engage school officials.

Barriers like these make it obvious that family involvement in the schools is not something that occurs naturally or easily when cultural, economic, political, or racial barriers are not addressed. Partnerships with parents must be purposely cultivated and planned. Professional learning communities can cultivate such involvement by bringing parents and other adults in to share their expertise and talents in meaningful ways and by creating parent-to-parent support networks. These schools recognize the value of the contributions that family members can make to the achievement of the school's educational mission.

Ways of encouraging meaningful parent involvement include

- Establishing a parent-to-parent outreach that contacts all parents to see what they can contribute to student learning;
- Inviting parents and community members to provide lessons in the language and/or culture of ethnic groups that are represented in the school community;
- Inviting parents and community members to provide leadership for extracurricular clubs based on special interests; and

Video Connection

www.corwin.com/ failureisnotan option3

In Video 9.2, teachers from Icenhower Intermediate School share how they "took it a step further" with personal invitations and visits after data showed they were reaching only a limited number of parents.

Think It Through: These teachers discuss creative ways to personally reach out to parents. They also note the danger of relying on online grade systems exclusively to communicate information. Consider how information is shared with parents in your district. What could you do to "take it a step further" and reach out to parents in more personal ways?

- Training teachers and the school receptionist in how to greet parents and conduct productive parent-teacher conferences.

One way to involve parents in the school is to keep them informed about what their children are learning—even to the point of offering parent workshops. Many schools tackle this objective by sending home a syllabus and posting it weekly online so parents can track exactly what students are learning each week. A middle school in Boston uses the quarterly report card as a time to celebrate student achievement by inviting parents to come in and meet teachers while the band plays music in the auditorium, food is served in the cafeteria, and friendly basketball games between teachers and students take place in the gymnasium.

Other school districts are taking similar approaches:

- Icenhower Intermediate School in Mansfield, Texas, offers "Culture Night" for families. Academic teams select geographic regions of the world and invite parents and families to sample the music, food, art, clothing, and geography of each region.
- Thornton Township High School in Illinois District 205 has a "Parent Academy" in each of its buildings to offer adult classes on topics ranging from word processing to Spanish language to swimming. Not only are the courses *attended* by parents and community members, but many courses are also *taught* by parent volunteers.
- Eagle Academy, an all-male public school in the Bronx, New York, offers weekend Parent Academies, with workshops on helping students apply to college, talking to teens about sex and drugs, and maintaining strong positive relationships. The workshops are consistently well attended because parents value the information that is made available to them.
- Fort Wayne Community Schools has a "Real Men Read Program" with Thursday story hours. Adults read a book to students and the children get to keep the book. This volunteer effort is so successful that summer sessions have been added.

Parents or community members can serve as translators to facilitate communication between the school and non-English-speaking families. They can also make presentations—talks, slide shows, or videotapes relevant to current events, areas, or subjects being studied. Principals and teachers who lack the language skills can also develop partnerships with local churches and community-based organizations to help in doing outreach and providing translation to immigrant parents.

Using Parents' Unique Abilities

At Pelham Road Elementary School in Greenville, South Carolina, parents use their abilities and experiences to enrich the lives of students through special-interest groups and clubs. Two bilingual parents volunteer their time twice a week to meet with the afterschool Spanish Club. Other parents, who have literary interests, work with the school's Authors' Club, to guide students through the process of writing and publishing a book. To meet the needs of Eritrean immigrants, one Oakland middle school hired a parent who had been a teacher in Eritrea to work at the school as an instructional assistant.

Getting parents into the school on a more formal basis can be an opportunity to provide a positive experience, expand the relationship, and encourage meaningful and helpful interactions between parents and their children. Teacher wisdom for maximizing parent-teacher collaboration includes asking parents to

- Mentor and tutor students who need extra help;
- Assist with classroom writing projects, science experiments, and so forth;
- Direct or assist with dramatic productions; and
- Present performances of puppet shows, musicals, dramas, or dramatic readings, to name a few (Shubitz, 2008).

Reaching out to parents and inviting them into the school—and especially into the classroom—can result in significant changes for teachers. Keep in mind that the vast majority of schools in affluent communities already feel a strong sense of accountability to the parents they serve. When low-income parents engage schools with a clear sense of what their children are entitled to as learners, and when they raise questions about the quality of education their children receive, schools are forced to be accountable. Of course, parents must be given clear guidance on what to look for in the classroom, and they must be given clear guidance about how to be involved when they volunteer so that they do not interfere with teachers. However, recognizing that the involvement of parents is important to improving school quality is absolutely essential to changing a school's culture. Embracing and valuing in-class volunteers is a prerequisite for an effective parent volunteer program. If the teachers don't accept the idea of having parents in the classroom, it won't work.

Reaching Out to Family and Community

In effective schools, teachers and administrators go the extra mile to reach those children and families whose problems stand in the way of their full involvement in schooling. Part of reaching out is simply by making staff members visible in the neighborhood, at fast-food restaurants, malls, and other places students and families are likely to visit.

Gary Burgess (HOPE Foundation, Video, 2002) says that *wherever* you meet parents—whether at the barbershop, the gym, the church, or the community center—becomes the locus of your campaign to get them into the school. In other words, recruiting parents is not an activity restricted to specific hours at specific places: it is a constant, ongoing process that is central to the operation of the school. Burgess recommends a "bring the mountain to Mohammed" approach for providing information about school activities and efforts to the com-

> **Video Connection**
>
>
> www.corwin.com/ failureisnotan option3
>
> In Video 9.3, Duane Thurston, the principal of Mary Orr Intermediate School, emphasizes the need to build a bridge to the community that can be crossed both ways.
>
> **Think It Through:** Often schools take important steps to make parents feel welcome in the building, but they neglect the vital step of also participating in the community. Consider whether or not the "bridges" in your district are designed to be crossed both ways. What further steps might you take to involve the school in the community?

munity. In his district, school principals hold periodic informational meetings at local churches and other public meeting places. He notes that these meetings are sometimes better attended than those held at the school because parents and community members perceive them as less threatening and more convenient. Burgess also uses a teacher log to record all parent contacts and then evaluates the information with teachers. By formalizing, valuing, and monitoring these contacts, he has been able to change teachers' behavior.

School as a Community Hub

A growing number of school leaders here and abroad are becoming more outward looking (Southworth, 2009). Some are returning to "wraparound" approaches from the 1980s as developed by James Comer, Ed Zigler, and others (e.g., Head Start and Co-Zi Schools, a collaborative initiative combining Dr. Comer's School Development Program [SDP] and Dr. Zigler's School of the 21st Century [21C]) (Comer, Haynes, Joyner, & Ben-Avie, 1996; Zigler & Muenchow, 1994).

These schools are in effect providing children a web of support to compensate for overstressed families. Since community services are often disjointed, these school leaders coordinate law enforcement and community agencies for the social, emotional, and academic success of their students. For example, programs might be devised to ensure that homeless children do not have to transfer to new schools throughout the year. As another example, at PS 28 in Brooklyn, the local YMCA runs the after-school programs based at the school, and youth on work release from Rikers Island have been trained to make repairs on the school as part of their rehabilitation.

Working With Local Agencies

Newport News School District in Newport News, Virginia, has worked with local agencies to create "Homework Clubs" for latchkey children. In 12 different locations throughout the city—including housing projects, shelters, and other community centers—the district has established quiet, safe places for studying after school. Each Homework Club is equipped with computers and classroom materials and is staffed by a teacher aided by a parent who has been trained as a teacher's assistant.

The district has also worked with housing projects in disadvantaged neighborhoods to create four computer labs for both parent and student use. In the evenings, the computers are available for student use. During the day, while students are at school, the labs are used to train adults in computer skills, with paid trainers teaching everything from computer maintenance to software design. These community resources, funded in part by a federal grant, serve both to prepare parents for the workforce and to help them become better teachers for their children.

Similarly, PS 28 in the Bedford Stuyvesant section of Brooklyn, New York, has developed an array of partnerships with local agencies to provide job training and ESL classes for parents and extended learning opportunities for students after school. These partnerships have made it possible for the school to provide its students with an enriched education that includes art, music, dance, and swimming lessons. Despite the fact that over 40% of the students served at PS 28 are homeless, it is also a high-performing school that has received numerous awards from the district and the state of New York. In explaining how the school has accomplished so much despite the odds it faces, school principal Sadie Silver says proudly, "Our parents are our partners. We can't do it without them."

Schools acting as a community hub can also benefit when they reach out to the local business community. Local businesses have a considerable stake in the quality of graduates that the schools produce—and they are often quite willing to contribute time, expertise, guidance, and funding. One middle school in Atlanta receives donations of blue jeans, backpacks, and sneakers each fall so that children have new gear at the start of school. David Douglas High School in Portland, Oregon, has an extensive array of partnerships with local businesses that provide internships and job training opportunities to students, some of whom go on to become future employees. In the San Francisco Bay Area, seven high schools, two community colleges, and one four-year college have formed a partnership with several leading biotech firms that is now in its 15th year. The partnership produces good-paying entry jobs and a pathway to college for the hundreds of students it serves.

What *Good* Looks Like

Each of the following scenarios offers an example of how schools can interact with parents and community members. Can you think of ways in which the interactions could be improved so that both parties come away with a more constructive approach to addressing the problem?

Scenario 1

Teacher: Marissa, this is the third time this week that you haven't had your homework done. The last two times, I gave you second chances—but you just don't seem to be trying.

Marissa: I'm sorry. I didn't have time again last night because I have to help take care of my brother on the nights my mom works.

Teacher: I understand that you have a responsibility, but I can't continue to overlook the fact that you aren't completing your work. From now on, if you don't turn in homework when it's due, I'm going to have to give you a zero for it.

Scenario 2

Parent: I am sorry to be registering my daughter a few days late for school but we just moved here and I had trouble figuring out what I needed to do. I understand that my daughter will be attending this school in the fall. I wondered if you'd mind giving us a tour.

Principal: We gave tours before school started. Now your daughter is already behind. That's not a great way to start the school year.

Parent: Well, it wasn't my intention for her to start late, but I didn't know what to do. I'm concerned that she may have a hard time adjusting now because she's new.

Principal: Well, this is a great school and we've got good kids and wonderful staff. The main thing is to get her caught up on her work. I hope we can count on you this year to do your part so that she doesn't fall behind.

Scenario 3

Teacher: Miguel, I've noticed that your mother has not been signing your weekly assignment sheets. Have you been showing them to her and asking her to help you check your work, as I asked?

Miguel: I did ask her, Mrs. Torphy, but she says her English isn't good enough to check my work. She says she doesn't understand most of my homework at all.

Teacher: I'm sorry, Miguel. Maybe you can translate it for her. Unfortunately, no one on our staff can speak Spanish.

What are your thoughts about each of these scenarios? We've provided our analysis in past chapters; now we're taking off the "training wheels." Have fun with this!

Implementation Guidelines

The National PTA lists the following six national standards for family involvement programs, along with associated practices:

> **Standard 1: Welcoming all families into the school community.** Families are active participants in the life of the school, and feel welcomed, valued, and connected to each other, to school staff, and to what students are learning and doing in class.

> **Standard 2: Communicating effectively.** Families and school staff engage in regular, two-way, meaningful communication about student learning.

> **Standard 3: Supporting student success.** Families and school staff continuously collaborate to support students' learning and healthy development both at home and at school, and have regular opportunities to strengthen their knowledge and skills to do so effectively.

> **Standard 4: Speaking up for every child.** Families are empowered to be advocates for their own and other children, to ensure that students are treated fairly and have access to learning opportunities that support their success.

> **Standard 5: Sharing power.** Families and school staff are equal partners in decisions that affect children and families and together inform, influence, and create policies, practices, and programs.

> **Standard 6: Collaborating with community.** Families and school staff collaborate with community members to connect students, families, and staff to expanded learning opportunities, community services, and civic participation (National Parent Teacher Association, 1998).

Challenges and Solutions

Teachers and administrators face numerous challenges as they work to strengthen school and community ties. Below are some of those challenges—and some of our suggestions for resolving them.

Challenge: "I've *tried* to reach out to the parents of my students . . . but most of them, especially the parents of the kids who are struggling, don't seem to care, and some are downright hostile. The ones who do care are generally parents of kids who are doing well and some are so overly involved that they second-guess my every move."

In many schools, the parents of students who do least well academically are also least likely to be involved. All of the research shows that reaching out to these parents can serve as an important step in improving the performance of these students.

Solution: Parents and administrators, and designated parent coordinators, need to actively reach out to parents and families not connected to the school. It is very important that the first communication not be a call home about bad behavior or poor academic performance. Make contact before problems occur. Demonstrate empathy and understanding to parents who may be struggling to make ends meet. Let them know that you value their support and that you truly believe their children can succeed if you work together. Meeting them in places where *they* feel comfortable facilitates the communication *and* the school professionals' empathy.

Challenge: "Our school has no problem communicating with parents! In addition to the full binder of material we send home with every student at the beginning of the year, we send weekly newsletters and calendars of upcoming events. Every teacher maintains a current 'homework hotline,' so parents can call in and check their children's assignments. And we post everything on our website and update it every two weeks."

Many schools mistakenly believe that communication flows in only one direction—that as long as they're getting information to parents, they're doing their part. Meaningful communication, however, must be two-way, constantly alternating between informing and listening.

Solution: Look into interactive modes of communication—including, but not limited to, voice mailboxes, suggestion boxes located both in the school office and in key locations around the community, parent surveys, and direct phone calls to ask for parent feedback and input.

Challenge: "We have some great parents, and I know they want to be involved in their kids' education—but they just don't seem to have a clue how to go about it."

Clearly, achievement is enhanced when students receive help with schoolwork at home. However, not all parents know how to help, and they may not feel qualified to offer guidance on subject matter that is unfamiliar to them.

Solution: Set up community-based homework support. Use students in the National Honor Society, students earning community service credit, and other peer tutors. Set up tutoring after school and during the weekends at the school, community center, or local library. Invite parents in and show them how best to help their children with homework. Remember that the children who most need the help often have parents who are not well prepared to provide the needed assistance.

Getting Started

As you begin preparing to open the lines of communication with parents and other community members, first take a moment to evaluate where your school currently stands with regard to community and parental involvement.

- How many community members participate as members of teams for various improvement activities in your school?
- How many parent volunteers does your school have?
- In what capacities are those volunteers used?
- Of the ethnic and cultural groups forming significant parts of the school population, how many are represented on school teams? As parent volunteers?
- What outreach initiatives have been undertaken to recruit community members?
- What forums or meetings have been organized to explain school-related issues and answer families' questions?

Consider these strategies for engaging parents in genuine partnerships:

- Change middle and high school handbooks so that they emphasize the positive, identity-building opportunities awaiting students. Feature interviews and stories with graduates. Place less emphasis on disciplinary infractions, but do present school rules that contribute to the positive identity of the school.

- Develop positive feedback systems to show appreciation of social-emotional intelligence, small amounts of progress, and academic success. Create progress reports about progress of all kinds, and change report cards to include indicators of life skills that parents will understand and appreciate.
- Provide parents with multimedia-formatted guidance explaining how parents can support the work of the school, at home.
- Create forums for dialogue about cultural and ethnic differences; create networks of parent liaisons composed of educators, parents, and community residents who can help new families of different ethnic groups adapt to the neighborhood.
- Create opportunities for community service and more meaningful, widely participatory student government. Publicize what happens in these contexts so parents can see what the school is doing and gain a better understanding of the interests and competencies of their teenagers.
- Provide forums for parent discussions and mutual support around the various developmental issues, familial stressors, and parent-child communication concerns that can be expected during the adolescent years (Elias, Bryan, Patrikakou, & Weissberg, 2003).

Moving Forward

This chapter has presented a variety of strategies and a framework for productively engaging family and community in the school. We included many examples of what successful schools are doing to engender broad-based support and to strengthen their entire school community in the process. The point of these examples is to show other educators that *it can be done.*

The next and final chapter addresses an issue that is crucial to sustaining the successes that arise from following the practices described in this and preceding chapters. Building sustainable leadership capacity at all levels enables school communities to maintain focus and continue to improve even while withstanding massive changes. Chapter 10 explains how this can be accomplished.

CHAPTER 10

Principle 6

Building Sustainable Leadership Capacity

Alan M. Blankstein with
Andy Hargreaves and Dean Fink

There is mounting evidence that if school leaders are to spread teaching and learning excellence beyond isolated classrooms, they need to create high-functioning instructional teams and distribute authority among staff members in the school building (including teacher leaders) to realize the vision, and then provide support to help others exercise their shared responsibility for improved learning.

—Wallace Foundation, 2010b, p. 12

Throughout this book, the focus has been on developing leaders capable of creating high-performing teams who in turn support effective teaching and learning. This is the route to sustainable student success and a vibrant, self-renewing school culture able to take on myriad challenges and mandates "du jour."

Authors' Note: This chapter includes text that has been adapted, with permission, from "Sustaining Leadership" by Andy Hargreaves and Dean Fink (2003, May), *Phi Delta Kappan, 84*(9), 693–700.

This final chapter focuses on three key words for long-term school success: *leadership, capacity,* and *sustainability.* Taken together, these words emphasize the importance of continually developing the human resources of the school community so that success lasts well beyond the initial implementation of school improvement efforts.

This implies a steadfast depth of commitment to change—a depth that comes from the commitment of the entire school community to a compelling *long-term* vision that impacts the school culture. When developed with care and forethought, sustainable leadership capacity enables school cultures to thrive despite challenges, including leadership transitions.

The following section addresses the *why* question—specifically, why should we build leadership capacity in our teaching staff? The current realities for principals and teachers are included here, as are obstacles to change and the means of addressing each.

This is followed by a definition of *leadership.* The summary of research leads us to propose a form of leadership that is enduring and outlasts any single *leader.*

Next, we address the issue of capacity. Building leadership capacity at all levels—including within the student body, family, and the community—is the ideal. Here, however, we focus on teachers as leaders. What does this mean? What roles would a teacher leader play? What examples exist? How can teacher leadership be instituted systematically? All of these questions are addressed in this section.

Finally, Hargreaves and Fink address sustainability using case studies from their multiyear projects in Finland; Ontario, Canada; and the United Kingdom, with attention given to "leadership of learning," "distributed leadership," and "leadership succession." In-depth Case Stories are provided to exemplify these critical components of sustaining leadership capacity.

Why Build Leadership Capacity?
The Job Is Too Big To Do Alone

Our proposed purpose of education—*sustaining high-achieving schools because failure is not an option for any student*—is a big job. Making the statement that all children will succeed (or learn to high levels) can be energizing. Trying to operationalize it as the sole leader of the school can be depleting. As referenced in the 2012 survey of California administrators from Chapter 2, and echoed in this National Association of Secondary School Principals survey, the distance between the ideal and the reality for building leaders is often great:

> Principals feel the most important aspects of their job are establishing a learning climate, dealing with personnel issues like hiring and evaluations, and providing curricular leadership. Yet, of the average 62 hours a week they work, only about 23 are spent on these activities. The rest are spent on parent issues, discipline, community relations, and school management. (Schiff, 2002)

Put briefly in today's context: "School leaders spend much of their days disconnected from the core business of better learning" (NSDC, 2010, p. 11). There is a chasm between the demands on educational leaders and what they are actually able to do. Often the instructional focus seems less pressing and visibly present than the organization and discipline of the school. In other words, while a few parents may complain about poor *instruction*, CNN cameras will show up if there is a major drug bust. For these reasons, plus those of traditional leadership training, and lack of content expertise (in how many subject areas in a good high school will the principal be the content "leader"?), it is understandable that "instructional leadership" can fall from the top of the pile.

In recent years, a number of reports depict the principalship as being in a state of crisis largely precipitated by two troubling factors: (1) School districts are struggling to attract and retain an adequate supply of highly qualified candidates for leadership roles (Knapp, Copland, & Talbert, 2003) and (2) principal candidates and existing principals are often ill-prepared and inadequately supported to organize schools to improve learning while managing all of the other demands of the job (Levine, 2005; Young, 2002).

The principal's job is too big and too complex to be done alone. Moreover, principals who try to "fly solo" often feel isolated and tend to burn out. It can be lonely at the top!

Yet giving up control and the traditional roles and views of authority is difficult and not often accomplished. This task requires the courage, described in Chapter 2, to take the risk of letting go of some control, trusting staff members to lead in major areas of decision making, as described in Chapter 4, and, in order to become a learner alongside your staff, admitting that you don't know everything.

Shared Leadership Develops Commitment and Yields Higher Student Achievement

Video Connection

In Video 10.1, school principals discuss the importance of sharing leadership and becoming "a leader of leaders."

www.corwin.com/ failureisnotan option3

Think It Through: Jo Ann Pierce states, "Leadership increases at all levels when the leader at the top lets go of the office, lets go of the position, and lets everyone else help run the show." What can you "let go of" to help share leadership and improve collaboration?

According to Leithwood and Jantzi (2000), teacher leadership has more significant effects on student achievement than principal leadership. Other benefits of teacher leadership include teacher efficacy, improved teacher quality (York-Barr & Duke, 2004), retention of good teachers (Hirsch, 2006; York-Barr & Duke, 2004), higher standards of achievement and responsibility for school reform at the classroom level (Childs-Bowen, Moller, & Scrivner, 2000); and extended principal capacity (Barth, 2001b).

When teachers are unwilling to take risks that go along with candid reflection, when they don't have many opportunities to come together over students' work, when they lack leadership or expertise at the school site, then community-building initiatives are hamstrung and commitment erodes during leadership transitions. (McGlaughlin & Talbert, 2006)

Merideth (2007) uses the acronym REACH to capture the values of teacher leadership: risk-taking, effectiveness, autonomy, collegiality, and honor. As articulated by teacher leader Mike Pringle of Brooks Wester Middle School in Mansfield, Texas,

The decisions at our school are driven, first of all, by our kids and secondly by the teachers. Our administration allows us to be a big part of what we do and have say in the process, which gives us the ownership that we need to make it work. (personal communication, 2009)

Challenges and Solutions

Although experience and the research clearly support the notion of teachers as leaders, the reality is that many teachers are reluctant to play that role. Their hesitancy arises from the following three areas.

Challenge: Teachers may not feel *able* to be a "leader." Their training has not been in this arena, and they have never considered themselves in that role. These teachers may ask, "What *exactly* do you want me to do, and how am I supposed to do *that?*" This request puts the teacher again in a role of follower and seems to minimize the risk of failure. This teacher may feel unable to meet the challenge.

Solution: Teachers who feel unable to rise to the challenge need first to understand the positive impact they have on student achievement by assuming an active role in the school.

Talking with teachers about the important role they can play *outside* their classroom to affect student achievement is one strategy. Specifically, principals can use the data provided earlier and the steps that were used to build the organizational mission, vision, and values.

Teachers who feel less than able to lead also need encouragement and peer support. Within the school, calling on early adopters to model the leadership role that can be played is perhaps the most powerful strategy for persuading others of its feasibility. In Mattoon, Illinois (HOPE Foundation, 2009c), teachers now design and lead professional development days and on their own develop ways to learn from one another (see Chapter 7).

Most important to success is the issue of relational trust (see Chapter 4). There is a high correlation between the trust and confidence in teachers displayed by the leaders and the amount of risk those teachers will take.

Challenge: Teachers cling to their traditional role as followers.

Solution: Administrators must recognize that the new and unaccustomed role of making and being responsible for decisions requires a major shift in thinking that increases over time. Steps should be taken to support hesitant teachers as the school moves beyond a top-down approach. In particular, there is little that creates more momentum for success than the power of support and shared commitment from one's peers. And the best way to create this forward momentum is to have teachers work *together* on an area of common interest. The tool provided in Resource 1 to create a rubric defining excellent instruction is an example.

The results are invaluable:

> Once we had the CLA [Courageous Leadership Academy] team at Williamston, everything wasn't coming from the principal anymore. Team members and colleagues were running our staff meetings and our inservices. We were the ones up there running people through the norms, talking about values, and looking at our mission. It had a different feel than your principal or administrator always giving you things from the top-down versus everyone invested in the system as a whole. (Laura Hill, personal communication, 2009)

> Our principal gives us responsibility so that we feel a valued part of what's happening. Before, I just did what I was told. . . . I just stayed in my classroom . . . but I didn't feel like I had any impact at the school level. Now I feel more involved. (Huffman & Hipp, 2004)

While teachers may not want to be "instructional leaders," they generally *do* want to lead instruction! Getting professionals started in work that is *their* passion—and building in the opportunity for them to take leadership of this work—is an excellent entry point to developing leadership in other areas as well. Again, the elements of success are:

- Tap people's interests and passions;
- Set up a road to success beginning with quick wins;
- Have the team endeavor that journey together;
- Provide feedback loops for them to see their own successes;
- Add celebrations and means for others to join the parade; and
- Institutionalize the processes in the culture (see discussion below).

The ultimate success is what we so often hear in our work: "I used to work here; now I help run the school!"

Challenge: Many teachers don't want to be leaders, at least not as leadership is traditionally defined. The charismatic, dynamic, highly public concept of a leader is much less appealing to many teachers than the role of humble yet courageous leader focused on curriculum and instruction.

Solution: A new definition of *leadership* is helpful for many of these teachers—one in which they can see themselves and thus feel impassioned. There are areas in which many teachers would pursue the opportunity to play a leadership role and make meaningful decisions. Many professionals with whom we work say, "I would like to be a part of deciding what we teach and how we teach it!" This desire is understandable, and it provides a good entry point for developing leadership and responsibility. Many appealing leadership roles for teachers are also listed in the later section about "Building Capacity."

Defining Leadership

Traditionally, the role of the leader has been that of a bold, action-oriented figure who solves most of the problems and draws others to his side in the effort. Think of John Wayne in the old westerns, and Will Smith, Bruce Willis, and countless others in their roles in today's shoot-em-up movies.

Although there may be some call for that style of leadership today, particularly in life-threatening crises, a growing body of research calls for a more participative approach in our schools (Fullan, 2011; Hargreaves & Fullan, 2012).

Specifically, principals "have to be [or become] leaders of learning who can develop a team delivering effective instruction" (Wallace Foundation, 2011, p. 4) that encompasses "five key responsibilities:

1. *Shaping a vision of academic success for all students* based on high standards

2. *Creating a climate hospitable to education* in order that safety, a cooperative spirit and other foundations of fruitful interaction prevail

3. *Cultivating leadership in others* so that teachers and other adults assume their part in realizing the school vision

4. *Improving instruction* to enable teachers to teach at their best and students to learn at their utmost

5. *Managing people, data and processes* to foster school improvement. (Wallace Foundation, 2011, p. 4, original italics)

These five key responsibilities are synergistic with the six principles that guide student achievement outlined in this book. Moreover, they are not developed as a checklist or as "one more thing to do!" but rather as a means of focusing the many initiatives currently under way, and enhancing those needing attention.

In the leadership system described by Jim Collins (2001), the most effective leaders are able to collaboratively create and uphold changes that *sustain* success through a combination of "intense professional will" and "humility." Likewise, when leaders are developed at every level of the organization, the responsibility for success shifts from one or two people to the entire learning community. This does not imply that everyone plays the same role, but that every role is important and that most entail some level of leadership. The next section of this chapter focuses on specific leadership roles played by teachers in high-performing schools.

Building Capacity

As we work toward developing teachers as leaders, we must move beyond the narrow definition of leadership and the minimal number of roles that it comprises. Districts that define leadership roles and encourage teachers to pursue one are well on their way to building vital leadership capacity.

Staff development has traditionally been delivered by outside experts. Today, there is a sense that leadership should be embedded in the school culture (Darling-Hammond, Wei, Andree, Richardson, & Orphanos, 2009). This happens through teacher mentors, teachers being recognized as content-area specialists, master teachers, and teachers leading curriculum writing teams, standards development teams, and professional development programs. In fact, beginning with "expert guidance" (McLaughlin & Talbert, 2006, p. 46) from an outside facilitator grounded in the research and practice that aligns with the schools' focus was essential in "all instances of significant school culture change that we found" (p. 40). This also builds internal capacity.

Building Capacity via Institutionalizing Processes, Routines, and Habits

It is helpful to institutionalize and systematize capacity-building approaches. By focusing on "keystone habits," the leader can cause widespread shifts through new, ongoing routines in the organization (Duhigg,

2012). These habits—when well selected—have ripple effects on myriad behaviors as well. For instance, "Families who habitually eat dinner together raise children with better homework skills, higher grades, greater emotional control and more confidence" (p. 109).

Forming key habits and routines also frees up the individual and collective "mental space," helping decisions become known patterns about everything from how to drive your car in the morning to what happens when the bell rings in every classroom. This in turn provides more time and mental capacity for those items that require deeper thought, while it simultaneously puts into place routines and habits that are critical to a high-performing school culture.

Selecting which habits to begin with is as much art as science. Where and how does the tone for the day or the key activities in your school get established? For children coming to school, it may well be the greeting from your bus drivers. If so, this may be a very high-leverage habit to formalize across all personnel involved with how that bus ride will unfold—including components such as the greeting, the seating, the ride itself, the leadership the driver provides in setting the "bus culture," and the transition from the bus to the school.

The formation of habits includes three elements:

1. **A cue**—the smell of coffee in the teacher's lounge;

2. **The routine**—everyone rushing to grab a mug and discussing how they feel about the school; and

3. **The reward**—which in this example is both the camaraderie and the rush of caffeine, sugar, and fat to the bloodstream.

The key to evaluating habits is in keeping the cue and the reward but reviewing the *routine*! Remember, *collectively* determining the desired change is vital because "your odds for success go up dramatically when you commit to changing as part of a group. Belief is essential, and it grows out of a communal experience . . ." (Duhigg, 2012, p. 93).

In most areas, habits already exist in your school. For instance, when the bell rings at the end or beginning of class, people play out their habits. The question is: do these habits center around routines that advance the culture of learning? If not, the intervention is in changing the routine.

Let's say that when the bell rings, the students run as fast as they can to their destinations, while teachers duck into their classrooms to avoid the melee. Here's what a hypothetical intervention might look like: The *cue* of the bell ringing would remain. The *reward* of energy release and laughter by the students would also need to remain in some form. The *routine* of running like crazy to the next class, however, would be altered if the school community decided together, for example, that it led to more fights in the hallway. The replacement might be a short "fun time" (energy release and laughter reward) for the students once they arrive at their next class. In this way, the new routine is most likely to have staying power since the cue and the rewards remain intact.

Routines exist in subsets of the school as well: team meetings, how or if teachers are collectively examining students' work, and so forth. The ideal result of working to institutionalize routines to support the learning culture is that everyone uses them. What happens in each teacher's class as soon as the bell rings (e.g., Is there a lesson on the board to get students started?)? What happens each time any member of the staff sees a child coming to school looking very upset? Is there a standard routine that is collectively agreed and acted on?

As the schools' values-based culture, framework for action, and routines become established, it is easier to add members to the staff who are likely to succeed. This clarity can become both a means of screening and of recruiting prospective job applicants. New employees would also be given both the expectation and the support necessary to become a part of a learning team and a project or endeavor that taps both their passions and interests in leadership.

At the Icenhower school, in Mansfield, Texas, for example, Principal Duane Thurston expected teachers to participate in the school's hiring decisions:

> When we interview any person for this staff, it's a team effort. We look for someone who has a heart for students and ask if that is someone we want to have as a part of our staff. It they don't have the six principles in their heart, they won't get hired to teach here. (personal communication, 2009)

In Mattoon, Illinois, similar learning community practices have led them to be inundated with applicants well beyond the norm for the region.

In the next section, Andy Hargreaves and Dean Fink define *sustainability* and provide Case Examples that demonstrate how some schools build it into their culture.

Sustainable Leadership

Andy Hargreaves and Dean Fink

In this section, we connect the concept of sustainability to the leadership literature in education and outline different interrelated principles that underpin the ideas and practices of "sustainable leadership." We draw on the *Change Over Times* study (Hargreaves & Goodson, 2003), as well as on very recent material on districts and countries that perform above expectations and where leadership is a key factor, along with preliminary findings from a study of succession management in three countries: Canada, England, and the United States (Hargreaves & Fink, in press). We use three positive and negative sets of Case Examples to illustrate our analysis of sustainability in leadership. Specifically, we focus on (1) leadership of learning, (2) "distributed" leadership, (3) leadership succession, and (4) integrating leadership.

Background of Sustainability

For many years, change theorists and change agents have been concerned with the problem of how to move beyond the *implementation* phase of change, in which new ideas and practices are tried for the first time, to the *institutionalization* phase, when new practices are integrated into teachers' repertoires and begin to affect many teachers, not just a few (Stiegelbauer & Anderson, 1992). "Institutionalization means a change is taken as a normal, taken for granted part of organizational life; and has unquestioned resources of time, personnel, and money available" (Miles, 1998, p. 59).

Many long-standing practices—the graded school; the compartmentalized, hierarchical, bureaucratized secondary school; tracking or streaming according to students' abilities; and didactic, teacher-centered teaching—are examples of policies and practices that have been institutionalized over long periods of time and that have become part of the "grammar" of schooling (Tyack & Tobin, 1994). The persistence of this grammar and of everyone's ideas of how schools should really work as institutions have repeatedly made it exceptionally difficult to institutionalize other changes, innovations, and reforms that challenge accepted practice, that imply a different and even deviant institutional appearance and way of operating for schooling (Meyer & Rowan, 1977).

Innovations that challenge the traditional grammar of schooling often arouse intense enthusiasm. They prosper and flourish in well-supported pilot projects, in specially staffed and charismatically led schools, or among an atypical minority of teachers and schools whose teaching careers and identities are characterized by risk and change (Fink, 2000a; Fletcher, Caron, & Williams, 1985; Riley, 1998; Smith, Dwyer, Prunty, & Kleine, 1987). But, typically innovations fade, light-house schools lose their luster, and attempts to spread initiatives across a wider, more skeptical system—to scale them up—meet with little success (Elmore, 1995). Even those few innovative settings that survive often serve as outlier exceptions—giving the system a safety valve where its most critical and questioning educators and their clients can be congregated together in one site (Lortie, 1975; Sarason, 1990).

In the face of the traditional grammar of schooling, and those whose interests are served by its abstract academic orientations, the vast majority of educational change that deepens learning and allows everyone to benefit from it neither spreads nor lasts. Sustainability, in the deeper sense, raises questions about the preoccupation of policy makers with short-term success over long-term improvement, statistical appearances that make them look good over sustained changes that ensure students learn well, and timelines for change that address electoral cycles of popularity rather than change cycles of durability.

Some contemporary discussions of sustainability in educational change repeat these traditional preoccupations with how to keep change going over time. In doing so, however, they often trivialize the idea of sustainability (Barber, 2001), reducing it to *maintainability*—to the question of how to make change last—but adding little to our understanding of change. Now, however, we have learned how to sustain change over time.

It also works against the type of systemic changes needed to sustain and expand major school improvements. The history of schools is strewn with valuable innovations that were not sustained, never mind replicated. Naturally, financial considerations play a role in failures to sustain and replicate, but a widespread "project mentality" also is culpable. Efforts to make substantial and substantive school improvements require much more than implementing a few demonstrations. Improved approaches are only as good as a school district's ability to develop and institutionalize them equitably in all its schools. This process often is called diffusion, replication, roll out, or scale-up.

The frequent failure to sustain innovations and take them to scale in school districts has increased interest in understanding systemic change as a central concern in school improvement.

Our interest in systemic change has evolved over many years of implementing demonstrations and working to institutionalize and diffuse them on a large scale (Adelman & Taylor, 1997, 2003, 2006a, 2006b; Taylor, Nelson, & Adelman, 1999). By now, we are fully convinced that advancing the field requires escaping "project mentality" (sometimes referred to as "projectitis") and becoming sophisticated about facilitating systemic change. (Adelman & Taylor, 2007)

Fullan emphasized that the leadership most needed is that which "motivates people to take on the complexities and anxieties of difficult change" (Fullan, 2005, as cited in Adelman & Taylor, 2007).

The Meaning of *Sustainability*

Sustainability is about more than endurance. It concerns more than the life and death of a change. Lester Brown, founder of the World Watch Institute, first coined the term *sustainability* in the environmental field in the early 1980s (Suzuki, 2003). He defined a sustainable society as one that is able to satisfy its needs without diminishing the opportunities of future generations to meet theirs.

We argue that sustainable educational leadership and improvement preserves and develops deep learning for all that spreads and lasts, in ways that do no harm to and indeed create positive benefits for others around us, now and in the future (Hargreaves & Fink, 2005).

Sustainable leadership is characterized by *depth* of learning and real achievement rather than superficially tested performance; *length* of impact over the long haul, beyond individual leaders, through effectively managed succession; *breadth* of influence, where leadership becomes a distributed responsibility; *justice* in ensuring that leadership actions do no harm to and actively benefit students in other classes and schools; *diversity* that replaces standardization and alignment with networks and cohesion; *resourcefulness* that conserves and renews teachers' and leaders' energy and does not burn them out; and *conservation* that builds on the best of the past to create an even better future (Hargreaves & Goodson, 2006).

What contribution can leaders make to sustainable improvement according to the sense of sustainability we have outlined? In our view, leaders develop sustainability by how they approach, commit to, and protect deep learning in their schools; by how they sustain others around them to promote and support that learning; by how they sustain themselves in doing so, hence they can persist with their vision and avoid burning out (see Chapters 1 and 3 also on sustaining your vision and yourself); and by how they try to ensure that the improvements they bring about last over time, especially after they themselves have gone (Fink, 2005; Hargreaves & Fink, 2005). We will now look at three particular aspects of what we call *sustainable leadership* that illustrate most of the different components of sustainability (and nonsustainability) that we outlined: leading learning, distributed leadership, and leadership succession. Last, we add final material from a district and a country to show how sustainable leadership is also integrating leadership that works beyond the school within and outside the immediate community.

The examples are drawn from our research reported in detail in the *Change Over Time* study (Hargreaves & Goodson, 2003), a special edition of the *Educational Administration Quarterly* (Hargreaves & Goodson, 2006), and the experience of working directly with four, then six, secondary schools over five years (1997–2002) to help them implement a major set of legislated changes in secondary school reform in ways that were consistent with principles of successful school improvement and with their own professional values as educators.

All of the schools were located in a large urban and suburban school district in Ontario, Canada, which funded the project in partnership with the Ontario Ministry of Education and Training. Two very recent examples are then added from the world's highest-performing country on many international tests—Finland—as well as *the most improved urban school district in England.*

The Canadian project design generated relationships of trust and candid disclosure among the schools and between the schools and the project team, and it accordingly built an authentic understanding of how teachers and leaders were experiencing and coping with reforms over a relatively long five-year period when other major changes were also affecting their schools.

Examples of Sustainability and Nonsustainability

Let's look now at the three paired examples of sustainability and failed sustainability in our project schools.

Leading Learning

The prime responsibility of all school leaders is to sustain learning. Leaders of learning put learning at the center of everything they do: student learning first, then everyone else's learning in support of it (Glickman, 2002; Stoll, Fink, & Earl, 2002). The leader's role as a leader of learning is put to the strongest test when his or her school faces demanding measures or policies that seem to undermine true learning or distract people's energies and attention away from it.

High-stakes testing can push teachers to deliver improved results but not necessarily to produce better learning. What educators do in this situation depends on their commitment to student learning and on their attitudes to their own learning. In 2001, the Canadian province of Ontario introduced a high-stakes literacy test in Grade 10. It was applied to virtually all students, and they were required to pass in order to graduate. High stakes, high pressure!

Two Approaches to High-Stakes Testing

Ivor Megson was the new principal at Talisman Park Secondary School. Promoted from being assistant principal at the school, Megson was dedicated to his work as a leader but did not like to rock the boat too much. Most of his staff had been at the school a long time. They liked being innovative in their own academic subjects but were skeptical and often cynical about larger-scale reform agendas. A coffee circle of embittered staff members met every morning before school to complain about the government's latest (almost daily) initiatives and announcements. Like many principals, Megson saw his responsibility as being to protect his staff from the deluge of reforms that descended on the school. This, he felt, was the best way he could help them.

With his staff, Megson therefore figured out the most minimal and least disruptive school response to the Grade 10 test—one that would produce the best results with the least amount of effort. Quickly, Megson and his staff began identifying a group of students who, on pretests, indicated they would fall just below the pass mark. The school then coached or "prepped" these students intensively in literacy learning so they would perform acceptably when taking the real test. Technically, the strategy worked. The school's results looked good.

(Continued)

(Continued)

But teachers' energies are finite, and as staff concentrated on those students near the cut-off point, the ones who really needed help with literacy, and had little chance of passing the test, were ignored. At Talisman Park, authentic literacy and learning for all—especially for the most needy— were sacrificed to appearances and results.

Charmaine Williams was the principal of Wayvern High School, just up the road from Talisman Park. Wayvern was a culturally and ethnically diverse school and had a high number of students for whom English was their second language. Wayvern had a lot to lose on the literacy test. Yet Williams' school made literacy, not the literacy *test*, one of their key improvement goals.

Williams engaged her staff in inquiry about how to improve literacy so it would benefit all students in the long term instead of focusing on how to manipulate the short-term scores on the test. Working with large staff teams, across disciplines, and with workshop training support, Wayvern undertook an audit of existing literacy practices in classrooms, researched effective literacy strategies that might be helpful, and undertook a gap analysis to see what improvements would be necessary.

Teachers shared their literacy strategies across subjects, then dedicated a whole month to a high-profile focus on literacy learning in the school and with the community. They also continued a successful literacy initiative they had already made where everyone in the school read together for 15 minutes each day. Williams harnessed her staff's learning in support of student learning. The immediate results were not spectacular (as is usual with more sustainable change), but together the staff and parents were confident that long-term improvement mattered the most. Wayvern teachers were convinced that in future years, scores would increase as genuine reflections of learning and achievement rather than because of cynical manipulations of the testing process (Nichols & Berliner, 2007).

One reform; two principals; two schools—but different outcomes! Especially in the most adverse circumstances, those principals who are leaders of learning make the most lasting and inclusive improvements for their students in their schools.

Distributed Leadership

Outstanding leadership is not just the province of individual icons and heroes (Saul, 1993). In a complex, fast-paced world, leadership cannot rest on the shoulders of the few. The burden is too great. In highly complex, knowledge-based organizations, everyone's intelligence is needed to help the organization to flex, respond, regroup, and retool in the face of unpredictable and sometimes overwhelming demands. Locking intelligence up in an individual leader creates inflexibility and increases the likelihood of mistakes.

But when we use what Brown and Lauder (2001) call "collective intelligence"—intelligence that is infinite rather than fixed, multifaceted rather than singular, and that belongs to everyone, not just a few—the capacity for learning improvement is magnified greatly. For these reasons, more and more efforts are being made to replace individual leaders with more distributed or distributive leadership (Harris, 2008; Institute for Educational Leadership, 2000; Spillane, Halverson, & Drummond, 2001). In a distributed system, leadership becomes a network of relationships among people, structures, and cultures (both within and across organizational boundaries), not just a role-based function assigned to, or acquired by, a person in an organization who then uses his or her power to influence the actions of others. Leadership is viewed as an organic activity, dependent on interrelationships and connections (Riley, 2000).

Different Leadership Styles; Different Outcomes

Mark Warne was the principal of North Ridge High School. Three years from retirement, Warne has a keen intellect and a deep knowledge about imposed change and its effects; he valued and was skilled at seeing the big picture of reform. When legislated reforms were announced, Warne produced detailed, thoughtful written and projected timelines for implementation responses that he circulated to staff members for comment. The response was disappointing, though, and Warne confided that his staff was generally apathetic about getting involved with change. His strength was his great intellectual clarity, but he could not develop the capacity among his staff to share his vision. The big-picture change belonged to Warne alone, not to everyone. His office was packed with policy statements, resources, and materials that might better have been distributed around the school.

Warne controlled the directions of his school through the line management of the department heads. The department heads were quite autonomous in their areas; staff involvement, therefore, depended on the leadership style of each head. One of his assistant principals (also close to retirement) performed traditional discipline and administrative roles. The other was battling with what sadly turned out to be a terminal illness.

(Continued)

(Continued)

Warne delegated to his subordinate department heads and accepted their advice in areas where they were more expert than he. The department heads generally described him as "supportive," "compassionate," and "well-intentioned." Yet the larger staff was excluded from decisions and ill-informed on important issues. They considered their principal to be "inde-cisive," "inconsistent," and "lacking a personal vision." At a school improvement workshop with the whole staff, they were the only school of the six to identify themselves as "cruising" (Stoll & Fink, 1996)—their mainly affluent students were getting good results, but the school lacked purpose and direction. The chief problem the staff chose to address at the workshop was "communications with the administration."

Soon after this, the school began to change dramatically, but not through a change of principal. In 1998, two new assistant principals were appointed. Together, they infused the school's administration with renewed enthusiasm, optimism, and focus. Diane Grant's athletic bearing and infec-tiously energetic style brought her sophisticated knowledge of curriculum and classroom assessment to the problem of reform. Before long, she was skillfully leading the staff in curriculum-gap analysis or having them share successful experiences in classroom assessment by seating them in cross-disciplinary tables at the staff picnic, where they scribbled their ideas as graffiti on paper tablecloths. Meanwhile, Bill Johnson, the other deputy, drew on his counseling skills to develop effective communications and rela-tionships with and among the staff. Grant aroused teachers' passions, and Johnson calmed them; as a team, they were able to set a common vision for the school and a more open style of communication. In this new style, the staff focused on collaborative learning, inquiry, and problem solving. Warne's strength was having the good sense to distribute the leadership of important classroom-related changes to his assistant principals, who in turn redistributed much of the leadership among the staff, who learned to be critical filters for government mandates rather than mere pipelines for implementing them.

Leadership Succession

Sustainable leadership outlives particular individuals. It does not disap-pear when the leaders leave. There is evidence that the departure of the initiating principal or a critical mass of early leaders from model or bea-con schools is the first symptom of decline (Fink, 2000b; Sarason, 1972). MacMillan (1996, 2000) has observed that the practice in some school districts of regularly rotating leaders between schools can harden teachers against change because they come to see the school's principalship as little more than a revolving door in a building where they are the permanent residents. Whether principal rotation is formalized or not, leadership succession always poses a threat to sustainable improvement.

How Two Schools Dealt With Leadership Succession

Bill Matthews was a tall, commanding figure who brought vision, energy, and intellectual rigor to his role. The son of a police officer, he believed strongly that students came first and pursued this belief with a sense of clear expectation and relentless determination. Some staff respected his commitment to children and his willingness to take action and put himself on the line for their sake. Prior experience of principalship buttressed his self-confidence, and in a teacher culture that reveled in argument and debate, his somewhat adversarial style (Blase & Anderson, 1995), which encouraged and entertained well-reasoned and supported opposition to his ideas, suited a sizable number of staff very well. It also stimulated some extremely lively staff meetings. Matthews led Stewart Heights School with firm expectations and clear example, accompanied by lively argument and considerable humor. The most outstanding instance of leading by example was when he personally solved the scheduling problems of 80 students to demonstrate that better service for students was indeed possible.

Matthews was quick to move to action by getting staff members to analyze data consciously and to make action plans on the basis of what they learned. He integrated several improvement teams to permit far greater voice and participation for teachers in the work of the school compared to the previous dominance of the department heads' council. In this culturally diverse school, Matthews encouraged the staff to initiate a range of changes that made students feel more included and parents feel more welcome. Structures, planning, and initiation, backed by his own personal interactions with people and his visibility around the school, were the ways in which Matthews brought about change. Many staff members, including most of those on the School Success team, warmed to his decisiveness and sense of direction. Staff referred to him as a "visionary," "change agent," and "efficient manager." Others, however—especially women—indicated they respected him but questioned his somewhat "authoritarian" style.

(Continued)

(Continued)

The two assistant principals offered complementary, indeed dramatically contrasting, approaches within Matthews' administrative team. One presented a quieter, more restrained, and more procedural version of masculinity in leadership than his more "up-front" principal. The other took a more relationship-centered approach to students, curriculum, and staff development, where caring, coupled with hard work and high expectations, played an important role. With their contrasting styles, they also fostered greater teacher participation in the work of the school.

Bill Matthews felt it had been a struggle to change the school culture to provide "a service to kids and the community." Yet when he presented the staff with survey data showing that 95% of staff members were satisfied with the school, but only 35% of students and 25% of parents were, this created a common problem that the staff had to work together to solve.

With more time to help staff members work through their doubts and difficulties, Matthews and his team may well have been able to convert the temporary success of short-term innovation into sustainable improvement. But by the end of his third year, changing circumstances within the school system resulted in his moving to a superintendency, one of the assistant principals to his first principalship, and the other to her second deputy principalship. Stewart Heights' new principal was new to the school and to the role; he had to feel his way carefully into both of them. Meanwhile, the mandated reform agenda was quickly gathering pace. The result of these converging forces was that the staff and their new principal turned their attention to implementation more than improvement. Observations at the school climate meetings indicated that with the previous principal's departure, student-centered policies now gave way to more conventional behavior-code initiatives. The early achievements of school improvement at Stewart Heights quickly began to fade. If school improvement is to be sustainable, one essential factor is continuity of tenure or at least longer tenure for the initial principal, as well as consistency in philosophy among those who come after.

By comparison, Blue Mountain School, an innovative model school established in 1994, planned its own leadership succession from the outset. The fate of most innovative schools is to fade once their founding principals have left. Blue Mountain's principal anticipated his own departure and worked hard to create a school structure that would survive his departure and "perpetuate what we are doing." He was especially alert to the threats posed by leadership succession (Fink, 2000b; Hargreaves & Fink, 2000; MacMillan, 2000), where an ensuing principal might import a different philosophy. He therefore "negotiated very strongly [with the district] to have [his] deputy principal appointed principal." After four years, the system moved the principal who founded the school to a large "high profile" school in the system and promoted his deputy in his place. In her words,

> We talked about [this move] and we talked about how we could preserve the direction that the school is moving in, and we were afraid that if a new administrator came in as principal that if he or she had a different philosophy, a different set of beliefs, then it would be quite easy to simply move things in that particular direction and we didn't want that to happen.

Blue Mountain is a rarity. In general, planned succession is one of the most neglected aspects of leadership theory and practice in our schools, and one of the most persistently missing pieces in the efforts to secure sustainability of school improvement.

Sustainable Leadership as Integrating Leadership

An Example From Finland

Finland is the world leader on results in the Program for International Student Assessment tests of sophisticated, applied knowledge in mathematics, science, and literacy, as well as on international ratings of economic competitiveness. It avoids shortsighted and unsustainable standardization along with national standardized tests altogether and reaches high levels of educational achievement and economic success (it ranks No. 1 in the world on economic competitiveness according to the International Monetary Fund) by attracting highly qualified teachers with supportive working conditions, strong degrees of professional trust, and an inspiring mission of inclusion and creativity.

With a team of colleagues, one of us reviewed the Finnish system for the Organization for Economic Cooperation and Development (Hargreaves, Halász, & Pont, 2008). We found that school principals were able to lead communities of highly qualified teachers who develop their school curriculum together within broad national guidelines.

They work in cultures of trust, cooperation, and responsibility, seeing themselves as one of a society of experts who work with fellow professionals and neighboring schools to achieve compelling and inspiring purposes together that rebuild their communities and their nation around knowledge, society, and principles of inclusiveness and creativity. Indeed, in the city of Tampere, high school principals told us that when they agree together on an important initiative for their community, if one school is short of resources, the principal can call the others and one of them will say, "We have a little bit extra, would you like some of ours?" Finnish teachers think about more than "me and my class." And Finnish principals think and act beyond "me and my school." It is not just teachers who need to stop operating as independent contractors. Principals do too!

An Example From London

If the culturally homogeneous and overwhelmingly "White" example of Finland seems irrelevant to the urban centers of America and elsewhere, the London borough of Tower Hamlets is an equally compelling example of sustainable leadership as integrating leadership. Tower Hamlets is improbably situated directly opposite the office towers of glass and steel that formed the setting for the G20's restructuring of the global economy in 2009.

The borough was originally the residence for the yeomen who guarded the Tower of London. For much of the 20th century, it was a prosperous working-class community of dockworkers. After the collapse of London's docking industry in the 1970s when supertankers and container ships could no longer navigate the tight bends of the River Thames, waves of immigrants moved into the newly impoverished area—many from rural areas of Bangladesh, one of the world's poorest countries. Despite the reconstruction of part of the Docklands into the fashionable global finance and media center of Canary Wharf, the white-collar workers who came and went on the new high-tech transit line were barely aware of the immigrant community in their midst.

Tower Hamlets' Bengali community suffered from high unemployment rates and some of the greatest incidences of poverty in the country, with more children on free school meals than almost anywhere else. Educators' aspirations for student achievement were startlingly low, and in 1997, Tower Hamlets was proclaimed the country's worst-performing Local Education Authority, with the lowest-performing primary school in the nation.

Ten years later, the transformation of the schools in Tower Hamlets is dramatic. The schools perform around and above the national average. On standardized achievement tests, high school examination results, and rates of students going on to university, the borough ranks as the most improved local authority in Britain. It has significantly reduced achievement gaps in relation to children with special educational needs, those from cultural minorities, and those on free school meals. These gains have been achieved with largely the same population and in comparison with the more modest national gains posted in the same time period.

Systemwide Turnaround

What explains this systemwide turnaround? In a research project codirected with Alma Harris, called *Performing Beyond Expectations,* one of us studied the secrets of Tower Hamlets' success (Hargreaves & Shirley, 2009). At the center of the story are the following components that relate to sustainable and integrating leadership:

- The *visionary leadership* of a new director (superintendent) who was a self-confessed workaholic and who believed that "poverty is not an excuse for poor outcomes," that aspirations should be extremely high, that efforts to meet these aspirations should be relentless, and that everyone should work on this together.
- The *successful succession* of this first driving leader by a more developmentally inclined, yet equally persistent, educator, with just a short period of instability in between.
- A commitment developed with and by the schools' leaders to set and reach ambitious *shared targets* for improvement in "a culture of target setting" so that "everybody owns them"—these were more ambitious than the targets imposed by government.
- *Active trust and strong respect* where "lots of our schools work very closely together and with the local authority" and where inspectors' reports refer to the "enthusiasm and high level of morale among the workforce."
- *Knowledge of and presence in the school* by all stakeholders to provide support, build trust, and ground intervention in consistent and direct personal knowledge and communication more than in the numerical data that eventually appear on spreadsheets.
- A commitment to *cross-school collaboration* so that when one of the authority's 13 secondary schools fell into the failing schools category after taking in Somali students from refugee families in a neighboring authority, all the other secondary schools rallied round to help.

- *Strengthening of community relations and engagement;* Tower Hamlets schools affect the communities that affect them. They have done this by working with faith-based organizations and forming agreements with imams from this largely Muslim community to counter the effects of children taking extended absence from schools to attend and then stay on after family events such as funerals in Bangladesh, by treating extended unauthorized absences as culpable truancy. Tower Hamlets also developed some of its schools into wraparound community centers that keep a school open from 8:00 a.m. until 10:00 p.m.—providing resources and recreation for both students and the community's adults. (See also Chapter 9 on schools as community hubs.) Last, the employment of large numbers of classroom assistants and other staff from the community to support teachers builds strong relationships and trust between professionals and community members and enables and encourages some of these community members to go on to become professionally trained teachers themselves.

In Tower Hamlets, as in Finland, leaders with a robust and resilient sense of purpose engage in successful, integrating, and sustainable system leadership that stays close to and is undertaken with schools and that is performed together in an ethic of schools helping schools and the strong supporting the weak. These leaders think and work sustainably beyond their isolated schools—with other schools and also with their surrounding communities.

Discussion of Implications

Our definition and dimensions of sustainability in education, along with the illustrations of what this looks like in practice, carry a number of implications for what it means to develop sustainable leadership.

1. The future of leadership must be embedded in the hearts and minds of the many and not rest on the shoulders of a heroic few.

We want dedicated and committed professionals in school leadership, not martyrs to management—severed heads whose all-consuming devotion to their work comes at the cost of their families, their lives, their health, and themselves.

School leadership is not the sum of its individual leaders, still less its separate principals. School leadership is a system and a culture. Schools are places where principals, teachers, students, and parents all lead. To sustain quality leadership, school systems must apply systems thinking to their mandate of leadership quality, qualifications, and development—not just by setting common standards and criteria but also by applying systems thinking to all initiatives. Leadership must be a culture of integrated qualities rather than merely an aggregate of common characteristics.

As we discussed in Chapter 1, school jurisdictions should see leadership as a horizontal system across space, where leaders can learn from each other within and across their schools through peer support groups, online dialogue, pairing of schools and their principals (Stoll & Fink, 1996), joint research and development projects, and so on. As we experienced in our school improvement project, one of the components most consistently valued by school leaders is the regular opportunity to meet and converse with each other to talk openly about shared professional, and sometimes personal, concerns.

2. Educational systems should see leadership as a vertical system over time.

The efforts of all leaders are influenced by the impact of their predecessors and have implications for their successors. No leader is an island in time.

Principals and their systems tend to put all their energy into what is called *inbound knowledge*—the knowledge needed to change a school, improve it, make one's mark on it, or turn it around. Little or no attention is devoted to *outbound knowledge*—the knowledge needed to preserve past successes, or keep initiatives going once the originating leader has left. The moment that head teachers and principals get new appointments, they immediately start to focus on their new school, their next challenge, or on how to ensure that their present achievements live on after their departure.

Few things in education are more fragile than leadership succession. Heroic heads do not plan for their own obsolescence. The emphasis on change has obliterated the importance of continuity. In inner-city schools, teachers see their principals come and go constantly; they learn quickly how to resist and ignore each new leader's efforts (MacMillan, 2000). The result is that school improvement becomes like a set of bobbing corks; many schools rise with one set of leaders, only to sink under the next. If we want *sustainable* as well as successful leadership, we must pay serious attention to leadership succession (Fink, 2000b). Leaders must be asked, and must ask themselves, these questions: What will be my legacy? How will my influence live on after my departure? The time for leaders to ask such questions is at the very beginning, not when their tenure is drawing to a close.

3. The promise of sustainable success in education lies in creating cultures of distributed leadership throughout the school community, not in training and developing a tiny leadership elite.

Amid today's contextual realities—sky-high expectations, rapid change, and a youthful profession in the first decades of the 21st century—teachers cannot be the mere targets of other people's leadership, but must see themselves as being, and encouraged to be, leaders of classrooms and of colleagues from the moment they begin their careers.

Distributed leadership means more than delegation. Delegation involves passing on lesser and often unwanted tasks to others. The individual leader decides what will be delegated and to whom. Distributed leadership means creating a culture of initiative and opportunity, in which teachers of all kinds propose new directions, start innovations— perhaps sometimes even challenging and creating difficulties for their leaders in the higher interests of the pupils and the school. In its fullest development, distributed leadership extends beyond the staff to pupils and parents. Distributed leadership gives depth and breadth to the idea and practice of leadership.

4. Recruiting new leaders means focusing on their potential rather than recycling their existing proficiencies.

At first glance, the challenge of leadership succession that faces most jurisdictions in the Western world can be viewed as strictly a problem of mathematical misalignment as the large baby boom generation slips into retirement to be replaced by a much smaller Generation X (Pont, Nusche, & Moorman, 2008). But the problem has more to do with politics and educational philosophy than with issues of supply and demand. A report for the Wallace Foundation (2003) states that "there is no shortage of qualified candidates for the principalship; it makes little sense to rely on strategies aimed solely at adding more candidates to the pipeline." The real challenge of leadership succession is to find and assign the right warm body to the right place, at the right time, for the right reasons. While timing and location may not always be controllable, hiring for the right reasons is always possible. Educational leaders, regardless of their roles, must see themselves as leaders of learning—their own, their teachers and other staff, and of course their students. They must be "passionately, creatively, and steadfastly committed to enhancing 'deep' learning for all students—learning for understanding, learning for life, learning for a knowledge society" (Fink, 2005, p. xvii). From this perspective, there is a succession challenge of major proportions looming in most Western countries to replace the vanishing leaders with new leaders who have the commitment, values, qualities, and intellect to advance student learning to new heights of genuine achievement and accomplishment.

The Wallace Foundation (2003) report suggests that school jurisdictions need to move beyond a replacement planning strategy designed to fill up the pipeline with certified people and focus far more attention and resources on reforming policies and practices to

- Adjust incentives and working conditions to enable noncompetitive schools and districts to attract qualified candidates;
- Bring local hiring practices into line with heightened expectations for principals' performance; and
- Redefine the job itself in ways that allow principals to concentrate on student learning above all else (p. 12).

Gradually, this advice is catching on. We are seeing a subtle but important shift in thinking over the past few years among some educational decision makers. Where once money spent on leadership recruitment and development was considered a cost, it is now viewed as an investment in the future, and as a result, some school authorities and districts have shifted focus from "replacement planning" in which specific people are identified as possessing the proficiencies to fill certain jobs, usually through open competition, to a "succession management" approach, which involves "the accelerated development of a select group of high-potential individuals for both current and future roles that may not be identifiable at present" (Busine & Watt, 2005, p. 225). Rather than "hire and hope," these school authorities have adopted a "grow your own" philosophy.

5. Sustainable leadership requires strategies of integrating development across school systems and networks, not just preparation of individuals. Sustainable leadership is systemic leadership (Hopkins, 2008).

It addresses how leadership spreads out in a school through distributed leadership, including teacher leadership rather than resting on the shoulders of the principal alone. It pays attention to how leadership is stretched out over time, from one leader to the next so that a school's success does not end with the exit of its leader. And last, it considers how schools and their leaders affect each other within and across their communities and addresses how to turn that to shared advantage. This positive interconnectedness of sustainable leadership occurs in several ways:

- **In networks of accreditation and evaluation.** In Rhode Island and Illinois, the School Accountability for Learning and Teaching project engages schools in developing self-evaluations, which are then connected to external evaluations administered by teams of peers drawn from other schools—improving capacity not only in the host schools but also in the teams who evaluate them.
- **In networks of learning and improvement.** More than 700 high schools in England's Raising Achievement/Transforming Learning project have improved at double the rate of the national average by networking schools that have experienced a dip in their performance with similar schools and with self-chosen mentor schools that have stronger records of performance with similar students, to exchange and develop short-term and long-term strategies of change related to student achievement (Hargreaves & Fink, 2005). The best networks and partnerships like these often begin with a distance among schools that are not in direct competition for clients.
- **In area-based cross-school collaboration** focused on the greater good of the shared community. Divided by district boundaries that reflect class-based or race-related residential patterns, opposed by the ruthless competition of the market, and isolated by the fear of betraying secrets to the enemy, schools in the same town or city are often the hardest to network of all. But as in Finland and Tower Hamlets, much is to be gained when stronger schools help weaker peers in similar demographic circumstances. Inspiring system leaders can appeal to the common commitment to the future of

the community. Funding formulae can encourage and incentivize area-based collaborations within and across local districts. Schools and their leaders can also learn that helping others increases their own confidence and capacity too.

10 Things That Are Sustainable About You

Sustainability sounds fine philosophically, but what does it mean practically? Here are 10 closing, practical ideas for developing sustainable leadership in your system or your school:

1. Refocus your curriculum, use of materials, and school design to include ecological sustainability as a core aspect of teaching and learning for all students. Consult UNESCO or the World Wildlife Fund for curriculum ideas on education for sustainable development. And look at schools that already employ this emphasis to deepen learning, raise achievement, and pay attention to the future of the planet (Senge, 2012).

2. Begin all discussions about achievement and how to raise it with conversation and reflection about the learning that underpins the achievement. Put learning first, before testing and even before achievement. Get the learning right and the other elements will follow.

3. Insist that all school improvement plans contain leadership succession plans. This does not mean naming successors, but it means having continuing conversations and plans, shared by the community, about the future leadership needs of the school or the district.

4. Make it a condition of professional employment that every teacher and leader is part of a learning team in his or her school district that meets within scheduled school time on a regular basis as well as outside of it. This focus of the learning teams should be self-guided, not administratively imposed.

5. Write your own professional obituary. It makes you think hard about the legacy you want to leave, and how, deliberately, you can bring that into being.

6. Form a three-sided partnership with a lower- or higher-performing district or school in your own country and with a school or district

in a less-developed country, so all are learning and inspired, everyone needs and gives help, and no one is top dog of everything.

7. Establish a collaborative of schools in your town or city, across district boundaries, to commit to community development initiatives beyond the interests of particular schools.

8. Create a system where principals and leadership teams in successfully turned-around schools can take on a second school or even a third (as well as their own), with dramatically improved salary (with resources being provided to maintain and replace capacity in their "home" schools), to develop administrative careers for administrators without having to abandon their close connections to learning, to provide peer assistance (rather than top-down intervention) to struggling schools, and to lighten district administration at the top in favor of more interconnected leadership within and across districts from below (England has already started this).

9. Coach a teacher who looks like they have little capacity for leadership—and not just ones who look like they already have leadership in them. All leadership is learned, even though some will struggle more than others to learn it. There will be little distributed leadership unless the pool of leaders is widened to include those who do not even yet aspire to lead.

10. Spend more time in schools (if you work in the district) or classrooms (if you are the principal in a school), not just to check up on people as in the overused management walkthrough, but as a way to develop genuine interest in, curiosity about, and knowledge of what teachers and students are doing. Know your people first. Check the data and spreadsheets second. Not the other way around.

Conclusion

I wrote the first edition of *Failure Is Not an Option*® with a dedication recognizing its simple history: a grandmother who was unwilling to give up on her grandson (Blankstein, 2004). This is similar to the untold story of so many of our successes with students in schools. One teacher, one principal, one cafeteria worker, or one janitor is unwilling to give up on a young person, who then succeeds as a result.

Taken independently, each of these courageous acts—these acts of the heart—are extraordinary. They have ripple effects that continue for generations. Creating a collective culture where courage is the norm—creating places where the entire school community can realistically expect sustained success for themselves and for all of their students—is what this book is about.

As demonstrated throughout this book, success is at hand! Schools and districts throughout North America and other parts of the world are overcoming real and perceived obstacles, using their moral outrage and courageous leadership to tackle both fears and traditions of failure.

Since that first edition of FNO was released, many of its more than 350,000 readers have stepped forward to "push the envelope" on what can be accomplished—not only in a school, but across a district, region, state, or province. This edition begins to capture their actions as well as the mentality that believes that success is the only option. Combined with research and practice from Canada, Finland, New Zealand, Australia, the United Kingdom, and the United States, this edition illuminates a more nuanced view of the precious *how to*, but, even more important, the *who* and the *why* of success. These small islands of possibility have now become oceans of hope, creating communities where failure is no longer an option.

With a clear focus on why we are in this profession, the development of our courageous leadership imperative, and information about how to create leadership teams capable of sustainable communities of learning, there is little that can stand in the way of our success; the research in this book now demonstrates that. Grandma wouldn't have had it any other way; and now with the additional motivation of little Sarah and baby Ava, neither can I. Thank you for making it this far and for all you do for our children.

Resources

 Resources also available for download at
http://www.corwin.com/failureisnotanoption3

Resource 1: Creating a Common Rubric to Define Excellent Instruction

Step 1: Brainstorm a List of Observable Indicators of Quality Instruction

1. Think of a lesson you have taught or observed that was highly successful in terms of participation and outcomes.

2. Think of these categories: teacher behaviors, student behaviors, and other indicators.

3. What were some of the key attributes of the lesson that contributed to its success in each category?

4. Individually, list teacher behaviors, student behaviors, and other indicators that you expect to see when quality instruction is present.

Step 2: Norm the Indicators of Quality Instruction as a Group

1. In teams or small groups, share your individual lists.

2. Combine and refine the lists to form one comprehensive list.

3. Continue combining and refining until you have a list of three to five indicators in each category (teacher behaviors, student behaviors, other indicators).

Some examples of possible indicators are student engagement, exploring students' ideas, thinking or reflection time, inquiry, and clear student expectations.

Step 3: Check Indicators of Quality Instruction

Be sure you have distinguished between indicators of quality instruction and lesson design and instructional strategies. For example, an indicator might be "student engagement" while one strategy the teacher is using to achieve engagement might be "cooperative learning."

Note: The research-based strategies from *Classroom Instruction That Works: Researched-Based Strategies for Increasing Student Achievement* (Marzano, Pickering, & Pollock, 2001) explain a number of strategies that have been proven to make a difference in student learning. Your lists should not include specific strategies as such, but rather should be what you can agree on as useful for describing and identifying effective instruction.

Step 4: Check for Understanding by Describing Each Indicator of Quality Instruction

Each indicator should have a description so that when looking for quality instruction, no one is confused regarding "what to look for."

When describing indicators of quality instruction, use observational language. What does each indicator look and sound like?

Examples of Indicator Descriptions of Student Engagement

The student is encouraged to participate and express ideas.

The student is seeking to understand and asks questions.

Examples of Indicator Descriptions of Setting Expectations

Students are informed regarding the objectives, standards, and concepts being taught.

Students have a clear understanding of what they are going to learn, how they will learn it, and why.

Instructional Learning Walks

Focus Principles

Principle 1. Common mission, vision, values, and goals

Principle 2. Ensuring achievement for *all* students—systems for prevention and intervention

Principle 3. Collaborative teaming focused on teaching for learning

Principle 4. Data-based decision making for continuous improvement

Principle 5. Gaining active engagement from family and community

Principle 6. Building sustainable leadership capacity

Objectives for This Session

Participants will

1. Build a shared understanding of quality instruction through the process of defining indicators of quality instruction.

2. Learn to define, describe, and identify indicators of quality instruction through the instructional learning-walk process.

3. Learn what quality instruction looks like and how it contributes to student success.

Agenda

1. Welcome and introductions

2. Instructional learning walks: Steps 1 through 7 (listed below under heading titled Purpose)

3. Plus/delta and next steps

4. HOPE evaluation

5. Closure

Group Norms

HOPE's Meeting Norms	Seven Norms of Collaboration
• Everyone has the right to be heard • Ideas, thoughts, and suggestions are generated with positive intentions • Starting and ending times are honored • Side conversations are avoided • Everyone focuses on group work and directions • Cell phones are on vibrate	• Pausing • Paraphrasing • Probing for specificity • Putting ideas on the table • Paying attention to self and others • Presuming positive intentions • Practicing a balance of inquiry and advocacy

Purpose

Instructional learning walks contribute to building shared understanding of quality instruction within the professional learning community through the process of defining indicators of quality instruction. The *instructional learning walk* process helps define, describe, and identify indicators of quality instruction. Learning what quality instruction looks like and including these practices into planned instruction contribute to student success.

Engaging in *instructional learning walks* is a professional development activity. Observing and defining indicators of quality instruction helps the work of developing a professional community by engaging in identifying the existence and frequency of the indicators of quality instruction. The classroom, name of teacher, and specific students are not important to the task.

Step 1: Brainstorm a List of
Observable Indicators of Quality Instruction

1. Think of a lesson you have taught or observed that was highly successful in terms of participation and outcomes.

2. Think of these categories: teacher behaviors, student behaviors, and other indicators.

3. What were some of the key attributes of the lesson that contributed to its success in each category?

4. Individually, list teacher behaviors, student behaviors, and other indicators that you expect to see when quality instruction is present.

Step 2: Norm the Indicators of Quality Instruction as a Group

1. In teams or small groups, share your individual lists.

2. Combine and refine the lists to form one comprehensive list.

3. Continue combining and refining until you have a list of three to five indicators in each category (teacher behaviors, student behaviors, other indicators).

Some examples of possible indicators are student engagement, exploring students' ideas, thinking or reflection time, inquiry, and clear student expectations.

Step 3: Check for Understanding by Describing Each Indicator of Quality Instruction

Each indicator should have a description so that when looking for quality instruction, no one is confused regarding "what to look for."

When describing indicators of quality instruction, use observational language. What does each indicator look and sound like?

Examples of Indicator Descriptions of Student Engagement

- The student is encouraged to participate and express ideas.
- The student is seeking to understand and asks questions.

Examples of Indicator Descriptions of Setting Expectations

- Students are informed regarding the objectives, standards, and concepts being taught.
- Students have a clear understanding of what they are going to learn, how they will learn it, and why.

Complete Steps 4, 5, and 6 onsite, and prepare to share at Courageous Leadership Academy (CLA) Session 3 debriefing.

Step 4: Prepare for the Instructional Learning Walk

1. Review the list of the indicators of quality instruction and your group's description of each.

2. Identify examples of the indicators of quality instruction and calibrate your group. This is done by practicing to make sure you are in alignment with each other regarding what you are looking for.

3. Record your group's indicators of quality instruction on the observation sheet.

Step 5: Do the Instructional Learning Walk

1. Go on an *instructional learning walk* as a group for 30 minutes.

2. Separate and walk through as many classrooms as you have time for with your observation sheet.

3. Look for indicators of quality instruction in each classroom you visit. (This activity does not expect you to identify either the teacher or students.)

4. Place a check mark next to each indicator that you observe.

Step 6: Debrief the Instructional Learning Walk

Tally the number of times you observed each indicator of quality instruction, first individually and then as a group. Consider the following questions as a form of data:

1. Which indicators were observed most frequently?

2. Which indicators were observed least frequently?

3. Which of the indicators were observed occasionally?

For each of the above questions (data points 1, 2, and 3), also consider

- What conclusions could you draw regarding the quality of instruction in your school?
- What questions are you asking about what you observed?
- What areas of quality would you especially like to celebrate?
- What suggestions do you have for "next steps" in communicating your observations?

Observation Sheet

Check if the behavior is observed in the classroom (CR)

Indicators: Teacher Behavior	CR 1	CR 2	CR 3	CR 4	CR 5	CR 6
Totals						
Indicators: Students Behavior	CR 1	CR 2	CR 3	CR 4	CR 5	CR 6
Totals						

Resource 2: Strategies for Making Time

- ☐ Share classrooms. Plan and schedule team teaching and multidisciplinary class time.

- ☐ Adjust daily schedule. Teachers agree to arrive sufficiently in advance of classes starting to allow for meeting time. Classes can also be started late one day a week to add 15 to 20 extra minutes to regular early meeting time.

- ☐ Bring classes together. Have classes exchange visits on a reciprocal basis (e.g., fifth graders visit first-grade classes to read or work with younger children, and first graders visit fifth graders on alternate weeks) and be supervised by one teacher, freeing up the other one.

- ☐ Use assemblies to free up time. Schedule buildingwide or schoolwide events (movies, assemblies, and so on) during which classroom teachers can meet while students are supervised by counselors, paraprofessionals, or administrators.

- ☐ Give common assignments. Several classrooms of students at the same grade level (or taking the same course) are given the same assignment or project simultaneously. Videos, library time, or other related activities are scheduled for all the classes at once, freeing their teachers to meet together while aides, volunteers, or others supervise.

- ☐ Use parent or business volunteers. Involve parents as aides or chaperones for appropriate activities. Invite local business representatives to share their particular expertise as they supervise classes.

- ☐ Free up the fifth day. Schedule all academic classes to take place four days each week, leaving the fifth day free for team meetings while students rotate to art, music, PE, technology, the library, and so on.

- ☐ Reduce the number of all-staff meetings, and replace them with smaller team meetings where the topics under discussion can be tailored to the needs of the group (Pardini, 1999).

- ☐ Use paraprofessionals, student teachers, and aides to cover classes on a regular basis.

- ☐ Allocate more staff positions to classroom teaching than to pullout teaching and/or support roles (Darling-Hammond, 1999).

☐ Implement schedules that engage students with fewer teachers each day for longer periods of time (Darling-Hammond, 1999).

☐ Free teachers from nonprofessional activities (e.g., playground, bus duty, and so on).

☐ Use professional development funding and time allocation for teamwork.

Resource 3: Self-Assessment

Do the Cultural Norms of Your School Promote School Improvement?

	Never	Rarely	Sometimes	Often	Always
1. **Shared goals.** "We know where we are going."	1	2	3	4	5
2. **Responsibility for success.** "We must succeed."	1	2	3	4	5
3. **Collegiality.** "We're working on it together."	1	2	3	4	5
4. **Continuous improvement.** "We can get better."	1	2	3	4	5
5. **Lifelong learning.** "Learning is for everyone."	1	2	3	4	5
6. **Risk taking.** "We learn by trying something new."	1	2	3	4	5
7. **Support.** "There's always someone there to help."	1	2	3	4	5
8. **Mutual support.** "Everyone has something to offer."	1	2	3	4	5
9. **Openness.** "We can discuss our differences."	1	2	3	4	5
10. **Celebration and humor.** "We feel good about ourselves."	1	2	3	4	5

Add the 4s and 5s

Source: Adapted from *Changing Our Schools,* 1996, by Louise Stoll and Dean Fink.

How Effective Is Your School?

	Never	Rarely	Sometimes	Often	Always
1. **Instructional leadership** (firm and purposeful, a participative approach, the leading professional)	1	2	3	4	5
2. **Shared vision and clear goals** (unity of purpose, consistency of practice)	1	2	3	4	5
3. **Shared values and beliefs**	1	2	3	4	5
4. **A learning environment** (an orderly atmosphere, an attractive working environment)	1	2	3	4	5
5. **Teaching and curriculum focus** (maximization of learning time, academic emphasis, focus on achievement)	1	2	3	4	5
6. **High expectations** (for all, communications of expectations, intellectual challenge for all)	1	2	3	4	5
7. **Positive student behavior** (clear and fair discipline and feedback)	1	2	3	4	5
8. **Frequent monitoring of student progress** (ongoing monitoring, evaluating school performance)	1	2	3	4	5
9. **Student involvement and responsibility** (high student self-esteem, positions of responsibility, control of work)	1	2	3	4	5
10. **Climate for learning** (positive physical environment, recognition, incentives)	1	2	3	4	5

Source: Adapted from Halton Board of Education (1988). Used with permission.

School Typology

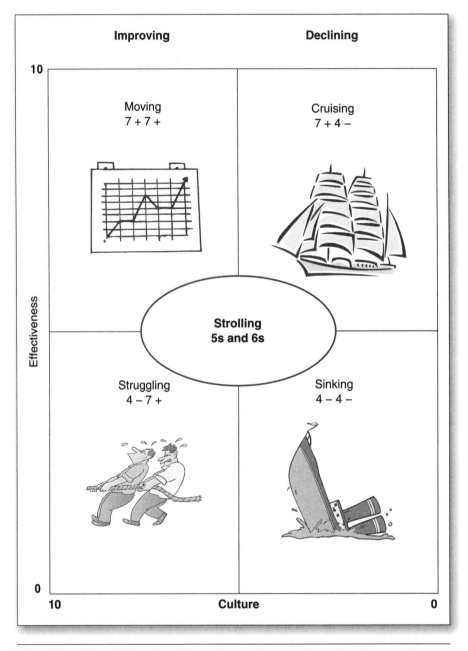

Source: Adapted from *Changing Our Schools,* 1996, by Louise Stoll and Dean Fink.

Three Strategies of School Development

III. Good Schools →	*II. Moderately Effective Schools* →	*I. Failing Schools* →
Keeping good schools effective and stimulated Becoming more effective		
✓ Build capacity ✓ Focus on teaching and learning ✓ Mainly work with existing leadership and support ✓ Some outside pressure/support ✓ Larger lesson periods to promote classroom creativity ✓ Broaden teacher leadership ✓ Listen and respond to students ✓ Motivate disillusioned staff ✓ Staff focused on purposes	✓ Extensive intervention and support ✓ Usually new leadership ✓ Target priorities for visible improvement, i.e., dress codes, attendance ✓ Building teacher competence and confidence in teaching strategies	✓ External partnerships ✓ Access to networks ✓ Exposure to new ideas/practices ✓ Consolidating collaboration ✓ Celebrating success ✓ Minimal external pressure

Source: David Hopkins, *School Improvement for Real* (2001). New York: Routledge/Falmer. Used with permission from Thomson Publishing Services.

Resource 4: Strategies for Dealing With Resistance

When faced with resistance, most people feel challenged. They feel that they must overcome the resistance in order to win their point. This instinct to overcome can actually lead to counterproductive behaviors. Some of these ineffective behaviors include

- **Use of power.** Meeting force with force to overcome the resistance
- **Manipulating those who oppose.** Finding subtle ways to apply pressure, or giving false impressions or partial information
- **Applying force of reason.** Overwhelming opponents with facts, figures, and flowcharts
- **Ignoring the resistance.** Failing to address it in the hopes that it will go away on its own
- **Playing off relationships.** Using friendships as leverage to get others to agree
- **Making deals.** Offering something in exchange for agreement (e.g., trade-offs)
- **Killing the messenger.** Getting rid of or bypassing the resistor
- **Giving in too soon.** Ceding your position before exploring the true level of resistance or the possibility of common understanding (Ontario Institute for Studies in Education at University of Toronto, 2001)
- According to research from the University of Toronto, these common responses actually increase people's resistance. Even if they are effective in the short term, the win may not be worth the long-term costs of sabotage, compliance versus commitment, or people opting out of the implementation phase.

We can better deal with resistance by remembering a set of core behaviors, or touchstones. As we develop strategies for dealing with resistors, each strategy should be consistent with these touchstones:

- **Maintain clear focus.** Don't let the fog of resistance obscure your vision of your original goal. Yet while never losing sight of the long-range goal, you must also keep an eye on the work of the moment. By maintaining a clear focus, you can switch your attention back and forth between what is going on at the moment and what you are ultimately trying to accomplish.

- **Embrace resistance.** Although it may seem counterintuitive, resistance can actually serve a positive purpose in your efforts to build consensus. If you are to overcome objections, you must know what they are—and resistance provides you with that information.
- **Respect those who resist.** Listen to what your resistors have to say with an open mind; do not automatically assume that they are uninformed, unjustified, or motivated purely by self-interest. Treat them with respect and dignity and be completely truthful.
- **Relax.** When someone pushes against us, it is instinctive for us to push back. It is that instinct, however, that prevents us from relaxing and embracing resistance. By relaxing—and not pushing back— you can allow your resistors to talk and tell you their thoughts. And once you understand their thoughts, you can use them to begin seeking common ground.
- **Join with the resistance.** By listening with an open mind and exploring the ideas of the resistors, you can begin to identify areas you have in common. Building support for your idea happens when you find this common ground—this merging of interests and concerns.

Source: Adapted from *Dealing With Resistance,* OISE/UT (2001). To read more about this topic, see Rick Maurer's (1996) *Beyond the Wall of Resistance: Unconventional Strategies That Build Support for Change.*

Resource 5: PLC Fidelity Checklist

Expectations	Dates									
Protocols are set and adhered to during meetings.										
The PLC team meets at a consistent time on a regular basis.										
An agenda is present and adhered to during the meeting.										
A strategy is in place to discuss items that are not on the agenda (Parking Lot).										
Meeting notes/minutes are posted in a place that is available to all members.										
All team members are present.										
All team members actively participate in discussions.										
There appears to be a shared vision for the team's work.										
The mission of the team supports the school's mission.										
Shared data may reference grades, behavior, quizzes, tests, attendance, or impact from instructional strategies.										
Instructional strategies are reviewed for effectiveness.										
Common assessments are regularly reviewed for relevance to curriculum/Essential Skills.										
Data from assessments drives reteaching.										
Incorporation of reading strategies into lessons is discussed.										

	Dates								
Expectations									
Levels of engagement are discussed with an emphasis on creating learning environments that facilitate learning, teaching and curriculum focus, and high expectations.									
Assessments are evaluated for percentage of critical-thinking questions.									
Assessments are evaluated for alignment to Essential Skills.									
Rubrics for written responses to Essential Questions are created/evaluated.									
There are set meetings for cross-curricular horizontal articulation (English/Foreign Lang/SS or Math/Science).									
There are set meetings for vertical articulation within the department.									
Teams review failures and near failures after each grading period.									
Use of time is maximized.									
Agenda topics are set for the upcoming meeting and there is closure.									
Top 5 PBIS data are reviewed/discussed monthly.									
PBIS Tracking Tool is shared with staff for review on a quarterly basis.									
Effective behavioral strategies used by team members are shared/discussed quarterly.									

Resource 6: Worksheet for Developing a School Improvement Plan

Work either singly or in small groups to achieve the following:

1. List all prevention and intervention strategies already in place at your school, grouping them in the following categories, which correspond to the ones in the pyramid below.

   a. Strategies for identified underachievers (entering ninth graders)

   b. Strategies for all ninth graders

   c. Strategies for persistent underachievers

   d. Strategies for fewer than 5% of underachievers

2. Evaluate each strategy carefully to determine whether it fits with your school's philosophical structure (i.e., mission, vision, values, and goals).

   a. Place a check mark beside each strategy that is already philosophically sound and does not need to be changed.

   b. Place a C beside those strategies that need to be modified to better fit into your school's philosophical structure.

3. Now, looking at your pyramid of interventions as a whole, identify any gaps in the structure that need to be filled (e.g., strategies to support specific subgroups). Add those strategies to your earlier list from Point 1, placing an N beside them to mark them as new.

Adlai Stevenson High School Pyramid of Interventions

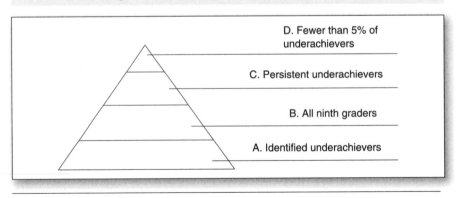

Source: Failure Is Not an Option® video series (2002).

Resource 7: Pyramid of Support at Coyote Ridge Elementary School

Purpose

To identify additional support systems at varying levels of intensity in order for students to perform at their academic and/or behavioral potential.

Green Level: No Additional Support Needed

Student is achieving at the desired level.

Yellow Level: Least Intensive

Individual Teacher

- Look at prior records and assessment information to determine student strengths and areas of need
- Converse informally with prior teachers
- Conference formally with parents two times per year
- Contact parents for additional conferences
- Provide midterm grades if below a C (depending on grade level)
- Provide additional reports to parents if student is failing
- Use classroom or grade-level volunteers to tutor small groups or individual students
- Continually assess students for movement in levels, for example, running records, district reading assessment, phonological awareness literacy service, basic reading inventory, math boxes, writing rubrics
- Complete and implement a literacy achievement plan
- Meet with administrator for support and suggestions
- Meet with specialists (PE, music, art, technology, teacher librarian) for support and suggestions
- Consult and set observations with special education specialists
- Use "buddy system" within classroom
- Use second-step curriculum
- Implement informal articulation therapy for speech
- Use informal occupational therapy and physical therapy strategies
- Establish consistent building rules and expectations that carry over into classroom expectations—taught, reinforced, posted

- Use classroom "contracts for success"
- Reinforce using classroom and buildingwide recognition, for example, Coyote of the Month, Coyote Howl Postcards, Positive Office Referrals
- Implementation of Coyote Ridge 3 (positive behavioral system) throughout the building

Grade Level

- Use groups within the school day based on academic need (reconfigure groups of students based on need between classes)
- Identify specific skills and concepts based on data from unit tests and reconfigure groups of students for review and reteaching activities
- Use district coaches, building student achievement coach, or gifted and talented coordinator to model lessons or help plan lessons using differentiation strategies
- Complete classroom data forms for identification of students not performing at level; discuss with administrator

Orange Level: More Intensive

Receive yellow support and consider the following:

Cross-Grade-Level, Specialist, and Volunteer Support

- Utilize special education staff to supplement (not supplant) instruction through best practices (e.g., multisensory)
- Provide math club for those struggling with basic concepts (Grades 3 and 4)
- Provide opportunities for students to move to an appropriate grade level for matched instruction (i.e., fourth grade to second, kindergarten to first)
- Utilize trained volunteers to support small groups or individuals in a variety of content areas
- Utilize literacy coordinator or interventionist for small-group instruction using best practices such as Success-Oriented Achievement Realized (SOAR) or Dynamic Indicators of Basic Early Literacy Skills (DIBELS).
- Provide or support summer school or tutoring opportunities
- See counselor on short-term basis
- Participate in *Learning Together* peer tutoring reading program, Grades 2 through 4 and 3 through 5

- Other:
  - Bubble Groups (those 10 points above or below cut scores) before or after school on state testing
  - Homework Club before or after school
  - College/high school students tutor additional groups or individuals
  - Individualized education plan less than 21% of the time out of the classroom

Red Level: Most Intensive

Provide yellow and orange support and consider the following:

Mentor System

- Provide short-term one-on-one counseling with school social worker or psychologist
- Implement intensive behavior support plans based on functional behavioral assessment
- Implement one-on-one intervention/enrichment
- Use student/staff member buddy system where the student meets with the staff member weekly to check on student progress
- Student may be referred to special education team for consideration for testing
- Collaboration with outside therapists/medical personnel
- Other:
  - Individualized education program (IEP) more than 21% of the time out of the classroom

Note: Special education, English language learners, gifted and talented, Section 504, and significant support needs students may be at any color on the Pyramid of Support based on the identified and implemented support being provided.

Consider the following for students on an IEP when placing them on the pyramid:

- Hours of support on IEP (certified and classified staff)
- Number of providers
- Outside support (family therapy, outside speech/language, vision therapy)
- Formal behavior plan
- Medical needs (identified by a doctor)

Source: Used with permission of Kari Cocozzella.

Resource 8: Developing a System of Prevention and Intervention

Begin the process by working with your colleagues to sketch plans or procedures on separate sheets of paper for (1) identifying students in need of extra support and attention; (2) monitoring such students intensively; (3) providing mentors, "good friends," or other adult support to these students; and (4) establishing intervention programs. List programs that already exist and note whether they need to be modified or expanded and, if so, in what ways. For new programs, state the specific goal and then address the following questions.

1. Identification

- What criteria, data, or information is used to identify incoming students who need extra attention?
- Who is responsible for gathering and evaluating this information?
- When is this done?
- What obstacles need to be confronted?

2. Monitoring

- What kinds of ongoing information or data about identified students are collected?
- How often is the information gathered?
- What is the vehicle for entering and transmitting the information?
- Who is asked to provide it?
- Who gathers and evaluates it?
- How promptly is it reviewed?
- What obstacles need to be confronted?
- What are some strategies for overcoming these obstacles?

3. Mentoring

- What kind of mentoring program is needed in our school?
- How can we ensure that every identified student has a "best friend" adult?

- Who is recruited to fill such roles? Certified personnel only? Clerical staff? Custodial staff? Kitchen workers? Parents and community volunteers? Also, what guidelines, orientation, or training is provided to these mentors?
- Who provides or leads the training?
- What is the procedure for pairing students with mentors? Should meetings between students and mentors be structured or allowed to develop naturally?
- What communication tree exists for mentors who become aware of problems?
- What obstacles need to be confronted?
- What are some strategies for overcoming these obstacles?

4. Intervention

- What is a reasonable and specific goal for each prevention or improvement program that we plan to implement?
- What resources are available for such programs (money, personnel, space, time, and so on)?
- What criteria are established for selecting students for the programs?
- Is the program mandatory or optional?
- What benchmark or standard do we hope to meet with each intervention, and what assessment and evaluation data determine the program's success?
- How often is each intervention program evaluated?
- What obstacles need to be confronted?
- What are some strategies for overcoming these?

Resource 9: FNO Tuning Protocols

What Are Tuning Protocols?

A *tuning protocol* is a staff-development process that is embedded in what a teacher does in the classroom, or what an educator does in a school. A group of colleagues comes together to examine each other's work, honor the good things found in that work, and fine-tune it through a formal process of presentation and reflection (Easton, 1999).

Tuning protocols provide a structure and process for professional dialogue to learn from our work. This process helps fine-*tune* educational practices using a *protocol* or formal process for examining our work in a supportive, problem-solving group.

Rationale

Four reasons to use tuning protocols are

1. Tunings provide accountability beyond test scores. We need to get different information from different kinds of data, not just comparisons against a population (norm-referenced tests) or comparisons to a standard (criterion-referenced tests). We need a repertoire. We also need a source of data that is less invasive than a test.

2. Tunings provide information useful in a classroom. By looking directly at student work, we learn what students really know and can do in the context of their real work—and why. We also learn what students do not know and cannot do. These are important insights for anyone educating young people.

3. Tunings build a learning community. They are content-rich since they focus on student work and educator practice. For these reasons, they ensure some level of application.

4. Tunings work.

   a. The process is relatively risk-free. The protocol does not permit attack-counterattack, pro-con, offense-defense, or statement-rebuttal discourse.

   b. These results are richer than those from a typical discussion. Individuals who debate each other sidetrack the group and prevent deep conversations and discussions.

c. Everybody learns from a tuning protocol. The tuning protocol allows everyone to think deeply about student work and educator practice, arrive at creative solutions, and connect with colleagues.

Source: Adapted from Easton, 1999, 2004, 2008.

Setting Up the Tuning Protocol

Table Roles

Each team appoints the following:

- **Presenter.** The presenter brings the samples, sets the context, and describes the teaching/learning situation.
- **Table Facilitator.** The table facilitator ensures that participants stay on task, checks for "airtime" midway in the discussion, ensures appropriate, nonevaluative questions are asked.
- **Timekeeper.** The timekeeper ensures that time limits are kept for each section.
- **Feedback Monitor.** The feedback monitor checks for warm and cool feedback, making adjustment suggestions if needed, and ensures feedback is focused on the process and not a critique of the presenter.
- **Key Question Monitor.** The key question monitor observes the degree to which the key question is addressed, making adjustment suggestions if needed.

Norms for the Tuning Protocol Process

- Engage fully by asking questions and clarifying your thinking.
- Actively listen to understand the perspective of your colleagues.
- Manage your personal needs.

Tuning Protocol Assumptions

- We want to improve in our work as educators.
- We want to be kind, courteous, thoughtful, insightful, and provocative.
- We are "in this together." This is a collaborative process.

Step 1: Presenter Role

1. Presenter sets the context and describes the teaching/learning situation.

2. Participants listen and take notes without interrupting the presenter.

3. Participants are given time to examine their copy of the student work being discussed.

4. Chart the one or two key questions that the participants pose.

Key Questions

What do these pieces of student work tell us about the following?

- Instruction
- Design
- Strategies
- Decisions
- Personalization

Step 2: Clarifying Questions

1. Participants ask nonevaluative questions about the presentation. For example,
   - What happened before X?
   - What did you do next?
   - What did Y say?

2. Participants must guard against asking questions that approach evaluation. For example,
   - Why didn't you try Z?

Step 3: Individual Writing

1. Review the information and samples pertaining to warm and cool feedback.

2. Participants, including the presenter, write feedback comments about the presentation, addressing the key question or questions.

3. This part of the protocol helps each participant to focus on what to say during the participant discussion.

Step 4: Participant Discussion

1. Review the responsibilities of the table facilitator, feedback monitor, and key questions monitor.

2. Presenter remains completely silent while taking notes, perhaps turning away to avoid eye contact.

3. Participants describe or explain what is to be tuned and improved, with the presenter listening in.

4. Participants discuss the issues raised during the presentation to deepen their understanding of the situation and seek answers to the key questions.

5. Participants should strive for a balance of "warm" and "cool" feedback.

6. Participants should strive to contribute to substantive discourse.

Step 5: Presenter Reflection

1. Participants remain silent and take notes on the presenter reflection.

2. Presenter reflects aloud on the participants' discussion, using the issues raised to deepen understanding, considering possible answers to the questions posed.

3. Presenter projects about future actions, questions, and dilemmas.

Step 6: Debrief the Tuning Protocol

Plus/Delta Activity (Classroom Assessment technique)

- What worked well?
- What did you learn?
- How will you use this in your professional collaborations and instructional learning?
- How would you improve the engagement of participants in the tuning protocol?

Next Steps

Record three implications for instruction that came from the tuning protocol.

Closure

After the table has debriefed, the room facilitator thanks the presenters and table monitors for stepping forward in those roles.

Critical Aspects of Doing a Tuning on Your Own

Do's and Don'ts

- ☐ Tuning protocols work best if participants and presenters think of their work as a collaboration to help students learn.

- ☐ Be vigilant about keeping time. Be sure to work through the entire protocol for the process to be effective. Do not let one person monopolize any part of the protocol.

- ☐ Try to gather the same group each time a protocol is done.

- ☐ If presenters come from within a group of people who will, themselves, do a protocol, they'll feel a little less intimidated about sharing the work they and/or their students are doing.

- ☐ The group should be somewhat protective of the presenter—by making their work public, presenters expose themselves to a critique.

- ☐ The room facilitator should help participants recast or withdraw inappropriate comments. The room facilitator can also ask how "tough" the presenter wants participants to be.

- ☐ Participants should also be courteous, thoughtful, and provocative. Be provocative of substantive discourse. Many presenters may be used to blanket praise. Without thoughtful but probing cool questions and comments, they won't benefit from the tuning protocol experience. Presenters often say they'd have liked more cool feedback (Cushman, 1995).

- ☐ Consider having an outside facilitator who does not participate in the process, at least for the first tuning.

- ☐ The facilitator should make sure all steps are followed, keep time, be sure that the group acts according to the assumptions, monitor airtime, check for the balance of warm and cool feedback, and make sure the group addresses the presenter's key questions. Without a facilitator, consider having participants take on these roles.

Warm and Cool Feedback

Joe McDonald, Coalition of Essential Schools, uses the terms *warm feedback* and *cool feedback*. Nothing is gained if participants only praise, but praise should be part of a protocol: What worked? Nothing is gained if participants only criticize, but a critique should be part of a protocol: What would help students learn better?

- *Warm feedback* consists of statements that let the presenter know what is working. Warm feedback takes the form of praise for what seems effective.
- *Cool feedback* consists of statements or questions that help the presenter move forward. They are less criticism than a critique of the work. They are oriented to improving the work and the work context. Cool feedback is never about the presenter—only about what the presenter brought to be tuned. The best cool feedback occurs through "What if . . ." questions such as, "I wonder what would happen if . . ."

Source: Powerful Designs for Professional Learning, Second Edition, by Lois Easton, NSDC, 2008. Reprinted with permission of the National Staff Development Council, www.nsdc.org. All rights reserved.

Resource 10: Checklist for Using Diagnostic (Preteaching) Assessments

If you have not been doing diagnostic assessments, use the following checklist to help you get started.

❐ I made an effort to learn about students' interests and learning styles, ideally at the beginning of the year or semester.

❐ I used the following methods (e.g., survey, observation, conversation):

Method	Date

❐ I recorded my results and observations (where?).

❐ I tried to determine my students' range of knowledge about the topic I'm about to teach.

Method	Date

❏ I tried to determine my students' misconceptions about the topic I'm about to teach.

Method	*Date*

❏ In response to my findings, I adopted the following teaching plans and adaptations:

❏ My students were informed about our learning goals for this topic or unit.

❏ My students were told about the assessments and criteria I use to conclude the unit.

❏ My students saw examples or models of the performances I expect of them.

❏ The methods I used are all nongraded and do not adversely affect students' self-esteem.

The use of diagnostic assessments caused the following changes in my instructional planning:

I would evaluate my experience using diagnostic assessments as follows:

Source: Reprinted with permission from *Failure Is Not an Option*® *3: Effective Assessment for Effective Learning* [Video series]. Bloomington, IN: HOPE Foundation, 2009b.

Resource 11: Checklist for Using Formative Assessments

If you have not been using formative assessments, use the following checklist to help you get started.

☐ I am providing feedback to the students frequently throughout the teaching unit. I plan to start teaching the unit on _____ and conclude it on _____. During that period, I will provide feedback by the following methods:

Date	Graded? (Y/N)	Strategies

☐ I make sure the feedback I provide is very specific.

☐ I make sure that the students clearly understand the feedback I give them. The information I gained has led me to modify my lesson plan in the following way:

☐ My students are given opportunities to show that they can correct and adjust the quality of their work.

❐ My students are beginning to learn to self-assess their own work. Evidence and comments:

My evaluation of my experience with using formative assessments:

Source: Reprinted with permission from *Failure Is Not an Option*® *3: Effective Assessment for Effective Learning* [Video series]. Bloomington, IN: HOPE Foundation, 2009b.

Resource 12: Checklist for Using Summative Assessments

My students will perform summative assessments on _____ *(name of teaching unit)* on _____ *(dates)*.

❏ Since the beginning of the unit, my students know what kinds of summative performance I expect. The assessments are aligned with the following learning goals:

❏ The assessments are authentic. The knowledge and skills that students display are transferrable in the following ways:

❏ I offered these options *(two or more)* to the students to display their learning, accommodate various learning styles, and target different learning goals:

Task	Learning Style	Targeted Learning Goal
1.		
2.		
3.		

☐ My students are aware of the criteria on which their work or performance is assessed. I used the following criteria to assess students' work:

Task	Rubric (Criteria)	Value (% of Grade)
1.		
2.		
3.		

I evaluated each of the assessment tasks as follows:

- Task 1:
- Task 2:
- Task 3:

Other comments:

Source: Reprinted with permission from *Failure Is Not an Option*® *3: Effective Assessment for Effective Learning* [Video series]. Bloomington, IN: HOPE Foundation (2009b).

Book Group Discussion Questions

Many schools across the country have selected *Failure Is Not an Option*® as the focus of book discussion groups for professional development. Most groups read one or two chapters before each group meeting. This section includes a list of questions that may be used to guide discussions.

Icebreaker

In no more than two sentences, complete the following statement: "I decided to become an educator because . . ." Share and discuss your responses.

Chapter 1. Why Failure Is Not an Option

1. This chapter highlights six lessons learned from leaders in the field. Which lesson inspired you most as you read the chapter? How does it apply to your particular situation—and what change would you like to see next?

2. In Case Story 1, the Fort Wayne Community School District used various approaches to maintain a collaborative culture while piloting a new approach to teacher assessment. What challenges are inherent to this situation? How is your school or district addressing these challenges? How did having the foundational Professional Learning Community (PLC) in place help Fort Wayne determine their course of action?

3. How does this case exemplify the "Lessons Learned" outlined earlier in the chapter? What processes did they use that would be helpful to address thorny issues in your school community? If you "transplant" the strategies Fort Wayne came up with to your learning community, would they work in the absence of the kind of culture those in the case study created?

4. Most schools have a "leadership team." What is the role of the team described in this chapter relative to the traditional leadership team?

Chapter 2. Courageous Leadership for School Success

1. Review the three cited principles of highly reliable organizations (HROs) shown on page 32. Brainstorm specific ways that schools could change to better meet these principles.

2. From your own experience, what are some reasons why leading change requires courage?

3. What might help skeptical, cynical, or burned-out educators recoup the idealism that led most of them into the profession at the beginning of their careers?

Chapter 3. 10 Common Routes to Failure, and How to Avoid Each

1. Review the 10 Common Routes to Failure. Recall and share situations in which you encountered resistance to a change or improvement you espoused. How did you handle the resistance? What other possible solutions might have worked?

2. Describe a planned change that is likely to arouse resistance. How might you use any of the strategies listed on in Figure 3.1, pages 46–47, to improve your chances of implementing the change?

3. Review Resource 2: Strategies for Making Time. Brainstorm additional strategies and discuss ways that some of these strategies could be implemented in your schools.

Chapter 4. Relational Trust as Foundation for the Learning Community

1. This chapter highlights the four components of relational trust: *respect; competence; personal regard for others;* and *integrity.* Discuss to what extent these elements currently exist in your learning community. If some do not, review the strategies for building trust on pages 67–69, and discuss how they might be used to elevate the level of trust that exists in your current situation.

2. This chapter raises three essential questions for creating a learning community: *What is a learning community in practice? What are the key elements for making such a community succeed? How do you know if you have succeeded in creating such a community?* Discuss your answers and identify some specific steps you can take to create and sustain a learning community in your school.

3. Look over the items in the box titled Trust and the Learning Community on page 72. Analyze each to show how the described situation reflects, or is founded on, a trusting interpersonal relationship. (You can skip the item about SMART goals, which is discussed in the next chapter.) Consider ways to create and support similar situations in your own school.

Chapter 5. Principle 1: Common Mission, Vision, Values, and Goals

1. Discuss, define, and list the values implicit in your school's or district's culture. If you have existing mission and vision statements, refer to them. Examine each implicit value that you list by asking, "Is this value consistent with our mission? Will this value help us realize our vision?" Discuss whether you need to rewrite or revitalize your mission, vision, values, or goals. Decide what steps need to be taken to begin the process.

2. Identify which goals are guiding your school's plans and actions right now. Are they consistent with your mission and vision? Are they SMART? (See Figure 5.4 on page 106.) How do they align with district goals? What types of peer-to-peer observation and support are practiced in your school or district? Discuss ways you can use peer feedback across the district to offer regular support to peers and to align and assess goals.

3. Review the guidelines for celebrating success in the bulleted list on pages 108–109 and discuss the kinds of events and achievements that are typically celebrated in your school. Should you rethink your policies and start celebrating other kinds of successes? Where should you begin?

Chapter 6. Principle 2: Ensuring Achievement for All Students—Systems for Prevention and Intervention

1. Discuss the mechanisms and prevention systems that are currently in place in your school to provide incoming students with a continuum of support. What systems are in place to align preK–12 philosophy and practice? To ensure all students' success? How do these systems help to identify those who are at risk for academic difficulties?

2. Review the discussion that occurs between the school principal and the science teacher on page 115. Does it seem as if the teacher is being asked to lower his standards? How can we reconcile maintaining high standards and still ensure success for all students? How should leaders respond to behaviors that conflict with the school's or district's vision, mission, and values?

3. Review Figure 6.5, "Four Cs . . .," on pages 126–127. Which column describes the practices in your school? Discuss steps you could take to ensure that your policies fall in the left-hand column to promote connection.

Chapter 7. Principle 3: Collaborative Teaming Focused on Teaching for Learning

1. Discuss some challenges you have encountered to creating a collaborative culture. What suggestions does the book give for ways these can be addressed? Brainstorm other ways these challenges could be addressed in the future.

2. Which of the four types of collaborative school culture are most prevalent in your school? How is team effectiveness measured in your school? How frequently and in what ways do staff members in your school work together to solve problems or plan improvements? How are conflicts handled? Discuss ways that each of these areas might be improved moving forward.

3. Consider a problem affecting your school or district that could be addressed by an effective team that is interdisciplinary (within a single school) or across two or more schools. Discuss who might join such a team, what needs would be addressed, and what steps you might take to put such a team in place. Schools in the Case Story from this chapter used a larger network to expand their learning opportunities. How were new initiatives introduced to minimize resistance? How did this initiative minimize overload and maximize cohesion? What is your district doing to provide a common system and framework for action that helps to ensure consistent implementation?

Chapter 8. Principle 4: Data-Based Decision Making for Continuous Improvement

1. In your school or district, what data besides test scores have guided recent decisions and planning? Can you think of other data sources that would have provided you with helpful information to make better decisions? Discuss ways to present and share data to get a comprehensive picture of each student.

2. In your opinion, how well do results of state tests reflect the quality of student learning? If you feel there is a discrepancy, what are some kinds of data you can collect or generate to determine what skills and knowledge the students have actually acquired? How should this be shared?

3. What data are most relevant to achieving your SMART goals? How often and by whom are these data reviewed? Share how you currently use data to inform your instructional practice, and discuss what additional steps you might take moving forward.

Chapter 9. Principle 5: Gaining Active Engagement From Family and Community

1. Do staff members know how to communicate effectively with parents of different racial, socioeconomic, and linguistic backgrounds? Do these parents feel welcome at your school? Discuss ways to improve relationships with these parents. How could your school make them feel more welcome or comfortable?

2. How do you respond to the idea of connecting with parents at community gathering places and events? What are some ways they could be made more visible? Discuss what else could be done at these events to improve school-community relationships.

3. Discuss the questions under the "Getting Started" section on pages 205–206. Now consider the strategies listed below those questions. Which strategies would work best for your school?

Chapter 10. Principle 6: Building Sustainable Leadership Capacity

1. Discuss instances in your school or district where teachers played leadership roles (obtaining grants for instructional initiatives; organizing professional study groups, mentoring programs, or other professional development activities; evaluating or developing curricula or local assessments; and so on). Brainstorm ways that teachers can be encouraged and supported in their efforts to exercise similar leadership.

2. Discuss the five implications listed in the "Discussion of Implications" section starting on page 230. How well does this list fit into the goals of your school or district? How can your school or district goals be adjusted to include the ideas from this list?

3. Review the "10 Things That Are Sustainable About You" on pages 235–236. How could your school or district implement these changes? What should the first steps be?

Wrap Up Your Reading With Reflection

When you have completed the series of group meetings on the chapters of *Failure Is Not an Option*®, answer the following questions, and then take time as a group to celebrate your hard work and mastery of school improvement theory and practice.

1. What is the most valuable lesson your school or district has learned from reading and discussing the book with your colleagues?

2. In light of what you have learned, what should be the two highest-priority actions for improvement in your school or district?

3. What actions will you, individually or with colleagues, take as a result of what you have learned?

4. Sketch out a possible timeline for the actions you listed in answering questions 2 and 3.

5. What, if any, follow-up activities would you like your group to undertake?

6. What have you learned about collaboration and teamwork as a result of the activities and discussions in this guide?

   a. What did you like about this process?

   b. What would you do differently if you were to do this again?

Set a date to get back together to exchange what you've done. As a result of this experience, identify how the group can help you in applying this reading to your practice.

References and Further Readings

Ackerman, R. H., & Maslin-Ostrowski, P. (2002). *The wounded leader.* San Francisco: Jossey-Bass.

Adelman, H. S., & Taylor, L. (1997a). Toward a scale-up model for replicating new approaches to schooling. *Journal of Educational and Psychological Consultation, 8,* 197–230.

Adelman, H. S., & Taylor, L. (2003). On sustainability of project innovations as systemic change. *Journal of Educational and Psychological Consultation, 14,* 1–26.

Adelman, H. S., & Taylor, L. (2006a). *The school leader's guide to student learning supports: New directions for addressing barriers to learning.* Thousand Oaks, CA: Corwin.

Adelman, H. S., & Taylor, L. (2006b). *The implementation guide to student learning supports in the classroom and schoolwide: New directions for addressing barriers to learning.* Thousand Oaks, CA: Corwin.

Adelman, H. S., & Taylor, L. (2007). Systemic change for school improvement. *Journal of Educational & Psychological Consultation, 17*(1), 55–77. doi: 10.1207/s1532768Xjepc1701_3.

Anthony, E. J. (1982). The preventive approach to children at high risk for psychopathology and psychosis. *Journal of Children in Contemporary Society, 15*(1), 67–72.

Anthony, E. J. (1987). Risk, vulnerability, and resilience: An overview. In E. J. Anthony & B. J. Cohler (Eds.), *The invulnerable child* (pp. 3–48). New York: Guilford Press.

Anthony, E. J. (1998, Fall). Attachment and belonging. *Journal of Emotional and Behavioral Problems, 7*(3).

Ariely, D. (2010). *Predictably irrational, revised and expanded edition: The hidden forces that shape our decisions.* New York: Harper Perennial.

Ash, K. (2012, Feb. 1). K–12 marketplace sees major flow of venture capital. *Education Week, 31*(19), 1.

Atkinson, A., Burgess, S., Croxson, B., Gregg, P., Propper, C., Slater, H., & Wilson, D. (2004). *Evaluating the impact of performance-related pay for teachers in England* (Working Paper). Bristol, UK: Centre for Market and Public Organization.

Bandura, A. (1986). *Social foundations of thought and action: A social cognitive theory.* Englewood Cliffs, NJ: Prentice-Hall.

Barber, M. (2001). High expectations and standards for all, no matter what: Creating a world class educational service in England. In M. Fielding (Ed.), *Taking education really seriously: Three years of hard labour.* London: Routledge/Falmer.

Bardwick, J. (1996). Peacetime management and wartime leadership. In F. Hesselbein, M. Goldsmith, & R. Beckhard (Eds.), *The leader of the future* (pp. 131–140). San Francisco: Jossey-Bass.

Barth, R. S. (2001a). *Learning by heart.* San Francisco: Jossey-Bass.

Barth, R. S. (2001b). Teacher leader. *Phi Delta Kappan, 82*(6), 443–449.

Barth, R. S. (2003). *Lessons learned: Shaping relationships and the culture of the workplace.* Thousand Oaks, CA: Corwin.

Barth, R. S. (2006). Relationships within the schoolhouse. *Educational Leadership, 63*(6), 9–13.

Barth, R. S., DuFour, R., DuFour, R., & Eaker, R. (Eds.). (2005). *On common ground: The power of professional learning communities.* Bloomington, IN: Solution Tree.

Barty, K., Thomson, P., Blackmore, J., & Sachs, S. (2005). Unpacking the issues: Researching the shortage of school principals in two states in Australia. *Australian Educational Researcher, 32*(3), 1–18.

Bennis, W. G. (1989). *On becoming a leader.* New York: Addison-Wesley.

Black, P., Harrison, C., Lee, C., Marshall, B., & Wiliam, D. (2003). *Assessment for learning: Putting it into practice.* Maidenhead, UK: Open University Press.

Black, P., Harrison, C., Lee, C., Marshall, B., & Wiliam, D. (2004). Working inside the black box: Assessment for learning in the classroom. *Phi Delta Kappan, 86*(1), 9–21.

Bland, J., Sherer, D., Guha, R., Woodworth, K., Shields, P., Tiffany-Morales, J., & Campbell, A. (2011). *The status of the teaching profession 2011.* Sacramento, CA: The Center for the Future of Teaching and Learning at WestEd.

Blankstein, A. M. (1992). Lessons from enlightened corporations. *Educational Leadership, 49*(6), 71.

Blankstein, A. M. (1997). Fighting for success. *Reaching Today's Youth: The Community Circle of Caring Journal, 1*(2), 2–3.

Blankstein, A. M. (2004). *Failure is not an option: Six principles that guide student achievement in high-performing schools.* Thousand Oaks, CA: Corwin.

Blankstein, A. M. (2007). Terms of engagement: Where failure is not an option. In A. M. Blankstein, P. D. Houston, & R. W. Cole (Eds.), *Engaging every learner.* Thousand Oaks, CA: Corwin.

Blankstein, A. M. (2010). *Failure is not an option: 6 principles for making student success the only option.* Thousand Oaks, CA: Corwin.

Blankstein, A. M. (2011). *The answer is in the room: How effective schools scale up student success.* Thousand Oaks, CA: Corwin.

Blankstein, A. M., DuFour, R., & Little, M. (1997). *Reaching today's students.* Bloomington, IN: National Educational Service.

Blankstein, A. M., Houston, P. D., & Cole, R. W. (Eds.). (2007). *Engaging every learner.* Thousand Oaks, CA: Corwin.

Blankstein, A. M., Houston, P. D., & Cole, R. W. (Eds.). (2008). *Sustaining professional learning communities.* Thousand Oaks, CA: Corwin.

Blankstein, A. M., Houston, P. D., & Cole, R. W. (Eds.). (2009). *Building sustainable leadership capacity.* Thousand Oaks, CA: Corwin.

Blankstein, A. M., Houston, P. D., & Cole, R. W. (2010). *The Soul of Educational Leadership series.* Thousand Oaks, CA: Corwin.

Blankstein, A. M., & Swain, H. (1994, Feb.). Is TQM right for schools? *The Executive Educator, 16*(2), 51–54.

Blase, J., & Anderson, G. (1995). *The micropolitics of educational leadership: From control to empowerment.* New York: Teachers College Press.

Block, P. (2002). *The answer to how is yes: Acting on what matters.* San Francisco: Barrett-Koehler.

Bolman, L. G., & Deal, T. E. (1991). *Reframing organizations: Artistry, choice, and leadership.* San Francisco: Jossey-Bass.

Bolman, L. G., & Deal, T. E. (2002). *Reframing the path to school leadership.* Thousand Oaks, CA: Corwin.

Bonstingl, J. J. (2001). *Schools of quality* (3rd ed.). Thousand Oaks, CA: Corwin.

Bowen, M., Cooley Nelson, E., Lake, R., & Yatsko, S. (2012). *Tinkering toward transformation: A look at federal school improvement grant implementation.* Seattle, WA: Center on Reinventing Public Education.

Bower, E. M. (1964). The modification, mediation, and utilization of stress during the school years. *American Journal of Orthopsychiatry, 34,* 667–674.

Bowser, B. A. (2001, May 24). Principal shortage. *Online NewsHour.* Public Broadcasting System. Retrieved July 28, 2009, from http://www.pbs.org/newshour/bb/education/jan-june01/principal_05-22.html.

Boykin, A. W., & Noguera, P. (2011). *Creating the opportunity to learn: Moving from research to practice to close the achievement gap.* Alexandria, VA: ACSD.

Bradsher, K. (2012, Sept. 3). Plan for change in schools stirs protest in Hong Kong. *The New York Times.* Retrieved from http://www.nytimes.com/2012/09/04/world/asia/plan-for-national-education-stirs-protests-in-hong-kong.html.

Brendtro, L. K., Brokenleg, M., & Bockern, S. V. (1990). *Reclaiming youth at risk: Our hope for the future.* Bloomington, IN: National Educational Services.

Brown, P., & Lauder, H. (2001). *Capitalism and social progress: The future of society in a global economy.* New York: Palgrave.

Brown, S., Choi, K., & Herman, B. (2011, March). *Exploratory study of the HOPE Foundation Courageous Leadership Academy: Summary of findings.* Washington, DC: American Institutes for Research.

Bryant, A. (2009, May 24). In a word, he wants simplicity (Interview with Eduardo Castro-Wright, vice chairman of Wal-Mart Stores). *New York Times,* Sunday Business Section, p. 2.

Bryk, A. S., Camburn, E., & Seashore Louis, K. (1999). Professional community in Chicago elementary schools: Facilitating factors and organizational consequences [Special issue]. *Educational Administration Quarterly, 35,* 751–781.

Bryk, A. S., & Driscoll, M. E. (1998). *The school as community: Theoretical foundation, contextual influences, and consequences for teachers and students.* Madison, WI: National Center for Effective Secondary Schools.

Bryk, A. S., Easton, J. Q., Kerbow, D., Rollow, S. G., & Sebring, P. A. (1994). The state of Chicago school reform. *Phi Delta Kappan, 76*(1), 74–78.

Bryk, A. S., Lee, V. E., & Holland, P. B. (1993). *Catholic schools and the common good.* Cambridge, MA: Harvard University Press.

Bryk, A. S., & Schneider, B. (2002). *Trust in schools: A core resource for improvement.* New York: Russell Sage Foundation.

Bryk, A. S., Sebring, P. B., Allensworth, E., Luppescu, S., & Easton, J. Q. (2010). *Organizing schools for improvement: Lessons from Chicago.* Chicago: University of Chicago Press.

Bryk, A. S., & Thum, Y. M. (1989). The effects of high school organization on dropping out: An exploratory investigation. *American Educational Research Journal, 26*(3), 353–383.

Buckingham, M., & Coffman, C. (1999). *First, break all the rules: What the world's greatest managers do differently.* New York: Simon & Schuster.

Busine, M., & Watt, B. (2005). Succession management: Trends and current practices. *Asia Pacific Journal of Human Resources, 43*(2), 225–237.

Cavanagh, S. (2012). Legislators reconvene with last year's battles in mind. *Education Week, 31*(15), 1, 21.

Challen, A., Machin, S., & McNally, S. (2008, Nov.). *Schools in England: Structures, teachers and evaluation* (Working Paper). Turin, Italy: Fondazione Giovanni Agnelli.

Champy, J. (1995). *Reengineering management.* New York: HarperCollins.

Childs-Bowen, D., Moller, G., & Scrivner, J. (2000). Principals: Leaders of leaders. *National Association of Secondary School Principals (NASSP) Bulletin, 84*(616), 27–34.

Clarizio, H. F., & McCoy, G. F. (1970). *Behavior disorders in school-aged children.* Scranton, PA: Chandler.

Clark, C. M. (1988). Asking the right questions about teacher preparation: Contributions of research on teaching thinking. *Educational Researcher, 17*(2), 5–12.

Cohen, D. K., & Moffitt, S. L. (2009). *The ordeal of equality: Did federal legislation fix the schools?* Cambridge, MA: Harvard University Press.

Cole, A. L. (1989, April). *Making explicit implicit theories of teaching: Starting points in preservice programs.* Paper presented at the Annual Meeting of the American Educational Research Association, San Francisco.

Collins, J. (1996). Aligning action and values. *Leader to Leader, 1*(1), 19–24.

Collins, J. (2001). *Good to great.* New York: HarperCollins.

Combs, A. W., Miser, A. B., & Whitaker, K. S. (1999). *On becoming a school leader: A person-centered challenge.* Alexandria, VA: Association for Supervision and Curriculum Development.

Comer, J. P., Ben-Avie, M., Haynes, N. M., & Joyner, E. T. (1999). *Child by child: The Comer process for change in education.* New York: Teachers College Press.

Comer, J. P., Haynes, N. M., Joyner, E. T., & Ben-Avie, M. (1996). *Rallying the whole village: The Comer process for reforming education.* New York: Teachers College Press.

Comer, J. P., Joyner, E. T., & Ben-Avie, M. (2004). *Six pathways to healthy child development and academic success.* Thousand Oaks, CA: Corwin.

Connelly, G., & Tirozzi, G. N. (2008, Sept. 10). A new leader, new school leadership support? *Education Week, 28*(3).

Connors, L. J., & Epstein, J. L. (1994). *Taking stock: The views of teachers, parents, and students on school, family, and community partnerships in high schools* (Report 25). Baltimore: Center on School, Family, and Community Partnerships at Johns Hopkins University.

Cooper, N. (2007, May 8). How to create meaning in the workplace. *Personnel Today, 29,* 362.

Cooperrider, D. L. (1990). Positive image, positive action: The affirmative basis of organizing. In S. Srivastva, D. L. Cooperrider et al. (Eds.), *Appreciative management and leadership: The power of positive thought and action in organizations.* San Francisco: Jossey-Bass.

Coopersmith, S. (1967). *The antecedents of self-esteem.* San Francisco: W. H. Freeman.

Corbett, D., Wilson, B., & Williams, B. (2002). *Effort and excellence in urban classrooms: Expecting—and getting—success with all students.* New York: Teachers College Press.

Costa, A. L., & Kallick, B. (Eds.). (2000). *Discovering & exploring habits of mind.* Alexandria, VA: Association for Supervision and Curriculum Development.

Covey, S. R. (1989). *The 7 habits of highly effective people.* New York: Simon & Schuster.

Cushman, K. (Ed.). (1995, Mar.). Making the good school better: The essential question of rigor. *Horace: The Journal of the Coalition of Essential Schools, 11*(4), 2.

Darling-Hammond, L. (1996). The quiet revolution: Rethinking teacher development. *Educational Leadership, 53*(6), 4–10.

Darling-Hammond, L. (1997). *The right to learn: A blueprint for creating schools that work.* San Francisco: Jossey-Bass.

Darling-Hammond, L. (1999). Target time toward teachers. *Journal of Staff Development, 20*(2), 31–36.

Darling-Hammond, L. (2007, Oct. 22). *Education leadership: A bridge to school reform.* Paper presented at the Wallace Foundation's National Conference, New York.

Darling-Hammond, L. (2012). Value-added evaluation hurts teaching. *Education Week.*

Darling-Hammond, L., Amrein-Beardsley, A., Haertel, E., & Rothstein, J. (2012, Feb. 29). Evaluating teacher evaluation: Popular modes of evaluating teachers are fraught with inaccuracies and inconsistencies, but the field has identified better approaches. *Phi Delta Kappan, Education Week.*

Darling-Hammond, L., Amrein-Beardsley, A., Haertel, E., & Rothstein, J. (2012, Mar.). Evaluating teacher evaluation. *Phi Delta Kappan, 93*(6), 8–15.

Darling-Hammond, L., & Baratz-Snowden, J. (Eds.). (2005). *A good teacher in every classroom: Preparing the highly qualified teachers our children deserve.* San Francisco: Jossey-Bass.

Darling-Hammond, L., & Lieberman, A. (2012). *Teacher education around the world: Changing policies and practices.* New York: Routledge.

Darling-Hammond, L., Wei, R. C., Andree, A., Richardson, N., & Orphanos, S. (2009). *Professional learning in the learning profession: A status report on teacher development in the United States and abroad.* Dallas, TX: National Staff Development Council.

Datnow, A., & Castellano, M. (2000). *An "inside look" at success for all: A qualitative study of implementation and teaching and learning.* Baltimore: Johns Hopkins University, Center for Research on the Education of Students Placed at Risk.

Davis, M. (2012). Canadian ed. dips into for-profit realm. *Education Week, Special Report, 31*(19), S10.

Davis, S., Darling-Hammond, L., LaPointe, M., & Meyerson, D. (2005). *School leadership study: Developing successful principals* (Review of Research). Stanford, CA: Stanford University, Stanford Educational Leadership Institute.

Deal, T. E., & Peterson, K. D. (1999). *Shaping school culture: The heart of leadership.* San Francisco: Jossey-Bass.

Deci, E. L., Koestner, R., & Ryan, R. (1999). A meta-analytic review of experiments examining the effects of extrinsic rewards on intrinsic motivation. *Psychological Bulletin, 125*(6).

deLisle, J. (2003, May 13). Asia's shifting strategic landscape: SARS, Greater China, and the pathologies of globalization and transition. *New York Times,* pp. 587–604. doi:10.1016/S0030-4387(03)00076-0.

Deming, W. E. (1986). *Out of the crisis.* Cambridge, MA: MIT Center for Advanced Engineering Study.

Dewey, J. (1927). *The public and its problems.* New York: Holt.

Dietz, M. E. (2002, Winter). Triangulated student data to inform instruction. *Portfolio Newsletter, NSDC Portfolio Network, 15.*

Donaldson, G., Jr. (2001). *Cultivating leadership in school: Connecting people, purpose, and practice.* New York: Teachers College Press.

Drucker, P. (1992). *Managing for the future: The 1990s and beyond.* New York: Truman Talley Books.

DuFour, R. (1991). *The principal as staff developer.* Bloomington, IN: National Educational Service.

DuFour, R. (2003, Winter). Leading edge. *National Staff Development Council, 24*(1).

DuFour, R., & Eaker, R. (1992). *Creating the new American school.* Bloomington, IN: National Educational Service.

DuFour, R., & Eaker, R. (1998). *Professional learning communities at work: Best practices for enhancing student achievement.* Bloomington, IN: National Educational Service.

Duhigg, C. (2012). *The power of habit.* New York: Random House.

Duke, D. (1988). Why principals consider quitting. *Phi Delta Kappan, 70*(4), 308–313.

Dweck, C. (2006). *Mindset: The new psychology of success.* New York: Ballantine Books.

Eaker, R., DuFour, R., & Burnette, R. (2002). *Getting started: Reculturing schools to become professional learning communities.* Bloomington, IN: National Educational Service.

Earl, L., & Katz, S. (2010). Creating a culture of inquiry: Harnessing data for professional learning. In A. M. Blankstein, P. D. Houston, & R. W. Cole (Eds.), *Data-enhanced leadership: The soul of educational leadership series.* Thousand Oaks, CA: Corwin.

Earley, P., Evans, J., Collarbone, P., Gold, A., & Halpin, D. (2002). *Establishing the current state of leadership in England.* London: Department for Education and Skills.

Eastman, C. (1902). *Indian boyhood.* New York: McClure, Phillips & Co.

Easton, L. (1999). Tuning protocols. *Journal of Staff Development, 20*(3), 55–56.

Easton, L. (2004). Tuning protocols. In National Staff Development Council & L. B. Easton (Ed.), *Powerful designs for professional learning* (2nd ed., pp. 239–240). Dallas, TX: National Staff Development Council.

Easton, L. (2008). *Powerful designs for professional learning* (2nd ed.). Dallas, TX: National Staff Development Council.

Easton, L. (2009). *Protocols for professional learning.* Alexandria, VA: Association for Supervision and Curriculum Development.

Edmonds, R. R. (1979). Effective schools for the urban poor. *Educational Leadership, 37*(10), 15–24.

Education Trust Fund. (1999). *Dispelling the myth: High poverty schools exceeding expectations.* Washington, DC: Author.

Education Trust Fund. (2002). *Dispelling the myth revisited.* Washington, DC: Author.

Elias, M. J., & Arnold, H. (Eds.). (2006). *The educator's guide to emotional intelligence and academic achievement.* Thousand Oaks, CA: Corwin.

Elias, M. J., Arnold, H., & Hussey, C. S. (Eds.). (2003). *EQ + IQ = Best leadership practices for caring and successful schools.* Thousand Oaks, CA: Corwin.

Elias, M. J., Bryan, K., Patrikakou, E. N., & Weissberg, R. P. (2003). *Challenges in creating effective home-school partnerships in adolescence: Promising paths for collaboration.* Chicago: Collaborative for Academic, Social, and Emotional Learning.

Elias, M. J., Frey, K. S., Greenberg, M. T., Haynes, N. M., Kessler, R., Schwab-Stone, M. E., & Shriver, T. P. (1997). *Promoting social and emotional learning: Guidelines for educators.* Alexandria, VA: Association for Supervision and Curriculum Development.

Elias, M. J., Friedlander, B. S., & Tobias, S. E. (1999). *Emotionally intelligent parenting: How to raise a self-disciplined, responsible, socially skilled child.* New York: Three Rivers Press.

Elias, M. J., Kress, J. S., & Novick, B. (2002). *Building learning communities with character: How to integrate academic, social, and emotional learning.* Alexandria, VA: Association for Supervision and Curriculum Development.

Elias, M. J., Ogburn-Thompson, G., Lewis, C., & Neft, D. (2008). *Urban dreams: Stories of hope, resilience, and character.* New York: Hamilton.

Elmore, R. F. (1995). Structural reform in educational practice. *Educational Researcher, 24*(9), 23–26.

Elmore, R. F. (1999–2000, Winter). Building a new structure for school leadership. *American Educator, 23*(4), 6–13.

Elmore, R. F. (2000). *Building a new structure for school leadership.* New York: Albert Shanker Institute.

Elmore, R. F. (2002). Hard questions about practice. *Educational Leadership, 59*(8), 22–25.

Empresarios colombianos no deben temerle a la competencia: Piñera. (2010, Nov. 27). *El Tiempo.*

Epstein, J. L., Sanders, M. G., Sheldon, S. B., Simon, B. S., Salinas, K. C., Jansorn, N. R., Van Voorhis, F. L., . . . Williams, K. J. (2009). *School, family, and community partnerships: Your handbook for action* (3rd ed.). Thousand Oaks, CA: Corwin.

Evans, R. (1996). *The human side of school change.* San Francisco: Jossey-Bass.

Ewing Marion Kauffman Foundation. (2002). *Set for success: Building a strong foundation for school readiness based on the social-emotional development of young children.* Kansas City, MO: Author.

Fenstermacher, G. D. (1986). Philosophy of research on teaching: Three aspects. In M. C. Wittrock (Ed.), *Handbook of research on teaching* (3rd ed., pp. 37–49). New York: Macmillan.

Ferguson, R. (2002). *What doesn't meet the eye: Understanding and addressing racial disparities in high-achieving suburban schools.* Oakbrook, IL: North Central Regional Educational Laboratory.

Financial Executive International (FEI). (2001). *Building human capital: The public sector's 21st century challenge.* Retrieved June 19, 2003, from www.fei.org.

Fink, D. (2000a). The attrition of educational change over time: The case of an innovative, "model," "lighthouse" school. In N. Bascia & A. Hargreaves (Eds.), *The sharp edge of educational change.* London: Routledge/Falmer.

Fink, D. (2000b). *Good schools/real schools: Why school reform doesn't last.* New York: Teachers College Press.

Fink, D. (2005). *Leadership for mortals.* London/Thousand Oaks, CA: Paul Chapman/Corwin.

Fink, D. (2010). *The succession challenge: Building and sustaining leadership capacity through succession management.* Thousand Oaks, CA: Corwin.

Fisher, R., & Shapiro, D. (2006). *Beyond reason: Using emotions as you negotiate.* New York: Penguin.

Flanigan, R. L. (2012, Feb.). U.S. schools forge foreign connections. *Education Week Special Supplement, 31*(19), S2–4.

Fletcher, C., Caron, M., & Williams, W. (1985). *Schools on trial.* Milton Keynes, UK: Open University Press.

Frankl, V. (1997). *Recollections.* New York: Plenum Press.

Frankl, V. (2000). *Man's search for meaning.* Boston: Beacon Press. (Original work published 1959.)

Friedman, T. (2009, June 28). Invent, invent, invent. *New York Times,* Sunday Opinion Section, p. WK8.

Fullan, M. (1991). *The new meaning of educational change.* New York: Teachers College Press.

Fullan, M. (1993). *Change forces.* New York: The Falmer Press.

Fullan, M. (1996). *What's worth fighting for in your school?* New York: Teachers College Press.

Fullan, M. (1997). *What's worth fighting for in the principalship?* New York: Teachers College Press.

Fullan, M. (2001a). *Leading in a culture of change.* San Francisco: Jossey-Bass.

Fullan, M. (2001b). *The new meaning of educational change* (3rd ed.). New York: Teachers College Press.

Fullan, M. (2003a). *Change forces with a vengeance.* New York: Routledge/Falmer.

Fullan, M. (2003b). *The moral imperative of school leadership.* Thousand Oaks, CA: Corwin.

Fullan, M. (2005). *Leadership & sustainability: System thinkers in action.* Thousand Oaks, CA: Corwin.

Fullan, M. (2006). *Turnaround leadership.* Hoboken, NJ: John Wiley and Sons.

Fullan, M. (2008). *The six secrets of change: What the best leaders do to help their organizations survive and thrive.* San Francisco: Jossey-Bass.

Fullan, M. (2009). *The challenge of change: Start school improvement now* (2nd ed.). Thousand Oaks, CA: Corwin.

Fullan, M. (2011). *Change leader: Learning to do what matters most.* San Francisco: Jossey-Bass.

Fullan, M. (2012). *Stratosphere: Integrating technology, pedagogy, and change knowledge.* New York: Pearson.

Fullan, M., Hill, P., & Crévola, C. (2006). *Breakthrough.* Thousand Oaks, CA: Corwin.

Fullan, M., & Levin, B. (2009, June 17). The fundamentals of whole-system reform: A case study from Canada. *Education Week, 28*(35), 30–31.

Fullan, M., & St. Germain, C. (2006). *Learning places: A field guide for improving the context of schooling.* Thousand Oaks, CA: Corwin.

Gabor, A. (2011, Sept. 22). Why pay incentives are destined to fail and how they could undermine school reform. *Education Week, 30*(4), 24, 28.

Galton, M. (2000). "Dumbing down" on classroom standards: The perils of a technician's approach to pedagogy. *Journal of Educational Change, 1*(2), 199–204.

Gardner, J. (1988). *Leadership: An overview.* Washington, DC: Independent Sector.

Gardner, J. (1991). *Building community.* Washington, DC: Independent Sector.

Garmezy, N. (1983). Stressors of childhood. In N. Garmezy & M. Rutter (Eds.), *Stress, coping, and the development in children.* New York: McGraw-Hill.

Garmezy, N. (1994). Reflections and commentary on risk, resilience, and development. In R. J. Haggarty, L. R. Sherrod, N. Garmezy, & M. Rutter (Eds.), *Stress, risk, and resilience in children and adolescents: Processes, mechanisms, and interventions* (pp. 1–18). Cambridge, UK: Cambridge University Press.

Gladwell, M. (2002). *The tipping point: How little things can make a big difference.* Boston: Back Bay Books.

Glasser, W. (1986). *Control theory in the classroom.* New York: HarperCollins.

Glasser, W. (1992). *The quality school: Managing students without coercion.* New York: HarperPerennial.

Glickman, C. (2002). *Leadership for learning: How to help teachers succeed.* Arlington, VA: Association for Supervision and Curriculum Development.

Glickman, C. (2003). *Holding sacred ground: Essays on leadership, courage, and endurance in our schools.* San Francisco: Jossey-Bass.

Goddard, R. D., Hoy, W. K., & Hoy, A. W. (2000). Collective teacher efficacy: Its meaning, measure, and impact on student achievement. *American Educational Research Journal, 37*(2), 479–507.

Goddard, R. D., Salloum, S. J., & Berebitsky, D. (2009). Trust as a mediator of the relationships between poverty, racial composition, and academic achievement: Evidence from Michigan's public elementary schools. *Educational Administration Quarterly, 45,* 292–311.

Goldstein, A. (2001, June 21). How to fix the coming principal shortage. *Time.* Retrieved July 28, 2009, from http://www.time.com/time/nation/article/0,8599,168379,00.html.

Goleman, D. (1995). *Emotional intelligence.* New York: Bantam Books.

Goleman, D., Boyatzis, R., & McKee, A. (2002). *Primal leadership: Realizing the power of emotional intelligence.* Boston: Harvard Business School Press.

Goodlad, J. I., McMannon, T. J., & Soder, R. (Eds.). (2001). *Developing democratic character in the young.* San Francisco: Jossey-Bass.

Goodlad, S. J. (Ed.). (2001). *The last best hope.* San Francisco: Jossey-Bass.

Govan, F., & Laing, S. (2010, Oct. 16). Miners came to blows, but swore to keep details secret. *The Daily Telegraph.*

Government of Western Australia. (2001). *Managing succession in the Western Australia public sector.* Retrieved June 29, 2003, from http://www.mpc.wa.gov.au.

Gregory, T. (2001). Fear of success? Ten ways alternative schools pull their punches. *Phi Delta Kappan, 82*(8), 577–581.

Guetzloe, E. (1994, Summer). Risk, resilience, and protection. *Journal of Emotional and Behavioral Problems, 3*(2), 2–5.

Hallowell, B. (1997). My nonnegotiables. In G. A. Donaldson (Ed.), *On being a principal: The rewards and challenges of school leadership.* San Francisco: Jossey-Bass.

Hargreaves, A. (2001). Beyond anxiety and nostalgia. *Phi Delta Kappan, 82*(5), 373.

Hargreaves, A. (2003). *Teaching in the knowledge society.* New York: Teachers College Press.

Hargreaves, A. (Ed.). (2005). *Extending educational change.* New York: Springer.

Hargreaves, A. (2010). *Leading beyond expectations: Inspiring examples of success from business, sports, and education.* Learning Forward Keynote Address, annual conference, Atlanta, GA, December 4–8.

Hargreaves, A., Earl, L., Moore, S., & Manning, S. (2001). *Learning to change: Teaching beyond subjects and standards.* San Francisco: Jossey-Bass.

Hargreaves, A., & Fink, D. (2000). The three dimensions of reform. *Educational Leadership, 57*(7), 30–34.

Hargreaves, A., & Fink, D. (2003, May). Sustaining leadership. *Phi Delta Kappan, 84*(9), 693–700.

Hargreaves, A., & Fink, D. (2004). The seven principles of sustainable leadership. *Educational Leadership, 61*(7), 8–13.

Hargreaves, A., & Fink, D. (2005). *Sustainable leadership.* San Francisco: Jossey-Bass.

Hargreaves, A., & Fullan, M. (1998). *What's worth fighting for out there?* New York: Teachers College Press.

Hargreaves, A., & Fullan, M. (2012). *Professional capital: Transforming teaching in every school.* New York: Teachers College Press.

Hargreaves, A., Fullan, M., Hopkins, D., & Lieberman, A. (Eds.). (2009). *The second international handbook of educational change.* Dordrecht, The Netherlands: Springer.

Hargreaves, A., & Goodson, I. (2003). *Change over time? A study of culture, structure, time and change in secondary schooling.* Project #199800214. Chicago: Spencer Foundation of the United States.

Hargreaves, A., & Goodson, I. (2006). Educational change over time? The sustainability and non-sustainability of three decades of secondary school change and continuity. *Educational Administration Quarterly, 42*(1).

Hargreaves, A., Halász, G., & Pont, B. (2008). The Finnish approach to system leadership. In B. Pont, D. Nusche, & D. Hopkins (Eds.), *Improving school leadership, Vol. 2: Case studies on system leadership* (pp. 69–109). Paris: OECD.

Hargreaves, A., Shaw, P., Fink, D., Retallick, J., Giles, C., Moore, S., . . . James-Wilson, S. (2000). *Change frames: Supporting secondary teachers in interpreting and integrating secondary school reform.* Toronto, ON: Ontario Institute for Studies in Education/University of Toronto.

Hargreaves, A., & Shirley, D. (2008, Oct.). The fourth way to change. *Educational Leadership, 66*(2), 56–61.

Hargreaves, A., & Shirley, D. (2009). *The fourth way: The inspiring future for educational change.* Thousand Oaks, CA: Corwin.

Harris, A. (2008). *Distributed school leadership: Developing tomorrow's leaders.* London: Routledge.

Harris, A., & Goodall, J. (2008). Do parents know they matter? Engaging all parents in learning. *Educational Research, 50*(3), 277–289.

Haynes, N. M., Emmons, C. L., & Woodruff, D. W. (1998). School development program effects: Linking implementation to outcomes. *Journal of Education for Students Placed at Risk, 3*(1), 71–85.

Heifetz, R. (1999). *Leadership without easy answers.* Cambridge, MA: Belknap Press of Harvard University Press.

Heifetz, R., & Linsky, M. (2002). *Leadership on the line: Staying alive through the dangers of leading.* Boston: Harvard Business School Press.

Henderson, A. (1987). *The evidence continues to grow.* Columbia, MD: National Committee for Citizens in Education.

Henderson, A., & Berla, N. (1995). *A new generation of evidence: The family is critical to student achievement.* Washington, DC: Center for Law and Education.

Hess, R. (2008, Dec.). The new stupid. *Educational Leadership, 66,* 12–17.

Higgins, G. (1994). *Resilient adults: Overcoming a cruel past.* San Francisco: Jossey-Bass.

Hill, N. E., & Tyson, D. F. (2009). Parental involvement in middle school: A meta-analytic assessment of the strategies that promote achievement. *Developmental Psychology, 45*(3), 740–763.

Hill, P. W. (2010). Using assessment data to lead teaching and learning. In A. M. Blankstein, P. D. Houston, & R. W. Cole (Eds.), *Data-enhanced leadership: Vol. 7. The soul of educational leadership* (pp. 31–50). Thousand Oaks, CA: Corwin.

Hirsch, E. D. (2006). *The knowledge deficit.* New York: Houghton Mifflin.

Hirsh, S., & Killion, J. (2007). *The learning educator: A new era for professional learning.* Dallas, TX: National Staff Development Council.

Hoffer, E. (1972). *Reflections on the human condition.* New York: HarperCollins.

HOPE Foundation. (2002). *Failure is not an option* [Video series]. Bloomington, IN: HOPE Foundation. Available from www.HopeFoundation.org.

HOPE Foundation. (2009a). *Evaluation of Courageous Leadership Academy I, conducted for Mattoon Community School District #2, Mattoon, IL.* Bloomington, IN: Author.

HOPE Foundation. (2009b). *Failure is not an option 3: Effective assessment for effective learning* [Video series]. Bloomington, IN: HOPE Foundation. Available from http://www.HopeFoundation.org.

HOPE Foundation. (2009c). *Courageous leadership for shaping America's future IV.* Bloomington, IN: Author.

HOPE Foundation. (2011, Aug.). *What highly effective school leaders do to sustain success.* New York: Author.

HOPE Foundation. (2012, Aug. 6). *Multiple ways of accessing student understanding.* Conference presentation. Ithica, NY.

Hopkins, D. (2001). *School improvement for real.* New York: Routledge/Falmer.

Hopkins, D. (2007). *Every school a great school.* Buckingham, UK: Open University Press.

Hopkins, D. (2008, June). Every school a great school: Realizing the potential of system leadership. *Journal of Educational Change, 9*(2).

Hord, S. M. (1997a). *Professional learning communities: Communities of continuous inquiry and improvement.* Austin, TX: Southwest Educational Development Laboratory.

Hord, S. M. (1997b). *Professional learning communities: What are they and why are they important?* Austin, TX: Southwest Educational Development Laboratory.

Hord, S. M., & Hirsh, S. (2008). Making the promise a reality. In A. M. Blankstein, P. D. Houston, & R. W. Cole (Eds.), *Sustaining professional learning communities* (pp. 23–40). Thousand Oaks, CA: Corwin.

Hord, S. M., & Sommers, W. A. (2007). *Leading professional learning communities: Voices from research and practice.* Thousand Oaks, CA: Corwin.

Houston, P. D. (1997). *Articles of faith & hope for public education.* Arlington, VA: American Association of School Administrators.

Houston, P. D., Blankstein, A. M., & Cole, R. W. (Eds.). (2009a). *Leaders as communicators and diplomats.* Thousand Oaks, CA: Corwin.

Houston, P. D., Blankstein, A. M., & Cole, R. W. (Eds.). (2009b). *Out-of-the-box leadership.* Thousand Oaks, CA: Corwin.

Houston, P. D., & Sokolow, S. (2006). *Spirituality in educational leadership.* Thousand Oaks, CA: Corwin.

Huffman, J. B., & Hipp, K. K. (2004). *Reculturing schools as professional learning communities.* Lanham, MD: ScarecrowEducation.

Institute for Educational Leadership. (2000). *Leadership for student learning: Reinventing the principalship.* Washington, DC: Author.

Interstate School Leaders Licensure Consortium (ISLLC). (2000–2008). *Standards for educational administration.* New York: Pearson.

Irlenbusch, B., & Ruchala, G. K. (2008). Relative rewards within team-based compensation. *Labour Economics, 15*(2), 141–167.

Jackson, K. (2000). *Building new teams: The next generation.* Paper presented at the Future of Work in the Public Sector conference, organized by the School of Public Administration, University of Victoria, British Columbia, Canada. Retrieved June 19, 2003, from http://www.futurework.telus.com/proceedings.pdf.

Johnson, D. (2001, Mar. 29). Maryland's strategy to lure new principals. *Washington Post*, B–2.

Jordán, R., Koljatic, M., & Useem, M. (2011). *Leading the rescue of the miners in Chile.* The Wharton School of the University of Pennsylvania and Pontificia Universidad Católica De Chile. Retrieved from http://kw.wharton.upenn .edu/wdp/files/2011/07/Leading-the-Miners-Rescue.pdf.

Joyce, B., & Showers, B. (1995). *Student achievement through staff development: Fundamentals of school renewal* (2nd ed.). White Plains, NY: Longman.

Kaiser, B., & Rasminsky, J. S. (2004). *Challenging behavior and social context.* Boston: Pearson Allyn Bacon Prentice Hall.

Kegan, R., & Lahey, L. L. (2001). *How the way we talk can change the way we work: Seven languages for transformation.* San Francisco: Jossey-Bass.

Kets de Vries, M. (1993). *Leaders, fools, and imposters: Essays on the psychology of leadership.* San Francisco: Jossey-Bass.

King, M. B., & Newmann, F. (2000). Will teacher learning advance school goals? *Phi Delta Kappan, 81*(8), 576–580.

Kleitman, S., & Gibson, J. (2011). Metacognitive beliefs, self-confidence and primary learning environment of sixth grade students. *Learning & Individual Differences, 21*(6).

Knapp, M. S., Copland, M. A., & Talbert, J. E. (2003, Feb.). *Leading for learning: Reflective tools for school and district leaders* (research report). Seattle, WA: Center for the Study of Teaching and Policy.

Kochanek, J. R. (2005). *Building trust for better schools: Research-based practices.* Thousand Oaks, CA: Corwin.

Korczak, J. (1967). *Selected works of Janusz Korczak.* Warsaw, Poland: Central Institute for Scientific, Technical and Economic Information.

Korczak, J. (1986). *King Matt the first.* New York: Farrar, Straus & Giroux.

Kotter, J. (1996). *Leading change.* Boston: Harvard Business School Press.

Kouzes, J. M., & Posner, B. Z. (1999). *Encouraging the heart.* San Francisco: Jossey-Bass.

Kouzes, J. M., & Posner, B. Z. (2010). *The truth about leadership: The no-fads, heart-of-the-matter facts you need to know.* San Francisco: Jossey-Bass.

Kozol, J. (2000). *Ordinary resurrection: Children in the years of hope.* New York: Crown.

Kranz, G. (2000). *Failure is not an option: Mission control from Mercury to Apollo 13 and beyond.* New York: Simon & Schuster.

Kruse, S., Seashore Louis, K., & Bryk, A. S. (1994). *Building professional community in schools.* Madison, WI: Center on Organization and Restructuring of Schools.

Kuhn, T. S. (1996). *The structure of scientific revolutions* (3rd ed.). Chicago: University of Chicago Press.

LaFee, S. (2003). Professional learning communities. *The School Administrator, 5*(60), 6–12.

Lambert, L. (1997). *Who will save our schools? Teachers as constructivist leaders.* Thousand Oaks, CA: Corwin.

Lambert, L. (2002). *The constructivist leader* (2nd ed.). New York: Teachers College Press.

Lambert, L. (2003). *Leadership capacity for lasting school improvement.* Alexandria, VA: Association for Supervision and Curriculum Development.

Land, D., & Stringfield, S. (Eds.). (2002). *Educating at-risk students.* Chicago: National Society for the Study of Education.

Langford, J., Vakii, T., & Lindquist, E. A. (2000). *Tough challenges and practical solutions: A report on conference proceedings.* Victoria, BC: School of Public Administration, University of Victoria. Retrieved from http://www.futurework.telus.com/proceedings.pdf.

Lawrence, D. (2009, Jan. 28). *Minnesota early childhood summit speech.* Retrieved July 28, 2009, from http://www.invisiblechildren.org.

Leana, C. R. (2011, Fall). The missing link in school reform. *Stanford Social Innovation Review.*

Leithwood, K., Day, C., Sammons, P., Harris, A., & Hopkins, D. (2006). *Seven strong claims about successful school leadership.* Nottingham, UK: National College of School Leadership.

Leithwood, K., & Jantzi, D. (2000). The effects of transformational leadership on organisational conditions and student engagement with school. *Journal of Educational Administration, 38*(2), 112–129.

Leithwood, K., & Mascall, B. (2008). Collective leadership effects on student achievement. *Educational Administration Quarterly, 44*(4), 529–561.

Leithwood, K., Patten, S., & Jantzi, D. (2010). The influence of principal leadership on classroom instruction and student learning: A study of mediated pathways to learning. *Educational Administration Quarterly, 48,* 626–663.

Leithwood, K., & Seashore Louis, K. (2012). *Linking leadership to student learning.* San Francisco: Jossey-Bass.

Leithwood, K., Seashore Louis, K., Anderson, S., & Wahlstrom, K. (2011). *Linking leadership to student learning.* San Francisco: Jossey-Bass.

Lepper, M. R., Greene, D., & Nisbet, R. (1973). Undermining children's intrinsic interest with extrinsic reward: A test of 'overjustification' hypothesis. *Journal of Personality and Social Psychology, 28,* 129–137.

Levine, A. (2005). *Educating school leaders.* Washington, DC: The Education Schools Project.

Lewis, A. C. (2000). Listening to adolescents. *Phi Delta Kappan, 81*(9), 643.

Livsey, R. C., & Palmer, P. J. (1999). *The courage to teach: A guide for reflection and renewal.* San Francisco: Jossey-Bass.

Lortie, D. C. (1975). *School teacher: A sociological study.* Chicago: University of Chicago Press.

Love, A., & Kruger, A. C. (2005). Teacher beliefs and student achievement in urban schools serving African American students. *Journal of Educational Research, 99*(2), 87–98.

Machiavelli, N. (1999). *The prince* (G. Bull, Trans.). London/New York: Penguin Books. (Original work published 1532.)

MacMillan, R. (1996). *The relationship between school culture and principals' practices during succession.* Unpublished doctoral dissertation, University of Toronto (OISE), Toronto, Ontario, Canada.

MacMillan, R. (2000). Leadership succession, culture of teaching, and educational change. In N. Bascia & A. Hargreaves (Eds.), *The sharp edge of educational change.* London: Falmer Press.

Marsh, J., Springer, M. G., McCaffrey, D. F., Yuan, K., Epstein, S., Koppich, J., . . . Peng, X. (2011). *A big apple for educators: New York City's experiment with schoolwide performance bonuses: Final evaluation report.* Santa Monica, CA: RAND.

Marx, A. (comp.). (1996). *Annotated bibliography: Research from the Center on Families, Communities, Schools and Learning.* Baltimore: Publications Department, Johns Hopkins University.

Marzano, R. J. (2003). *What works in schools: Translating research into action.* Alexandria, VA: Association for Supervision and Curriculum Development.

Marzano, R. J. (2007). *The art and science of teaching: A comprehensive framework for effective instruction.* Alexandria, VA: Association for Supervision and Curriculum Development.

Marzano, R. J., Pickering, D. J., & Pollock, J. E. (2001). *Classroom instruction that works: Research-based strategies for increasing student achievement.* Alexandria, VA: Association for Supervision and Curriculum Development.

Marzano, R. J., Waters, T., & McNulty, B. A. (2005). *School leadership that works: From research to results.* Alexandria, VA: Association for Supervision and Curriculum Development.

Mason, S. (2002, Apr.). *Turning data into knowledge: Lessons from six Milwaukee public schools.* Paper presented at the annual conference of the American Educational Research Association, New Orleans, LA.

Masten, A. S. (2001). Ordinary magic: Resilience processes in development. *American Psychologist, 56,* 227–238.

Mattern, K. D., & Shaw, E. J. (2010). A look beyond cognitive predictors of academic success: Understanding the relationship between academic self-beliefs and outcomes. *Journal of College Student Development, 51*(6), 665–678.

Maurer, R. (1996). *Beyond the wall of resistance: Unconventional strategies that build support for change.* Austin, TX: Bard Press.

McKenna, J. (2009a). Data without fear. Using relational trust to overcome fear of data. *What's Working in Schools Newsletter, 2*(8).

McKenna, J. (2009b, Apr. 1). From red-flagged to blue ribbon: Using data and collaborative teaming for school success. *What's Working in Schools Newsletter, 2*(4).

McLaughlin, M. (1993). What matters most in teachers' workplace context. In J. W. Lilly & M. McLaughlin (Eds.), *Teachers' work: Individuals, colleagues, and context.* New York: Teachers College Press.

McLaughlin, M. W., & Talbert, J. E. (2006). *Building school-based teacher learning communities.* New York: Teachers College Press.

McTighe, J., & O'Connor, K. (2005). Seven practices for effective learning. *Educational Leadership, 63*(3), 10–17.

Meier, D. (1995). *The power of their ideas: Lessons for America from a small school in Harlem.* Boston: Beacon Press.

Mendler, A. N. (1992). *What do I do when . . . ? How to achieve discipline with dignity in the classroom.* Bloomington, IN: Solution Tree.

Merideth, E. M. (2007). *Leadership strategies for teachers* (2nd ed.). Thousand Oaks, CA: Corwin.

Meyer, J. W., & Rowan, B. (1977). Institutional organizations: Formal structures as myth and ceremony. *American Journal of Sociology, 83,* 340–363.

Miles, M. (1998). Finding keys to school change. In A. Hargreaves, A. Lieberman, M. Fullan, & D. Hopkins (Eds.), *International handbook of educational change* (pp. 37–69). Dordrecht, The Netherlands: Kluwer Press.

Mintzberg, H. (2004). *Managers not MBAs: A hard look at the soft practice of managing and management development.* San Francisco: Berrett-Koehler.

Montgomery, A. F., & Rossi, R. J. (1994). Becoming at risk of failure in America's schools. In R. J. Rossi (Ed.), *Schools and students at risk: Context and framework for positive change.* New York: Teachers College Press.

Mullen, C. A., & Schunk, D. H. (2011, Fall). The role of the professional learning community in dropout prevention. *AASA Journal of Scholarship & Practice, 8*(3), 6–29.

Murphy, J., Jost, J., & Shipman, N. (2000). Implementation of the interstate school leaders licensure consortium standards. *International Journal of Leadership in Education, 3*(1), 17–39.

NAACP Report. (2009). *Misplaced priorities: Over incarcerate, under educate.* Washington, DC: National Association of State Budget Officers.

Nanus, B. (1992). *Visionary leadership.* San Francisco: Jossey-Bass.

National Academy of Public Administration. (1997). *Managing succession and developing leadership: Growing the next generation of public service leaders.* Washington, DC: Author.

National Association of Secondary School Principals. (2001). *The principals shortage.* Retrieved June 19, 2003, from http://www.nassp.org.

National Council of Teachers of Mathematics (NCTM). (2012). *Differentiated learning.* Reston, VA: Author.

National Education Goals Panel. (1995). *National education goals report executive summary.* Washington, DC: Author.

National Parent Teacher Association. (1998). *National standards for parent/family involvement programs.* Chicago: Author.

National Parent Teacher Association. (n.d.). *National standards for family-school partnerships.* Retrieved August 1, 2009, from http://www.pta.org/documents/National_Standards.pdf.

National Staff Development Council (NSDC). (2010, Apr.). Leadership. *JSD, The Learning Forward Journal, 31*(2).

Nespor, J. (1987). The roles of beliefs in the practice of teaching. *Journal of Curriculum Studies, 19,* 317–328.

Newmann, F. M., & Wehlage, G. (1995). *Successful school restructuring.* Madison, WI: Center on Organization and Restructuring of Schools, School of Education, University of Wisconsin–Madison.

Nichols, S., & Berliner, D. (2007). *Collateral damage: How high-stakes testing corrupts American schools:* Cambridge, MA: Harvard University Press.

Noer, D. M. (1993). *Healing the wounds.* San Francisco: Jossey-Bass.

Noguera, P. A. (2003). *City schools and the American dream: Reclaiming the promise of public education.* New York: Teachers College Press.

Noguera, P. A. (2009). *The trouble with black boys: And other reflections on race, equity, and the future of public education.* San Francisco: Jossey-Bass.

Noguera, P. A., & Wing, J. Y. (Eds.). (2008). *Unfinished business: Closing the racial achievement gap in our schools.* San Francisco: Jossey-Bass.

Novick, B., Kress, J. S., & Elias, M. J. (2002). *Building learning communities with character.* Alexandria, VA: Association for Supervision and Curriculum Development.

O'Connor, K. (2007). *A repair kit for grading: 15 fixes for broken grades.* Portland, OR: Educational Testing Services.

Organization for Economic Cooperation and Development (OECD). (2001). *Schooling for tomorrow: What schools for the future?* Paris, France: Author.

Organization for Economic Cooperation and Development (OECD). (2010). *Programme for international student assessment (PISA) rankings.* Washington, DC: Author.

Ovando, M. N. (1994). *Effects of teachers' leadership on their teaching practices.* Paper presented at the Annual Conference of the University Council of Educational Administration, Philadelphia.

Palmer, P. J. (1998). *The courage to teach: Exploring the inner landscape of a teacher's life.* San Francisco: Jossey-Bass.

Pardini, P. (1999). Making time for adult learning. *Journal of Staff Development, 20*(2).

Pascale, R. (1997–1999). Conversations with change practice consulting teams of Price Waterhouse Coopers and Anderson Consulting, Oxford, England, and Colorado Springs, Colorado.

Pascale, R. (1998, March). Personal communication with David Schneider, partner, North American Change Practice, Price Waterhouse Coopers, Santa Fe, New Mexico.

Pascale, R. T., Millemann, M., & Gioja, L. (2000). *Surfing the edge of chaos.* New York: Three Rivers Press.

Pedler, M. (2011). Leadership, risk and the imposter syndrome. *Action Learning: Research & Practice, 8*(2), 89–91.

Peters, T. (1999). *The circle of innovation: You can't shrink your way to greatness.* New York: Vintage.

Pianta, R. C., & Walsh, D. I. (1998). Applying the construct of resilience in schools: Cautions from a developmental systems perspective. *School Psychology Review, 27*(3), 407–417.

Pink, D. (2009). *Drive: The surprising truth about what motivates us.* New York: Riverhead Books.

Pintrich, P. R. (1990). Implications of psychological research on student learning and college teaching for teacher education. In W. R. Houston (Ed.), *Handbook of research on teacher education* (pp. 826–857). New York: Macmillan.

Pont, B., Nusche, D., & Hopkins, D. (2008). *Improving school leadership: Vol. 2. Case studies on system leadership.* Paris: OECD.

Pont, B., Nusche, D., & Moorman, H. (2008). *Improving school leadership: Vol. 1. Policy and practice.* Paris: OECD.

Porter, A. C., Murphy, J., Goldring, E., Elliott, S. N., Polikoff, M. S., & May, H. (2008). *Vanderbilt assessment of leadership in education: Technical manual, Version 1.0.* Nashville, TN: Vanderbilt University.

Porter, A. C., Polikoff, M. S., Goldring, E., Murphy, J., Elliott, S. N., & May, H. (2010). Investigating the validity and reliability of the Vanderbilt assessment of leadership in education. *Elementary School Journal, 111,* 282–313.

Portin, B. S., Knapp, M. S., Dareff, S., Feldman, S., Russell, F. A., Samuelson, C., & Yeh, T. L. (2009). *Leadership for learning improvement in urban schools.* Seattle, WA: Center for the Study of Teaching and Policy.

Posner, B. Z., & Westwood, R. I. (1995). A cross-cultural investigation of the shared values relationship. *International Journal of Value-Based Management, 11*(4), 1–10.

Programme for International Student Assessment. (2012, May). *Does performance-based pay improve teaching?* Paris: Organisation for Economic Co-operation and Development (OECD).

Pungello, E., & Ramey, C. (2012, Jan. 19). *Benefits of high quality child care persist 30 years later.* Abecedarian Project. Chapel Hill, NC: The University of North Carolina.

Purkey, W. W., & Novak, J. M. (1996). *Inviting school success.* Belmont, CA: Wadsworth.

Putnam, R. D. (2000). *Bowling alone: The collapse and revival of American community.* New York: Simon & Schuster.

Putnam, R. D., Leonardi, R., & Nanetti, R. Y. (1993). *Making democracy work: Civic traditions in modern Italy.* Princeton, NJ: Princeton University Press.

Ravitch, D. (2011, Mar. 29). Thoughts on the failure of merit pay. *Education Week* [Web log comment].

Raymond, M. (2009). *New Stanford report finds serious quality challenge in national charter school sector.* Stanford, CA: Center for Research on Education Outcomes (CREDO).

Reeves, D. B. (2000). *Accountability in action.* Denver, CO: Advanced Learning Press.

Reeves, D. B. (2002a). *Making standards work* (3rd ed.). Denver, CO: Advanced Learning Press.

Reeves, D. B. (2002b). *The leader's guide to standards: A blueprint for educational equity and excellence.* San Francisco: Jossey-Bass.

Riley, K. (1998). *Whose school is it anyway?* London: Falmer Press.

Riley, K. (2000). Leadership, learning and systemic change. *Journal of Educational Change, 1*(1), 57–75.

Robelen, E. W. (2012). Advocates say creativity index may foster curriculum balance. *Education Week, 31*(21), 1.

Rogers, E. M., & Rogers, E. (2003). *Diffusion of innovations* (5th ed.). New York: Free Press.

Rossi, R. J., & Stringfield, S. C. (1997). *Education reform and students at risk.* Washington, DC: Office of Educational Research and Improvement, U.S. Department of Education.

Sanders, L. (2003, Mar. 16). Medicine's progress, one setback at a time. *New York Times Magazine,* 29.

Sarason, S. (1972). *The creation of settings and the future societies.* San Francisco: Jossey-Bass.

Sarason, S. (1990). *The predictable failure of educational reform.* San Francisco: Jossey-Bass.

Saul, J. R. (1993). *Voltaire's bastards.* Toronto, ON: Penguin Books.

Schiff, T. (2002, Jan.). Principals' readiness for reform: A comprehensive approach. *Principal Leadership, 2*(5).

Schlechty, P. C. (1992). *Schools for the 21st century: Leadership imperatives for educational reform.* San Francisco: Jossey-Bass.

Schmoker, M. (2004). Tipping point: From feckless reform to substantive instructional improvement. *Phi Delta Kappan, 85*(6), 424–431.

Schorr, L. B. (1988). *Within our reach: Breaking the cycle of disadvantage.* New York: Anchor Press/Doubleday.

Schorr, L. B. (1998, Summer). Searchlights on delinquency. *Journal of Emotional and Behavioral Problems, 7*(2).

Seashore Louis, K. (2008). Creating and sustaining professional communities. In A. M. Blankstein, P. D. Houston, & R. W. Cole (Eds.), *Sustaining professional learning communities* (pp. 41–58). Thousand Oaks, CA: Corwin.

Seashore Louis, K., & Kruse, S. D. (1995). *Professionalism and community: Perspectives on reforming urban schools.* Thousand Oaks, CA: Corwin.

Seashore Louis, K., Kruse, S. D., & Marks, H. M. (1996). Schoolwide professional community. In F. Newmann and Associates (Eds.), *Authentic achievement: Restructuring schools for intellectual quality.* San Francisco: Jossey-Bass.

Seashore Louis, K., Kruse, S. D., & Raywid, M. A. (1996). Putting teachers at the center of reform. *NASSP Bulletin, 80*(580), 9–21.

Seashore Louis, K., Leithwood, K., Wahlstron, K. K., & Anderson, S. E. (2010). *Investigating the links to improved student learning: Final report of research findings. Learning from the Leadership Project.* St. Paul, MN: University of Minnesota, Ontario Institute for Studies in Education, Wallace Foundation.

Segalla, M. (2009). How Europeans do layoffs. *Harvard Business Review.* Retrieved from http://blogs.hbr.org/hbr/hbr-now/2009/06/how-europeans-do-layoffs .html.

Senge, P. M. (1990). *The fifth discipline: The art and practice of the learning organiza-tion.* New York: Doubleday/Currency.

Senge, P. M. (2010). Education for an interdependent world: Developing systems citizens. In A. Hargreaves, A. Lieberman, M. Fullan, & D. Hopkins (Eds.), *The second international handbook of educational change.* Dordrecht, The Netherlands: Springer.

Senge, P. M. (2012). *Schools that learn: A fifth discipline fieldbook for educators, par-ents, and everyone who cares about education.* New York: Doubleday.

Senge, P. M., Ross, R., Smith, B., Roberts, C., & Kleiner, A. (1994). *The fifth disci-pline fieldbook: Strategies and tools for building a learning organization.* New York: Doubleday.

Sergiovanni, T. J. (1992). *Moral leadership: Getting to the heart of school improve-ment.* San Francisco: Jossey-Bass.

Sergiovanni, T. J. (1994). *Building community in schools.* San Francisco: Jossey-Bass.

Sergiovanni, T. J. (2000). *The lifeworld of leadership: Creating culture, community, and personal meaning in our schools.* San Francisco: Jossey-Bass.

Shockley-Zalabak, P. S., Morreale, S., & Hackman, M. (2010). *Building the high-trust organization: Strategies for supporting five key dimensions of trust.* San Francisco: Jossey-Bass.

Shubitz, S. (2008, Sept. 1). 20 Rules for great parent-teacher conferences. *Instructor, 118*(2). Retrieved August 09, 2009, from http://www.thefreelibrary.com/20+ Rules+for+great+parent-teacher+conferences.-a0187 672975.

Simkin, L., Charner, I., & Suss, L. (2010). *Emerging education issues: Findings from The Wallace Foundation Survey.* New York: The Wallace Foundation by the Academy for Educational Development.

Singleton, G. E., & Linton, C. (2006). *Courageous conversations about race: A field guide for achieving equity in schools.* Thousand Oaks, CA: Corwin.

Smith, L. M., Dwyer, D. C., Prunty, J. J., & Kleine, P. F. (1987). *The fate of an innova-tive school.* London: Falmer Press.

Smith, R. (2000, Oct.). *The School Administrator.* Retrieved September 17, 2012, from http://www.aasa.org/SchoolAdministratorArticle.aspx?id=14390.

Soder, R. (2001). *The language of leadership.* San Francisco: Jossey-Bass.

Soder, R., Goodlad, J. I., & McMannon, T. J. (2001). *Developing democratic character in the young.* San Francisco: Jossey-Bass.

Solmo, R. (1995, Feb.). Meetings—management; consensus (social sciences). *Social Policy, 44*(2).

Southworth, G. (2009). *Courageous leadership for shaping America's future: A syn-thesis of best practices guiding school leadership for 21st century education.* Bloomington, IN: HOPE Foundation.

Sparks, D. (2002). *Designing powerful professional development for teachers and prin-cipals.* Oxford, OH: National Staff Development Council.

Sparks, D. (2007). *Leading for results.* Thousand Oaks, CA: Corwin.

Sparks, S. (2012, Oct. 17). IES to Start 'Continuous Improvement' Study Program. *Education Week,* 10.

Spillane, J. P., Halverson, R., & Drummond, J. B. (2001). Investigating school leadership practice: A distributed perspective. *Educational Researcher, 30*(3), 23–28.

Spiro, J. (2010, Apr.). Winning strategy: Set benchmarks of early success to build momentum for the long term. *Journal of Staff Development. Leaning Forward, 33*(2).

Springfield, S. C. (1995). Attempts to enhance students' learning: A search for valid programs and highly reliable implementation techniques. *School Effectiveness and School Improvement, 6,* 67–96.

Standing Bear, L. (1933). *Land of the spotted eagle.* New York: Houghton Mifflin.

Sternberg, R. J. (1996). *Successful intelligence: How practical and creative intelligence determine success in life.* New York: Simon & Schuster.

Stiegelbauer, S. M., & Anderson, S. (1992). *Seven years later: Revisiting a restructured school in northern Ontario.* Paper presented at the American Educational Research Association Meetings, San Francisco.

Stiggins, R. (2004). *Student-involved assessment for learning* (4th ed.). Upper Saddle River, NJ: Prentice Hall.

Stiggins, R., Arter, J. A., Chappuis, J., & Chappuis, S. (2007). *Classroom assessment for student learning: Doing it right—using it well.* Upper Saddle River, NJ: Prentice Hall.

Stoll, L. (1999). Raising our potential: Understanding and developing capacity for lasting improvement. *School Effectiveness and School Improvement, 10*(4), 503–532.

Stoll L., & Fink, D. (1996). *Changing our schools: Linking school effectiveness and school improvement.* Buckingham, UK: Open University Press.

Stoll, L., Fink, D., & Earl, L. (2002). *It's about learning (and it's about time).* London: Routledge/Falmer.

Stoll, L., & Temperley, J. (2009). Creative leadership: A challenge of our times. *School Leadership and Management, 29*(1), 63–76.

Stringfield, S., & Land, D. (Eds.). (2002). *Educating at-risk students.* Chicago: National Society for the Study of Education.

Stringfield, S., Reynolds, D., & Schaffer, E. (2008). Improving secondary students' academic achievement through a focus on reform reliability: 4- and 9-year findings from the High Reliability Schools project. *School Effectiveness and School Improvement, 19*(4), 409–428.

Suzuki, D. (2003). *The David Suzuki reader: A lifetime of ideas from a leading activist and thinker.* Vancouver, BC: Greystone Press.

Swartz, R. (2012, Sept. 13). *New York Times second annual schools for tomorrow conference: Building a better teacher.* Hosted by the National Center on Education and the Economy, New York.

Talbert, J., & MacLaughlin, M. (1994). Teacher professionalism in local school contexts. *American Journal of Education, 102,* 123–153.

Taylor, L., Nelson, P., & Adelman, H. S. (1999). Scaling-up reforms across a school district. *Reading and Writing Quarterly, 15,* 303–326.

Teddlie, C., & Stringfield, S. (1993). *Schools make a difference: Lessons learned from a 10-year study of school effects.* New York: Teachers College Press.

Test of wing damage called "smoking gun." (2003, July 8). *redOrbit*. Retrieved July 30, 2009, from http://www.redorbit.com/news/general/16681/test_ of_wing_ damage_called_smoking_gun/index.html.

Tough, P. (2011, Sept. 14). What if the secret to success is failure? *The New York Times*, p. 19.

Tschannen-Moran, M. (2001). Collaboration and the need for trust. *Journal of Educational Administration, 39*, 308–331.

Tschannen-Moran, M. (2004). *Trust matters: Leadership of successful schools*. San Francisco: Jossey-Bass.

Tyack, D., & Tobin, W. (1994). The grammar of schooling: Why has it been so hard to change? *American Educational Research Journal, 31*(3), 453–480.

Tyler, R. W. (1949). *Basic principles of curriculum and instruction*. Chicago: University of Chicago Press.

Wagner, T. (2008). *The global achievement gap: Why even our best schools don't teach the new survival skills our children need—and what we can do about it*. New York: Basic Books.

Wagner, T. (2012). *Creating innovators: The making of young people who will change the world*. New York: Scribner.

Wallace Foundation. (2003). *Beyond the pipeline: Getting the principals we need where they are needed most*. Seattle, WA: Center on Reinventing Education.

Wallace Foundation. (2010a). *Investigating the links to improved student learning: Final report of research findings. Learning from the Leadership Project*. New York: Author.

Wallace Foundation. (2010b). Reimagining the job of leading schools: Lessons from a 10-year journey. *Journal of Staff Development, 31*(2).

Wallace Foundation. (2011). *The school principal as leader: Guiding schools to better teaching and learning*. New York: Author.

Walsh, M. (2002, June 27). Supreme Court upholds Cleveland voucher program. *Education Week, 21*(42). Retrieved July 28, 2009, from http://www.edweek.org.

Walton, G., & Dweck, C. (2011, Nov. 27). Willpower: It's in your head. *The New York Times*, p. SR8.

Weinstein, C. S. (1989). Teacher education students' preconceptions of teaching. *Journal of Teacher Education, 40*(2), 53–60.

Werner, E. E., & Smith, R. S. (1977). *Kauai's children come of age*. Honolulu, HI: University of Hawaii Press.

Werner, E. E., & Smith, R. S. (1982). *Vulnerable but invincible: A longitudinal study of resilient children and youth*. New York: McGraw-Hill.

Wiggins, G. (1998). *Educative assessment: Designing assessments to inform and improve student performance*. San Francisco: Jossey-Bass.

Wiggins, G., & McTighe, J. (2005). *Understanding by design* (2nd ed.). Alexandria, VA: Association for Supervision and Curriculum Development.

Wiggins, G., & McTighe, J. (2007). *Schooling by design: Mission, action, and achievement.* Alexandria, VA: Association for Supervision and Curriculum Development.

Wilcox, K. C., & Angelis, J. I. (2009). *Best practices from high-performing middle schools: How successful schools remove obstacles and create pathways to learning.* New York: Teachers College Press.

Wilker, K. (1983). *The Lindenhof* (S. Lhotzky, Trans.). Sioux Falls, SD: Augustana College. (Original work published 1920.)

Williams, M. P. (2002, Sept. 25). Reading by the second grade is a strategy to fight crime. *Richmond-Times Dispatch,* p. H4.

Williams, T. (2001). *Unrecognized exodus, unaccepted accountability: The looming shortage of principals and vice-principals in Ontario public school boards.* Toronto, ON: Ontario Principals' Council.

Wilmore, E. (2007). *Teacher leadership: Improving teaching and learning from inside the classroom.* Thousand Oaks, CA: Corwin.

Woods, E. G. (1995). *School improvement research series, close-up 17: Reducing the drop-out rate.* Portland, OR: Northwest Regional Educational Laboratory.

World Commission on Environment and Development. (1987). *Our common future.* New York: United Nations General Assembly.

Yeager, D. S., & Walton, G. M. (2011). Social-psychological interventions in education: They're not magic. *Review of Educational Research, 81*(2), 267–301.

York-Barr, J., & Duke, K. (2004). What do we know about teacher leadership? Findings from two decades of scholarship. *Review of Educational Research, 74*(3), 255–316.

Young, M. D. (2002, Feb.). *Ensuring the university's capacity to prepare learning-focused leadership.* Report presented at the meeting of the National Commission for the Advancement of Educational Leadership, Racine, WI.

Zigler, E., & Muenchow, S. (1994). *Head Start: The inside story of America's most successful educational experiment.* New York: Basic Books.

Index

CORWIN

A SAGE Company

The Corwin logo—a raven striding across an open book—represents the union of courage and learning. Corwin is committed to improving education for all learners by publishing books and other professional development resources for those serving the field of PreK–12 education. By providing practical, hands-on materials, Corwin continues to carry out the promise of its motto: **"Helping Educators Do Their Work Better."**

The HOPE Foundation logo stands for Harnessing Optimism and Potential Through Education. The HOPE Foundation helps to develop and support educational leaders over time at district- and state-wide levels to create school cultures that sustain all students' achievement, especially low-performing students.